SIX FRENCH CITIES

Onion soup

©Photography by Celestine Cooley

SIX FRENCH CITIES

My Magical Medieval Journey

A French Memoir Series

Celestine Cooley

 Cooley Communications

Six French Cities, My Magical Medieval Journey
Copyright © 2025 Celestine Cooley
First Edition, January 2025

All rights reserved. No part of this book may be reproduced in whole or in part without written permission from the publisher, except by reviewers who may quote brief excerpts in connection with a review in a newspaper, magazine, or electronic publication; nor may any part of this book be reproduced, stored in a retrieval system, copied, distributed or transmitted in any form by any means of electronic, mechanical, photocopying, scanning, recording, or other means, without written permission from the publisher. It is illegal to copy this book, or post it to a website.

No portion of this work may be used or reproduced in any manner for training large language models or similar artificial intelligence (AI) systems. The author reserves all rights to license uses of this work for generative AI training and development of machine learning language models.

Cover Design & Cover Photography by Celestine Cooley
Print ISBN: 978-0-615-2995-8
Printed in the United States

https://celeste-cooleycommunications.com/

To my talented daughter, Alexis Nichele Pauling, who shares my dream. To my sister Patricia Somerville, my nephew, Galileo Ryan Somerville, and my supportive extended family across the USA.

TABLE OF CONTENTS

INTRODUCTION i
My Lifelong Dream i
CHAPTER ONE 1
First Things First 1
Removing The Biggest Obstacles 11
Tying Up Loose Ends 18
It's Time to Move On 22
Learning French and French History 27
CHAPTER TWO 32
Executing the Scouting Plan 32
CHAPTER THREE 42
Not A Simple Plan 42
CHAPTER FOUR 62
Exploring Six Cities 62
CHAPTER FIVE 72
Exploring Bordeaux 72
CHAPTER SIX 121
Discovering Biarritz 121
CHAPTER SEVEN 126
Exploring Toulouse 126
CHAPTER EIGHT 148
Exploring Nice 148

CHAPTER NINE 190
Exploring Lyon 190
CHAPTER TEN 208
Exploring Paris 208
CHAPTER ELEVEN 261
Choosing A French City 261
FRANCE 263
BORDEAUX 265
BIARRITZ 268
TOULOUSE 271
NICE 273
LYON 276
PARIS 278
EPILOGUE 280
Old Endings, New Beginnings 280
ACKNOWLEGEMENTS 283
ABOUT THE AUTHOR 284

SIX FRENCH CITIES

Six French Cities

INTRODUCTION

My Lifelong Dream

BIENVENUE! means "WELCOME!" in French, which is how I felt in the spring of 1985 on my very first trip to France. Immediately, this country stole my heart. Back then, I was working for a newly appointed Federal Judge in downtown Los Angeles.

Five years earlier I reluctantly traded my first invigorating entertainment industry job for regular working hours (8 am to 4:30 pm) to provide my daughter with more stability. She would soon be entering kindergarten. We needed to spend more quality time together in the evenings. Subsequently, I would return to the entertainment industry a few years later.

My first role working for the Federal Clerk's Office for the Central District of California started as a criminal docket clerk, managing schedules and maintaining court records. Less than a year later, I was promoted to the position of Courtroom Deputy Clerk (the first black candidate to make it) after going through a rigorous training process.

Before this job, I had been working long and crazy hours, up to

12 hours a day in Television production for the Dinah Shore show. I loved that job and learned so much about the behind-the-scenes workings of a TV variety show.

While working steadily on these two jobs, I had not taken any kind of break or vacation in seven years. When an opportunity arose to go to France, I jumped at the chance to travel abroad. Luckily, my vacation time had accumulated during those five years at the Court enabling me to take a 30-day vacation.

Visiting London, where I also had family, was worked into my schedule and of course I had to see Paris, its iconic museums, monuments, and the Seine. My daughter, now ten years old, would camp out with her dad in L.A. while I travelled to visit Europe.

Originally my plan was to travel with my best friend, Betty Henson, but she dropped out at the last minute. So, I asked another girlfriend, Renée, to take her place. When I met Renée in 1976, I was not working but attending college full time on the G.I Bill to obtain a degree in Broadcast Technologies. Our daughters were the same age and in the same preschool daycare program for low-income single parents in Los Angeles.

A program sponsored by the Thalians, which was a Beverly Hills charitable organization. This exceptional day care program was called HomeSafe; we paid a weekly fee according to our income. Having very little money for daycare while attending college, I was grateful to have found this daycare program through a referral.

Jump ahead eight years later, we are 34 years old and going on our first non-stop TWA flight from Los Angeles to London. From London's Heathrow airport, we took an airport bus into the city, then caught a cab to a cheap boutique hotel on Cromwell Street near

Six French Cities

Kensington.

We could walk everywhere; a park, shops, and restaurants were nearby. I meticulously created this trip from a European Travel Guide purchased from a Crown book store along with a French language phrase book (which I still have today). But mostly, we traveled by the seat of our pants, carefreely going where the wind took us without a real plan, except for Cannes.

That whimsical trip seemed so much easier to organize than this one planned for 2023 to scout six French cities. Literally, when leaving the UK for France, we traced the exact same route by train as described in that guide book. It felt like a true adventure and it began the moment we boarded our flight from Los Angeles.

Londoners were kind and helpful, always asking if we were Americans. At Buckingham Palace, we tried our best tactics but failed to make the Stoic Palace Guards smile. Having our pictures taken with those guards in front of this magnificent palace and visiting my aunt were two of the many highlights of our trip to Britain.

After staying in London for three days, we caught our train from London's Victoria Station riding in coach to Dover, England. Then we grabbed the Ferry to Calais, France where we boarded the night train into Paris. We could not imagine what lied ahead on this fun adventure as we enjoyed each moment we experienced abroad.

At the Dover Ferry Station's bar, we met two cute Australian guys our age who were surfing around Europe, and other young adults from different countries who were also going to France. We spent our time chatting, laughing, having whisky shots, snacks, and hanging out with this hilarious group throughout our ferry ride and then on our train ride to Paris.

In our train car were a handful of musicians who broke out their instruments and began playing Motown songs. We were amazed and impressed especially when passengers from the other cars started piling into our car to listen to the music. Every one of us sang the songs while some kids danced in the aisles; that night no one slept on the train in our car due to the hours we spend enjoying the unexpected musical entertainment.

This European trip happened by coincidence after receiving an invitation to the French Film Festival in Cannes. My Hollywood connections made that Cannes experience possible. On a Thursday night late winter in 1984. Betty and I were at the West Hollywood Improv Comedy Club, as usual sitting at owner Budd Friedman's big round table along with him and other Hollywood insiders.

We're listening to a Film Festival discussion when I jokingly said,

"I wish I could go to Cannes."

Well, it appears that unforeseen miracles do occur because a film marketing executive responded to my statement. That night, I unintentionally rubbed an invisible magic lamp, *abracadabra*, my wish was granted. The executive whom I had just met gave me his business card and wrote down the Cannes Festival information I needed like whom to contact to arrange my visit.

He said, "Bring your friend too."

"Okay!" I replied in disbelief.

Was this conversation real? It was one of those crazy moments of being in *the right place at the right time* scenarios. I never expected to get that kind of a response to my statement. I was excited and did not want to miss my chance of going to Cannes so I followed through a few days later to make those French connections and get the information I'd need to go to France.

Of course, I'd have to get to Cannes on my own dime to realize that magic wish. Truly a hallowed moment at the Improv when I decided to grab this surprising opportunity and take this once in a lifetime trip abroad that next year. Realistically, I had only four months to request my vacation in May and make some quick travel plans for myself and Betty using my TWA Getaway credit card.

As a kid, traveling to Europe is what I wanted to do after reading numerous books that took me to faraway places. I was desperate to see those towns and villages for myself. My family traveled to the Caribbean and all around the US often by car in caravans but never ventured abroad.

On that first trip to France, our good luck and street smarts kept us safe. The moment we walked out of the Gare du Nord (train station) in Paris, I felt comfortable, free, and so much at home. The sun was shining, the weather was mild, and the city was alive. Amazed and delighted to see how big, beautiful, dirty, and tall were the famous Haussmann buildings. The wide boulevards and small cars. The French people moving about and speaking fast French.

We slowly walked down lots of gritty cobblestoned streets, through some of the twenty districts, viewing the incredible city sights, shops, restaurants, and the smell of fresh baked bread were sensory overloaded experiences like no other; and the French people's quiet resolve created my instant love for France. In my heart I knew that one day I would call France my home. Paris is a lot different today though.

Celestine Cooley

Without a clue as to where we were going, with my guidebook in hand and some very helpful recommendations from locals, we found a perfectly cute 2-star boutique hotel and reserved a small room with twin-beds. This hotel was a classic six-story hotel in an old stone building with a winding interior staircase. It had no elevator.

Located in the classy 1st arrondissement on Rue de Richelieu. Just a stone's throw away from the Louvre. At that time, the currency exchange rates were favorable for us at ten Francs per one U.S. dollar. Our hotels, meals, and transportation were very cheap during that trip. We could not have timed this trip better. Perfect from the beginning, it unfolded like an old newspaper without wrinkles, tears, or stains. Our journey seamlessly continued for the duration of this trip without any big unsolvable issues at all.

We ventured all over Paris on foot, by bus, and on the metro *(subway)* accumulating a pile of metro tickets and several new French friends. Our chance encounters in Paris where were positive. At first, we met two very cute French males who were supportive. Although these guys were younger than us, they respectfully treated us like two French Queens.

They took us on fabulous walking tours that tourist would not see through Paris neighborhoods on the outskirts of the city. Inviting us to parties at private clubs and just being good new friends and fun companions during much of our stay in this city. They spoke French and English. We were quite impressed.

During the day, Renée and I lived on cheap sandwiches of thinly sliced ham *(Jambon)* with butter *(beurre)* tucked inside crusty baguettes. We drank boxed Rosé wine from paper cups in the park,

Jardin des Tuileries. At night, we had marvelous French dinners and went dancing in nightclubs. We learned so much about French culture while immersing ourselves and experiencing life in Paris like locals with locals.

We did not speak much French. My high school French equivalent wasn't going to get us very far. We tried our best to communicate in French by using my phrase book. Along the way we met English speakers, helpful foreigners, and a community of African Americans. Mailing postcards at La Poste was another unforgettable experience due to our limited language skills. We also tried making phone calls to the USA, but found it nearly impossible to connect.

After spending four glorious days in Paris, it was time to head south. We rented a new Volkswagen Golf economy car from Hertz. A small white compact with a black interior; we chose a manual transmission. Our paper Michelin map guided us south to Cannes. Renée drove crawling onto the expensive A6 toll road out of Paris. We soon rushed off that costly tollway to find a free alternative route.

Making our way south, we used the back roads on some single 'suicide passing' lanes that twisted through lovely medieval villages which unfolded like ancient story books. While further down the road, like turning another page of that book, we found ourselves saturated in the lush beauty of the scenic French countryside, some areas touched by miles of vineyards stretching across the landscape that beckoned our full attention. So amazing!

A few hours later, we're cruising along the big beautiful Mediterranean coast known as the Cote d'Azur or French Riviera. This route reminded us of Southern California's iconic seacoast with breath-taking scenic views along Pacific Coast Highway, both are so tranquil.

Along the way on a dark mountain road in the Alps outside Antibes, we had a flat tire. We pulled off to the side of the road to change the tire when two kind young and handsome Gendarmeries *(French National Police)* drove up behind us. Courteously, they changed our flat tire. We were so grateful, expressing many Merci's.

When we arrived in Cannes it was 1:00 am without any hotel reservations during a raging rainstorm. So, we needed to make a few calls to find a room. Parking near a partially covered phone booth, we ran to it to skim through a French yellow page directory while being saturated by heavy pellets of rain. After dialing countless local hotels of various star ratings, we found one, The Sofitel Mediterranean, which had one available room. The hotel fairies did it again.

The sweet French woman who answered our call spoke English, thank goodness. This hotel sat on the Marina adjacent to the Boulevard de la Croisette and in walking distance to the Palais des Festivals. The receptionist could move us daily from room to room, because the guests were arriving at stagnant times throughout the week. We were not far from this hotel and jumped back into the car.

Our small twin-bedded room on the third floor had a great view of the Marina and the cityscape. We could not have been luckier to find this available room at the beginning of the Cannes Film Festival. I hadn't booked European hotel reservations in advance. My naiveté resulted from a lack of foreign travel and travel planning at all. After settling into our Cannes hotel, we crawled into our twin beds and fell fast asleep.

That next morning, we woke early to catch breakfast at the hotel's restaurant. Never missing the free breakfast included at all our hotels. After breakfast, eager to start our day, we checked in with my contacts and met other industry people; all of whom offered us a room from the reserved room blocks they held at their hotels. Crazy! But we opted to stick it out at the Sofitel. Attending numerous activities during the day with a tour guide on call made us feel like celebrities.

We had so many fun experiences while in Cannes, lunch in a Monastery on an Island, driving the wrong way on narrow streets, screening new movies, meeting producers, mingling with celebrities, dining out and drinking high priced Champagne in fancy expensive restaurants with other attendees at private parties at the Hôtel Martinez and Carlton Hotel, unforgettable memories.

The long-term friendships and contacts we developed were priceless and surreal. Grateful for all the wonderful and wild adventures we had that began in London, carried on into Paris, and then culminated in Cannes. Because we were in France, drinking wine from a box made us laugh. The warm reception, the kind and respectful treatment we received from everyone we met on this trip made us feel so very special. The French people's care and generosity throughout our stay made us not want to leave this dazzling dream.

Still, we could not lose ourselves completely to France, our young daughters, jobs, family, and friends awaited us in the United States. Once home, I rethought my career ambitions, resigned from my Courtroom Deputy Clerk's job to pursue work once again in the entertainment industry, but this time in film production.

Then I found a French Tutor for my ten-year-old Daughter, so she could learn to speak French. She was already plenty fluent in Spanish. I figured one of us had to know French very well to live in that country. Her Tutor was an older guy named George, who was French and from Marseille, France. He was a professor teaching the

French language at our local community college. He spoke English well. My daughter took private lessons from him twice a week for an hour and a half.

Six months later she graduated from sixth grade, and as the Student Council President, spoke and understood enough French to give her graduation speech in both French and English. A French couple at the graduation were so impressed they asked her how long she had been speaking French, and was surprised to learn, not long. Her pronunciation was so good. After her French lessons ended, we maintained our friendship with George for many years. He went back to Marseille a few years later and we'd correspond with him through letters.

I knew that Alexis would pick up that language quickly. My daughter learned to speak Spanish not from taking a formal class but from the various Mexican babysitters I had hired to care for her while I worked when she was a toddler up to five years old. My nephew, Ryan, also learns languages easily. He is fluent in Spanish, learned Italian, and continues to learn more languages too.

Enrolled Alexis in kindergarten at an Episcopalian school the required her to be tested. Her test results indicated an IQ level of 150. Astounded but I then understood why she learned everything so quickly like reading entire books by the time she was three years old, learning languages, and solving complicated puzzles. Had to us psychology just to relate to her level of understanding for practical situations. My life has been a roller coaster of coincidences.

This book reveals some of the early challenges I faced in my life. Then illustrating all the steps, I took to prepare for this scouting trip. Soon I would take on this French adventure to find a city to call home. Thus, helping to make my decades old dream of living in France come true.

Six French Cities

CHAPTER ONE

First Things First

Past circumstances in my adult life and a renewed sense of self led to this "it's now or never" decision to take this scouting trip to France in the fall of 2023. Over four decades, I never dismissed the idea of moving to and living in France. I always believed in the possibility and merely postponed that dream for a while. Over fifty years ago I pursued two other big dreams, the first, to move to California and the second, to work in the entertainment industry.

After living this manifested life in Hollywood that I loved, I'm grateful for the varied experiences that those realized dreams provided. Although I was content back then with my happily fulfilled life, an ever-growing career in a business I adored, a great kid, and my wonderful friendships curated in Southern California, deep down in my soul was a free loading feeling of longing.

While growing up in Chicago, I often dreamed of living in Los Angeles, Southern California's warm sunny city, especially during the brutal winter Chicago months. The West Coast sunshine, beaches, and laid-back lifestyle appealed to my sense of adventure at a very young age. Plus, this city was home to Hollywood and

Disneyland. I never understood why my Jamaican grandmother moved her family from Jamaica to Florida and then to such a cold Northern climate where only polar bears, not people should live. Later I found out her move was after my grandfather's tragic yet historical death, so that she and her children could be closer to their Jamaican family living in the windy city.

When I was 15, I volunteered as a Candy Striper at a nearby hospital assisting the nursing staff and where I had enrolled in a Nurse's Aide training program. In high school I aspired to become a Registered Nurse after my mother rebuked my desire to be a writer. She didn't think I'd make enough money writing; instead, I would need a viable career backup plan. During my junior year in high school, Chicago experienced a debilitating snow blizzard that shut down the entire city adversely affecting the southern suburbs where we lived.

I was fed up with this weather and no longer wanted to endure the cold harsh winters, ice glaciers, and snow drifts. I wanted out, wanted to travel, and be in a warmer climate. I imagined myself sitting on a California beach with the hot sun beating down on me. That cold crazy Illinois weather motivated me to find a way to leave Chicago. At 17, I applied for my social security number with two girlfriends, Roz and Susie. Then Susie and I applied for a cashier's job at a local retail store to earn a small income and save money.

Two years later, I was ready to get out from under my mother, leave my stilted teen life, our sleepy little town, and my junior college behind. I dropped out of college but would return a few years later. Many of my friends from high school went off to colleges, were getting married, and having babies. Older now, I did not want that seemingly expected lifestyle. My sights were set higher; my dreams were bigger. My growing independence and an aching to escape my teenage home motivated me to leave. I just wanted to live my life on my own. For years I had a deep desire to see the world, find adventure, and experience what else life had to offer me. But how? I needed a gap year or two or three.

In mid-December of 1969, at 19, I made my break from home by joining the United States Navy. The war in Vietnam was still raging. I happened to walk by an armed forces recruitment office in Harvey, Illinois, backed up and went inside to inquire about joining the Navy. Influenced by the fascinating stories my step-dad, Tommy told me about his time spent on ships in the Navy during World War II. That day, I joined on the spot and after signing my freedom away, my Naval recruiter said that I'd be shipping out in two weeks, leaving for Boot Camp at the US Navy Training Center, Recruit Training Command in Bainbridge, Maryland.

'That's fast,' I thought, but I was ready to go. The sooner the better. I didn't tell anyone that I had joined the Navy, not even my mother. I enlisted for three years; my military experience was worth the time spent serving my country. After my enlistment ended, I was honorably discharged and received my VA benefits. As a young adult, I learned so much more about myself and life after making that leap. I gained discipline and an atypical education from leaving home, joining the Navy, and venturing out on my own.

In the Navy, I met people from all over the U.S. and the Philippines. I evolved and matured much in those three years. During and after Bootcamp, this lifestyle was an experience similar to living on campus at a university and going to classes. We learned about military history, the laws of military Justice, and so much more. In Service school, it was about medicine.

So many trees (the nickname given to the enlisted young men attending service schools) whom while in bootcamp, us recruit WAVES were discouraged from having any kind of contact with them during our sequestered ten-week training.

We were strongly instructed and reminded daily by our company Commanding Officer, "Don't look at the trees and don't talk to the trees." Yet with all our young raging hormones, it was very hard not to look at the abundant forest surrounding us daily on the field and in the mess hall during all those secluded weeks of basic training. You know I made contact and the other girls followed my lead. Such a rule breaker.

After boot camp, I was sent to service school in Great Lakes, Illinois, where for six months I trained to be a Hospital Corpsman working in the medical field. During my three years of enlistment, I dated many young sailors and a very tall and handsome Marine officer. He was ten years older than me and drove a very cool restored black Corvette. In the company of all these young men, I was treated well, felt protected, and was very much respected.

To my surprise after that medical training, the Navy sent me to Southern California. When my plane finally landed at Los Angeles International airport (LAX,) and we disembarked, I was so excited to be in Los Angeles, I kissed the tarmac out of gratitude. It was a big "WOW!" moment for me. I was thrilled that my first big dream of moving to California had now by chance come true.

Back then in my youth, all I had was a hope and a dream but I knew in my heart that somehow and someway, I would move to California one day. This girl was genuinely ready to begin living her new life in this sunny and magnificent State, working at the U.S. Naval hospital, and embarking on a new life full of potential and different kinds of adventures. Now away from my family and childhood home, alone, and almost on my own, I felt truly unrestricted to be me and do whatever I wanted to do, even write. Instantly, I knew I could never return to my old life in Chicago to ever live there again, and I never returned except to visit.

I reported to my first duty station, the Naval Hospital at Camp Pendleton near Oceanside, California in the Fall of 1970. This is where my fully immersed and intensive medical training with seasoned doctors began. Stationed on base with the US Marines who practiced war games training all night long, so even in our barracks we could hear (load bombs blasting in air) coming from the distant mountains. Nerve racking at first. Yet I wanted to be in the Field Med Service (like in Mash) working as a Corpsman out in the trenches in Vietnam. No girls allowed.

Once settled on the base at Camp Pendleton, I could not wait to jump on a Greyhound Bus to make my way up to Los Angeles for a weekend visit. I was eager to see Hollywood, the stars on the walk of fame, handprints in cement at Grauman's Chinese Theatre, cruise through Beverly Hills, Venice Beach, and Malibu, and all the other city sites I had imagined seeing. Then dash off to Disneyland in Anaheim just south of L.A for a day of fun.

On my first full work day at the hospital's emergency room, I had my very first patient, a 19-year-old Marine who arrived in a body bag; a casualty of those war games. He had picked up a grenade that he thought was a dud, it wasn't. I won't describe what I saw inside that bag which I had to unzip; it was horrendous (an image that never leaves you).

Next patient, on the same day, was a six-month-old baby boy who arrived blue and unresponsive, and doing CPR, I could not revive. He was a victim of SIDS. So many emergencies, dependent families and military, arrived at that hospital.

Later, I was taught to perform minor surgeries. Rotating through several different hospital departments, I assisted the nurses and doctors in the Psychiatric department, on the surgical and medical ICU wards, in the lab drawing and analyzing blood and urine samples, performed inhalation therapy, and rehabbing mostly male patients in the recovery ward.

I witnessed many major injuries and devastating deaths while working on that base. A day after we participated in mass casualty training, one of the men's barracks on base caught on fire, injuring some servicemen; we quickly set up a triage outside that building to assess and treat injured while the firemen worked at putting out the fire.

My second duty station brought milder work experiences, also putting my clerical skills to the test typing up medical reports and assisting my Commanding Officer, at the Medical Center, MCRD (Marine Corps Recruit Depot) in San Diego. There I lived off base in a small bungalow I rented in Point Loma. I worked as an Xray and Medical Technician on base. We treated the Marine recruits for various injuries and ailments. I had to multi-task. We were busy.

Soon I was promoted to an NCO (non-commissioned officer), getting my first stripe as a Petty Officer Third Class. My CO suggested sending me to Officer's Candidate Training School in

Annapolis, Maryland but I didn't want a career in the Navy. I had Hollywood aspirations to be a writer and producer after my military enlistment ended. A year before my enlistment ended I bought my CO's used Oldsmobile through the Navy Federal Credit Union where I had my checking and savings accounts.

I made many weekend trips to Los Angeles and developed new friends there during my three-years serving in San Diego. I've always been extremely adventurous and fearless on my own. Self-sufficient, an introvert, and a loner by nature but highly social. Easily making friends in both cities quickly. Eventfully moving to L.A. in 1974.

My love of Hollywood's movies especially from the 30s, 40s, and 50s turned me into an avid film history buff. I loved watching those dramas, comedies, and musicals. The snappy dialogue of those early films really caught my ear and attention which later helped me develop my own writing style.

On Sundays, during my pre-teens, when my family went to their Episcopalian Church's early mass, I went to the movie matinees (that's another story). I wanted to know more about the people whose names scrolled by on the credits at the beginning and end of films. Although we had a movie camera at home, I never used it to make short movies, it never occurred to me because my focus was not on directing but on writing and producing for TV and Film.

So, I became an in-depth researcher, and then spent much time devouring all that I learned about Hollywood, the actors, writers, producers, directors, the set crews, and production staff. Scoured encyclopedias and books to read celebrity biographies and studio histories. To keep track of the Hollywood happenings, I bought and subscribed to Hollywood fan magazines and publications devoted to celebrities during the 60s and 70s like Screen Stories, Modern Screen, Flip, Jet, Ebony, and Soul Newspaper (whose owners I would later meet).

In the 70s and 80s, reading People, Essence, Premiere, the Hollywood Reporter, Variety, TV Guide, GQ, and more helped me stay in touch with the inner 'goings on' of Hollywood. Later, I purchased reference books about TV shows and Films, even seeking out industry directories for production companies and literary agencies. I built a massive entertainment resources library of my own. I knew a lot about Hollywood back then, still do today.

Thoroughly captivated by the filmmaking process, I ached to go to Hollywood to work in the film industry and learn how movies were made first hand. I did not know how difficult it would be to break into show business but I did and my knowledge about the business was invaluable. Ultimately becoming a writer and producer was my main goal.

This longing to work in TV materialized in the 1970s after my resume reached Norman Lear's company which resulted in me working for Dinah Shore. While working in Hollywood, I had many wonderful experiences, met many talented people, made tons of friends, and accomplished other goals on my long 'must do and experience' list.

Even though my life took many dramatic twists and turns, the one thing I never lost was hope, my humor, my dreams, and my love for life. I'm a drifter who also likes stability but not being tied down. I get bored easily. So, I've learned many skills, worked at many jobs, learned to adapt to adverse situations and perform effectively in many different roles over the decades. I'm autodidactic with an eidetic (photographic) memory, still at my age. So, I learn and remember tasks quickly.

Thus, I was never the type of person who could ever work for one employer or do the same task for thirty years. Bravo to those who can, I'm just too curious and spontaneous. I like being busy, it's mentally stimulating. I must have variety in my life or boredom sets in. I always had a deep desire to learn something new every day, figure things out like a dog with a bone, and continue working on my personal development. Meeting new people, having loads of fun, and gaining new insights and experiences are important to me. Probably why I love traveling so much. Ambitious, resilient, and persistent are the three words to best describe me.

I started writing and jotting down my thoughts from the moment I learned how to read and write. I was precocious and inquisitive, always asking "Why?" Growing up in a large Jamaican family on Chicago's West side, we had many immigrant neighbors *(Polish, German, Italian, Irish, Jewish, Jamaican, and Mexican)*. I learned firsthand about those cultures. Playing with our neighbors' kids, I learned their traditions, ate their cuisines which ignited my desire to try different foods and inspired my future adventures.

My big Jamaican family stretched across the country, the Caribbean, and into the UK. We loved to travel; usually by car on roads and highways all around the United States. Sometimes in multiple car caravans, visiting our extended family while learning the history of America. I was the navigator, the map keeper. Maps were much easier for me to understand.

My love for history and travel was cultivated early by all those annual family adventures around the USA. We also went to three World Fairs in the 1960s, *(Seattle '62, New York '64 and Montreal '67)*. My life growing up was full of fun and educational activities.

Another opportunity to visit France came about in the winter of 1996. This time traveling with my daughter, Alexis to her College Orientation at the American University in Paris on a scholarship to study art and photography. She applied for this French study aboard program through Clark University in Worcester, Massachusetts where she was enrolled and studying Psychology.

I wanted her to study on the east coast so she could experience living away from home on her own. She has always been inquisitive and creative. I raised my daughter to be strong and independent. Alexis is a polyglot, fluent in French; she speaks six other languages, including American Sign Language (ASL) which she began learning on her own by watching a show on PBS when she was seven years old. Decades before she took a college course in ASL. She's exceptionally artistic too.

After our joint experience in Paris, neither of us wanted to leave. Sadly, I returned home after an enjoyable week, while my daughter stayed in Paris to study for a year. I was so happy that she was able to have this life changing experience of studying and living in France. Hiring, George, the French tutor, all those years ago was a blessing. Alexis' early language learning and years of taking French throughout high school and college really paid off. Another small dream realized.

Removing The Biggest Obstacles

By 2015, I felt the time had come to realize my third big dream. Before I could even think about leaving the country, I had to resolve a few things first. As I began putting my plan to relocate into motion, I knew I had to get a divorce but I couldn't afford to hire an attorney.

Therefore, I would have to pay the court fee, fill out all the paperwork, and file those documents myself. After which I could restore my maiden name and then update my last name on all my separate personal and financial accounts including Social Security, a process once started would take several months to accomplish.

Also, my Passport and Global Entry would have to be renewed with my maiden name change. Not only was I excited and unafraid to begin this journey, but relieved to be closer to my dream. At long last I was more determined than ever to see this goal through. Tying up the loose ends meant I had much work to do before I could ever leave the country. It would take eight years before I finalized my divorce and fully restored my finances.

Externally, no one knows anyone's unusual life circumstances or even what someone deals with in a relationship, or the inner personal struggles you may face daily. People can only see what you offer to show externally, some may speculate or judge. Before I tied the knot in 1990, my life was drama free and going very well.

I was extremely happy living my fast-paced single life in L.A. Working as an executive assistant in the entertainment industry, I had a wonderful career that I loved. I raised my daughter and spent quality time with my family and friends. My daughter and I traveled a great deal. Having already accomplished a lot of goals in my 30s, my life was one of contentment. I even saved money without a 401K plan, which I don't think existed back then wasn't offered in my benefits package.

Towards the end of 1989, I had everything I wanted but not a loving relationship. Although I had dated a few fun guys to be around, none were husband material. I was looking for like mindedness and stability in a life partner not an immature party animal. Someone intelligent with a sense of humor and a strong work ethic who wasn't a substance abuser.

All qualities that were hard to find in many men living in Los Angeles. People come to this town to run away from something, or to become something, or to reinvent themselves. I just wanted a no nonsense, well-adjusted, mature, and normal male who didn't want to be in show business.

Then in April 1990, on a blind date arranged by a friend who thought we had a lot in common; I met a guy who looked like an older George Clooney, soon fell in love, and got engaged. We married within four months of meeting. I threw caution to the wind, even when people asked, "Why the rush?" If I didn't marry now, I probably would never marry anyone, I thought.

This was my first marriage. I was 40 and my daughter was turning 15. Her dad, Clarence Paul, was a former Motown Producer, Composer and Writer, and 22 years older than me. We met in a recording studio and dated for a while. After our daughter was born, he asked me to marry him several times; and each time I said no. I was very goal oriented and more focused on my career.

Back then I wasn't ready for marriage and especially not to someone who was older, had already experienced a lot in life, and was set in his ways. Plus, he attracted a Harem of women. I was young but not foolish. We never married, lived our separate lives, co-parented, and remained very close friends for over two decades until his death in 1995. My daughter is the executor of his estate.

Finally, with this new guy, I thought I had met *"the one."* However, within a few months of our marriage, I knew it was a big mistake. This man was not the same charming person he had portrayed himself to be in the beginning of our courtship. He had a very dark Dr. Jekel/Mr. Hyde personality.

He arrived in my life carrying lots of heavy baggage, a criminal history, two disgruntled ex-wives, and two older children from his first marriage whom he had withdrawn from entirely. He had no lose ties or close friends like a normal person. Sadly, he missed a lot of the precious moments and memories that life produces from having those connections we make with our families and friends.

I brought no baggage or drama into our marriage; I had a clean slate, very strong, intact, and loving outside relationships. So, I had no clue that my fantastic little curated world was about to collapse completely, like a building imploding and being brought down from a single blast.

Foolishly, I did not get out of that strained marriage earlier when I had an opportunity to leave. Instead, emotionally invested, I tried to help him be a better person. Over time, I realized that I couldn't fix the relationship or my husband. Nor was I responsible for his behavior or his past life. My married life was a disaster and not what I had expected or wanted. Somehow, I was stuck in a huge rut, bonded by emotion and misplaced loyalty. Repeating my mother's pattern of engaging in bad relationships. I knew better.

Still not one for giving up, I stayed *as many do* and tried to make the marriage work. I could not do it alone though. Early in our marriage, I sought individual therapy for him. We also attended couples counseling together but our irreparable relationship was doomed from the start. He didn't want to continue therapy, nor did he continue the court ordered anger management sessions resulting from an earlier incident he had with a neighbor. Our marriage was broken like an old car that I kept trying to fix with old spare parts from a junk yard. This relationship like a lemon car was never going to work.

My husband abused illegal drugs and alcohol which I didn't know until well after our marriage. I didn't use drugs and I detested drug use. He was deceptive, a master liar; good at hiding his ill deeds, and his infidelity. He was also a volatile alcoholic, angry, verbally abusive, and more unfaithful than I could have imagined. From his medical visits, I soon learned that he was Bipolar; a mental disorder that he continued to deny. However, his erratic behavior, mood swings, bad judgement, and his medications confirmed that diagnosis.

Our relationship was very toxic and explosive at times. I felt deceived by him and was very disappointed. Not a partnership at all. I endured mental, emotional, and sometimes physical abuse for years. I fought back though, I'm no victim. The police became a constant fixture in our lives. Still, I stayed but not because I wanted to, I had to for a while. Financially, I had no clear way out. My savings dwindled paying for his bad acts and behavior. Our only working partnership was from the various short term business ventures we started together.

People can be critical and think it's easy to walk away from an abusive relationship, well it isn't. Usually, there are too many underlying factors and binding ties; strong emotional bonds, fear for self and others, finances, and mingled personal property. Also, a misplaced sense of loyalty or sense of security in an unsafe space. So, if you've never walked in those shoes, you can't even imagine just how uncomfortable, painful, and difficult it can be just trying to exist. However, recognizing my mistakes, nonetheless, I dealt with these issues for three decades.

Finally, one day my mental exhaustion caused me to shut down and go on strike. I refused to do anything. All I could do was go to work, come home, and go straight to bed. He could fend for himself. Over time, my optimistic outlook and positive personality were no match for his dark arrogance, depraved ethics, and pessimistic attitude about life. I had many friends, he had none. I was close to my family; he was estranged from his own, except for his mother whom I adored.

I thought I loved him, and at first, I did, but as those layers of his personality shed like the summer skin of a snake, I saw a different and darker side of this man which I did not like nor could I continue to love. He was narcissistic, manipulative, and he tried to control me, but I was stubborn, defiant, and had an inner strength that he could not penetrate nor dismantle no matter how much he tried. I'm a warrior. I can't give up.

Eventually his frustration, threats, and actions toward me finally ended our marriage but not peacefully at first. In the beginning, I was embarrassed to tell anyone about my house of horrors. Not wanting my family to get involved, I remained silent. How could I be in this position? And how do I get out of it? I needed to leave him; needed an exit plan.

It took time to untangle my life from his and to break free. The first step was to remove my name from all our joint accounts: banking, credit cards, and household bills. During this marriage, I attempted to have a normal life and maintain a stable environment for my daughter while combating his demons. My fading mental and emotional health made me realize that I had to break completely free of him to save myself. Once I no longer cared about the marriage, that was my breaking point. I was done with his erratic actions, mental breaks, and disgusting behavior, still it wasn't easy to untie that knot. Becoming less committed, I had nothing left to contribute to him or that faded relationship.

Finally in 2015, he had another violent psychotic break that affected my safety which finally ended this marriage and our living together. Faced with a life and death turn of events, he was out of my life. We separated permanently. He went to prison again. The malicious circumstances leading up to that incident resulted in me getting from the court a ten-year protective order that expires in 2025, he could not have any contact with me at all. Still, I asked the Judge for limited phone contact to divide up our personal property and assets.

My facial expression showed my relief and happiness to be alive and away from him for good. That protective order was the gift that freed me completely from the emotional and physical bond that held me hostage to that man for way too long. I thank the female judge who laid it on the line, admonished him in court for his rotten behavior toward me which he admitted to. It was the turning point that set me free.

Now on my own and feeling safer, I had renewed confidence. I moved on and had no intention of ever returning to that marriage, him, or that life ever again. I kept that promise. I wanted more out of life and I tried to pick up where I had left off before we were married. It wasn't easy at first but I continued to pave a new path and reconnect with lost friends.

More confident and feeling safer, I began restructuring my single life and getting back on my feet. Still not solvent, I was determined to bounce back and turn my life around once more. Although not legally separated or divorced yet, I felt content to now be living alone. After my 25-year marriage ended in separation, divorce was looming. Over time I restored my credit, finances, and my mental health. It took nearly a decade before fully recovering emotionally and financially, but so worth the time it took for me to succeed.

The one thing I learned from all of my crazy experiences was my capacity to stay strong and believe. I did not allow the bad times to bring me down. I held onto all of my dreams, kept working toward my goals and achieving them one step at a time. Deep down I knew I'd survive and that one day I'd see this dream true.

Celestine Cooley

Tying Up Loose Ends

Letting go of my two lingering and obligations, my dysfunctional marriage and my travel business were priorities which would set me free completely. Then I could focus on my plans to leave the country. At age 62, I applied early for my social security retirement, rather than waiting until my official retirement date, a mistake I now regret.

During those early years from 2013-2017, I focused on slowly rebuilding my travel business. Realistically an additional income was needed while trying to get this business off the ground. Although I thought my corporate working days were behind me, they weren't. Ultimately, I would have to go back to work in entertainment to achieve my financial goals. Determination to fulfill my goals guided me.

The separation led me to seek a few months of trauma therapy. I was taking anxiety medication to help me cope and feel much better mentally. Now, I could focus and continue operating my homebased travel agency full-time while living on my retirement income for two years. By mid-2017, I had grown increasingly tired of struggling, I was miserable, exhausted, and my travel business had become unfulfilling. The escalating costs of everything left me conflicted and concerned about my future.

Although I had loved living in Los Angeles for the last 50 years, it was time to move on. Realistically, I knew after retiring that my Social Security income alone would not allow me to continue living in this city or maintaining the same lifestyle I had while working in entertainment. I did not want to work forever, I had already worked too long. My life and living situation would have to change and fast.

In the meantime, I created a way to generate a passive income on the side by building a website to sell my business forms and documents to travel agents. It did well by word of mouth and with very little marketing. Mentally exhausted I needed a break from my travel business, which no longer brought me the same joy or success it had in the beginning back in the mid-90s. Even though I love traveling and enjoyed helping others travel. My heart was no longer in it. Instead, I was longing to write. Still too many distractions.

By now, I needed a real change, no job, no business, just rest to figure out my next steps. I wanted to be a full-time writer, but I needed a steady substantial income. My current financial situation certainly would not qualify me for a French Visa. That dream had to wait again. Instead of taking a break, I started working temporary administrative positions for various corporate executives in the entertainment industry to rebuild my finances and survive the high cost of living in this city. It was the next step-up I needed to take.

My therapist suggested that I get a canine companion. Colonel came into my life in 2016 by coincidence. Then he was two years old and belonged to my disabled wheelchair bound neighbor who lived in our apartment complex across the courtyard from me. I knew Colonel's mother, Princess, and saw him right after his birth. Feeling sorry for Colonel, I agreed to walk him about three times a day. Often puppy sitting duties for Colonel whenever his owner spent time in the hospital.

It was fall and I had just returned from a trip to Costa Rica, while rolling my suitcase towards my apartment, Colonel's owner approached me in his wheelchair, and said,

"Here, Colonel is your dog now."

Then he handed me the little dog with his leash and harness. I wasn't surprised, but knew it would only be a matter of time before the owner gave me his dog. Colonel and I had already bonded and we loved each other. He enjoyed going on our walks. This dog was now secure and very content living with me. And I was happy to have him in my life.

His presence was impactful. The timing of our unity was right for us both. We needed each other. I missed our German Shepards. Dogs do offer good therapy and companionship. Colonel had not been properly trained at all. Over several months I trained him to be my service dog. He learned obedience and commands quickly, understanding his task and how to assist me.

Between 2017 and 2018, my time was very flexible so I began alternating my temporary work assignments between three studios, Universal Studios, Dick Clark Productions, and MGM Studios. Usually working in various departments like Labor Relations and VFX (visual effects) as an Executive Assistant for film and TV executives.

Often requested by the other assistants who needed me to sit in for them temporarily. Just the type of variety that I enjoyed which kept my mind from drifting too far off into the future. I also worked for various corporations in sales and marketing as a temporary EA (executive assistant) in the early years of my marriage.

In 2016, my sister and I began taking sister trips together each year going to Canada, Mexico, Seattle, Sonoma, Napa, and San Francisco. Over time, I realized that I didn't enjoy traveling with other people. I preferred renting a car and taking solo trips to wineries around California. I'd visit family in San Diego, and in Nevada with Colonel as my companion.

Now working steadily, I felt better about my quality of life in Los Angeles, still I knew it wouldn't last. I couldn't work forever nor did I want to. I am older now, near 70, tired, and so very ready to retire and move on. Early in 2019, I was recommended for a temporary job by MGM's Human Resources to work for a newly hired MGM Executive in Consumer Products located in Beverly Hills. This temp job would eventually become a permanent Administrative Assistant position.

For many years I worked steadily through the Friedman Personnel Agency thanks to my account executive and close friend, Luise Hamaguchi who always kept me employed. Luise is a very talented Actress and singer too. She called me about the MGM Consumer Products position and to set up an interview with the newly hired EVP, Robert Marick. We hit it off right away.

At the time, I was uncertain about my future. So, this job occurred when I needed it the most. My income increased, accelerating my savings. My stability, happiness, and sense of security was restored. I loved working in Consumer Products at MGM with Robert, my seasoned new boss, and our knowledgeable and very talented teammates *(Tricia, Lynn, Karol, Meghan, Julie, Ricardo, Sandee, Ben, Shannon, Laurie, Matt G, Matt S, Andrew, Pamela, Shant, and Denny)*. We all had so much fun working together! Soon my stress diminished, I thought I could hold out for five years from my hire date. After which I could comfortably retire and move to France.

Celestine Cooley

It's Time to Move On

Working full time for a year now, I'm finally being paid a decent salary. For eight years, I lived without owning a car thanks to y ex. Instead, I would rent cars when I needed to take a trip or attend a travel agent function far away.

By now, I had grown tired of taking the bus to and from these studio jobs and dealing with public transportation's continuous cast of characters disrupting the bus service in some way nearly every day. My 15-mile commute by two buses each way to work from the San Fernando Valley to Beverly Hills usually took about 90 minutes, sometimes longer. Fed up, I wanted a new car not some used junker.

So, in November of 2019, I went to the LA Auto Show to have a thorough look at the cars I had an interest in buying. Then in December to celebrate all my big achievements, I ordered my car online, and three weeks later purchased it from a local Chevrolet dealership. I selected a shiny new black Metallic 2020 Chevy Equinox LT Turbo 2.0 SUV, fully loaded. It was my dream car, the same model that I admired at the auto show a month earlier.

This small SUV was roomy, safe, mechanically sound, and served its needed purpose. My new car was a Christmas present to myself. It was expensive and came wrapped with a big red bow and ribbon. Thrilled to have a car again. I'd come a long way financially in those four years since my separation, I was so proud of myself.

When Covid-19 hit in March 2020, all travel and other public activities came to a standstill. While isolated and working from home my attitude about my present life situation had changed again greatly. Pretty much done with my old life but hanging in there just a while longer to meet my financial goal. I concentrated not only on work but on myself, my future in retirement, and this nagging dream to relocate to France sooner. A strong feeling I could not shake.

My passion for being a travel agent faded completely, I announced the closing of my agency in 2021. Then during mid-March of 2022, Amazon purchased MGM Studios. As the studio began to reorganize and change significantly, my thoughts about retiring later also changed.

After working so diligently, I had rebuilt my single life and became financially secure. At least, I would have enough savings to begin the next chapter of my new life which would include being a writer I thought with the time to write.

My road trips to Central California's wine country, attending wine festivals, and experiencing a different environment, stirred my imagination about what it would feel like to live in France, while enjoying a different lifestyle surrounded by similar vineyards. I wanted that simpler life in retirement. This faster pace was beginning to wear me down. I was exhausted most days.

Older now and with fewer obligations, I begin to seriously research and plan my dream move to France. Diligently, I studied French as I wrapped my head around the idea of living in a country where I would have to learn the language. I wasn't aging in reverse. If I was really going to relocate to France then I better start preparing for that move right now.

So, to stay organized and map out my plan I created a time line chart in excel with the "things to do" like when to contact shipping companies for quotes, when to start looking for short term accommodations, and when to make various appointments for myself and Colonel's healthcare. Through the pandemic, I was so restless. All I could think about was living in France and constantly being badgered by "you should make this move now!" thought every single day.

Still separated from my husband, the shadow of that marriage weighed heavily on my mind. I didn't feel totally free. By July 2022, I had grown weary of dragging that chain and ready to file for divorce. Downloading the divorce forms was easy. I filled them out completely, prepared the copies for the court and copies to send to my husband, and then made the short trip to the Clerk's Office at the Courthouse in Van Nuys to file those papers.

My husband was on board after we had an earlier conversation about legally ending our marriage. He agreed. Surprisingly, our divorce was amicable, neither one of us wanted any financial support from the other. Our personal assets and all property had been divided up years before.

By January 2023, my divorce was finalized. Happiness! Free at last. I shed the "Mrs." title for good by restoring my maiden name, Cooley, on all my accounts. Quickly, I left that old life behind, never looked back, and reemerged like an impatient butterfly from a sturdy cocoon. The divorce restored my maiden name, my freedom, and my sense of self. Unexpectedly, my last name change would play an important role in my French residency.

As the threat of Covid lifted, my co-workers and I were summoned back to the office a few days a week. I took Colonel with me since Amazon allowed dogs at work. Working from home remotely through Covid meant that Colonel became accustomed to being by my side every single day. We were inseparable. He had severe separation anxiety when left home alone for too long. Which gave me anxiety just by watching his anxious behavior on my home security camera.

He'd spend most of the day pacing, barking, howling, and running to the front door. Then jumping on a chair near my front window, sticking his nose through the blinds to look outside and bark some more. He'd take a nap then awaken to start that anxiety drill again throughout the day. Talking to him on my security camera only escalated his behavior, making him more anxious.

This reaction was a trauma stemming from being left alone for four days in his old owner's apartment. We didn't know how long he had been without food or water. He was in distress. His incessive barking woke me up at 1:00 am one morning. So, I went to see why he was crying and barking so much. Knocking on my neighbor's door, no one answers. I wake up the apartment manager who tells me that the owner is in the hospital. The manager called animal services, he would not let me take care of Colonel until the owner returned. The next day I tracked down Colonel's owner at a nearby hospital. Then got him to sign a letter authorizing me to retrieve Colonel from the animal shelter. I don't like leaving my dog alone, we both get anxious and he knows I need him and he needs to be with me all the time.

Once again, I started taking risks, trying new things, traveling more, and reconnecting with old friends. Happier now and ready to move forward with my retirement plans to live out my dream. I could feel a new chapter in my life unfolding. Suddenly one day I felt totally at peace knowing I had cleared that slate, my obligations, and the emotional bond that once held me hostage for 32 years, now broken forever.

During the strains of that marriage, I learned a lot about myself; how to channel my inner strength, and my ability to tolerate the intolerable. Through it all, I held tightly onto my self-esteem, my sense of humor, and most of all my dream. Also, through all the drama and madness of that relationship I managed to raise a smart, strong, beautiful, compassionate, and independent daughter, now an adult. We still have a very close bond. I love Alexis very much.

Newly single, and with no other ties or obligations outside of my job, I could laser focus on leaving the country, to make my own decisions, and do whatever I wanted to do on my terms. It was now, "all about me." Finally, I could exhale, walk tall, and move on. This new lease on life was about to get much better.

Six French Cities

Learning French and French History

I still had many questions. Plus, I wanted to know how other expats who relocated adapted to living in France, so I began following YouTuber, like Oliver & Lina Gee (The Earful Tower Podcasts), an Australian, Jay Swanson (Paris in my Pocket) from Spokane, and other Americans who live in Paris. Then in late 2023, I began following An and Jeff Scott, (Postcards from Our Golden Years) retirees from Florida who were preparing for their move to France.

They are all thriving in France. I found these influencers to be very creditable and knowledgeable about the relocation process. Most helpful in every way, they answered many of my questions which made planning my exploratory trip a lot simpler.

An and Jeff moved to Nice around the same time that I moved to France. Much of their information, expertise, and experience helped me to make the right decisions about my relocation planning throughout this journey. I've connected with them all and still follow their channels. I enjoy their fun and informative Vlogs about living in France. You will too.

The biggest question I had was whether I needed to speak French fluently? Should I enroll in French language classes now? Of course, I wasn't at all fluent in French, nowhere near that level. Out of curiosity, I took the free online French language assessment through Alliance Française in Pasadena. I wanted to see how much French I actually remembered from High School.

Surprisingly, I tested at the A2 intermediate level. My high school French along with various French language learning tools I used over time helped with that assessment. Since I was working in Beverly Hills, taking their night French classes across town in Pasadena was logistically impossible. I did not want to take those classes online.

Still this A2 level, although intermediate, is basic French not conversational. Sure, I could identify words and phrases but I was unable to understand spoken French or to have a basic conversation. I needed to resume my French studies. Instead of taking an in-classroom French language course, I preferred to learn on my own. My daughter suggested I try the language learning App Duolingo to review the French basics and learn more French.

Starting with the free Duolingo course, then after a year in 2021, I moved on to the paid Super Duolingo course. Learning French on my own was easier using Duolingo than other audio courses I tried, removing the pressure of trying to keep up in a traditional immersive class for now. Daily I could move through Duolingo lessons at my own pace.

To enhance my self-learning, I bought French short stories, flash cards for words and phrases, a 501 French Verbs book, Dictionaries, and workbooks to learn verb conjugation; plus, more grammar, and practiced my pronunciation. It became a frustrating ordeal to learn French quickly. There is no quick way to learn French. It takes years.

Still, my lack of knowing this language well was not a barrier to my goal. I was persistent and consistent in my studies and in my desire to migrate to France sooner. I knew that more French people spoke English even if they didn't want to.

Feeling I knew enough to get by on my limited French for a

little while. For French pronunciation, YouTube University was helpful, watching videos in French, and listening to the sounds of words. I learned more vocabulary, phrases, and language etiquette from French speakers. I watched French cartoons online as my daughter had suggested.

Plus, I listened to audio books and podcasts in French. I watched films, newscasts, and television series all in French at first with English subtitles. I began speaking French aloud in my voice recorder to listen to how I pronounced French words and sentences, if correctly or not. It's an ongoing exercise. My pronunciation is going to take time, which I will have a lot of to learn French.

As my vocabulary grew, I was able to switch to French subtitles on TV. Listening to spoken French helped me recognize some words and phrases I knew more often. In the beginning, I couldn't understand any spoken French whatsoever. The French speak very fast, and the words we learn in school or on these apps are not the same way that the French speak, often abbreviating or cutting off words. In different regions there are different French dialects to understand too. However, all the methods I used really helped to improve my French.

My ability to speak French has not come easy, along with some comprehension. Being able to read and write in French helps a lot. I continue to learn. Although I understand French better, not being my native language, it's still a challenge when not using it daily.

French is a difficult language to learn at any age. So, I use two translation Apps, Google Translate and Deepl when needed in a crunch. Google translate now has a new learning feature where you can practice speaking everyday phrases for getting around a city, using scenarios shown on that platform. It's a handy new tool that was in the beta testing phase.

There are other language Apps like Babel and Rosetta Stone which are great tools to use in the beginning as well. Immersive French language courses which aren't cheap are available either privately or in a classroom. Taking a French language course in a classroom setting to learn this language is probably more ideal for most people and it is the best way to learn any language if you want to comprehend and carry on conversations. However, if you've never studied French or have a minimum knowledge of it then being in an immersive classroom to learn it could be a frustrating experience for beginners.

Over these years, I have spent a great deal of time and effort dedicated to learning French on my own. So far, my efforts have paid off since I've reached the A2-B1 intermediate level. Still, I am not very adept at French conversation. I don't feel confident enough to carry on a full discussion in French. Fluency is at level C2 under DELF and CEFR proficiency tests. My goal is to become fluent in French.

Alternatively, I plan to take a formal French course at a university in France. At my age learning this language is no longer a requirement to live in France. But it is a requirement for me, since I've always wanted to be able to speak French well. I will someday.

There are French language level requirements for obtaining some French Visas which constantly change. However, I'm not going to explain what level is needed for what Visa type, since that information can be found online through the French Consulate's website which gets updated occasionally. It's a good place to start researching if you are interested in moving to and living in France.

Additionally, I was curious to learn more about French history and culture. So, I purchased Audiobooks to listen to on my drive to and from work about the history of France, events, and of very prominent historical figures. I researched the country's various regions and smaller cities in France. Years before, when this idea of moving to France resurfaced, I considered moving to Paris. But after watching Paris YouTube videos I realized that Paris was a big, hectic, crowded, and noisy city like Los Angeles.

Instead, I should look at smaller cities with the same appeal as Paris. So, I watched videos about other French cities too. After all my research and attempts to relearn French, I had lots of information to digest. My excitement grew stronger over the possibility of realizing this now activated dream.

Accordingly, I also knew this move would involve much planning and expense before jumping on a flight to France. Consequently, I decided to take this scouting trip to fulfill that promise I made to myself decades ago. Now with a clearer vision I felt more confident in my decision. Without hesitation, I began putting together the pieces of my exploratory trip and scheduling it for the fall of 2023.

The following chapters of this book cover my planning and execution of this journey to explore six smaller cities in France. I recount my whirlwind experiences of traveling by train with Colonel through five regions of France, stopping to explore city after city on my list and then finally choosing a French city in which to live and why.

Celestine Cooley

CHAPTER TWO

Executing the Scouting Plan

Before I could even think about moving or putting down roots, I knew I had to go to France and explore a few cities. Although I had researched the options for moving to France, such as the type of Visa I needed and the financial requirements to live in France, I had not decided on a city in which to live. Even after reading about other expats who also made the leap, I needed to learn more about relocating and living in France.

Personally, how could I know what living in France was like without experiencing it myself? It meant spending some time exploring that country to find out if I could adapt to living there now. Assessing the time needed, I figured I would need at least a three-weeks minimum to size up French cities, and ultimately finding the one that best suited my list of needs and wants.

The Corona Virus caused many countries like France to close their borders in 2020 and 2021, but now two years later foreign travel to Europe was slowly beginning to ramp up again. Aggravated with myself that I'm still working at my age which was never in my life's plans before I had gotten married. Still, I'm determined to retire sooner than my original five-year plan. However, the pending question remained, where to live in France? So many potential expats find themselves in this same predicament before planning a move and taking a scouting trip.

France is a large country consisting of 18 regions with different climates, dialects, and traditions. Each French city or village is unique with their individual histories and traditions. So, there was much for me to consider when choosing a place to live in France. This trip to France wasn't going to be just a leisurely vacation.

Although I would be a tourist, my goal was to live like a local to find out how suitable a city would be for me. It would be like a working vacation. I would not be lying on a beach all day or partaking in many tourist activities for the heck of it. Nope, my time there would be more purposeful and intentional. Looking for the ideal place to live was going to take a lot of planning. After this trip, I would be returning to France not as a tourist but as an expat residing in France permanently. So, I had to be certain about where I wanted to land.

Originally, I had planned to take this trip in May of 2023. Since 2019, my accumulated vacation time allowed me to take much time off from work. This trip would require more than two weeks to properly plan and arrange such an intricate trip, the necessary components (transportation, lodging, tours) needed for traveling and bringing my dog along.

So, I pushed the date up to September. I didn't want to rush through the planning process because of its complexity involving several cities. Instead, opting for a three-week litmus test to immerse myself into the culture and prove whether I could acclimate and enjoy living in France or not, even with my limited French and limited income. I wanted to find the city that spoke to me loudly and checked all my 'must have' boxes.

Of course, this trip would also answer the many questions stuck in my mind about making this transition. For instance, could I live comfortably and navigate successfully through France with my limited language skills? Could I live without the simple creature comforts I'd grown accustomed to having in the US?

What about adapting to the French customs that are much different from mine? Would the French locals be friendly and accepting? Would I feel safe and secure? Could I find an apartment to rent easily? I wasn't interested in buying property. Could I live without a car? Find a doctor? Get my same medications? Find a good Veterinarian for Colonel? Feel connected? So many questions needed answers.

France is not Paris. There are many more cities to consider. What region would be most ideal for me? And the climate is important too? I like warm weather, not too hot or too cold. Sure, I was aware of the larger cities like Strasbourg and Marseille but what about the smaller ones? The Suburbs? The Countryside?

Which cities should I visit on this trip? I knew living in a Village would be too remote, I'd need a car to get to resources like larger supermarkets, doctors, and hospitals found in the surrounding cities. I needed a walkable city, a quiet neighborhood, and good public transportations to conveniently get around town.

All these questions and considerations raced around in my mind. I wanted answers before I could pack up and leave the United

States all alone at my age. I could not answer these questions by sitting on my couch in L.A. It was those real-life experiences and the cultural immersion that one can only get by going to a place.

And I had to be realistic because moving is expensive, laborious, and it also takes a huge leap of faith. Moving abroad is an enormous life changing experience. I would be on my own across an ocean and thousands of miles away from my family and friends. Once I made the decision to move to France there would be no turning back on my part. France was going to be my home for the remainder of my life. Confident to make this move, I just had to make sure that I made the right decision about the city because this dream was no whim.

Weighted down with these logical and logistic questions, I picked up my physical Michelin paper map of France, spread it out on my dining table and began selecting cities to visit. As a former travel agent, and from my prior research and visits, already I knew a lot about the various regions and smaller cities in France. Still, I wasn't certain about which region or city would be ideal for me.

Accordingly, I commenced planning my route in a logical way to make traveling easier when going from one city to the next. I was leaning toward traveling by train since the time I'd have to spend scouting through France was short. Desperately growing tired of my country's divisiveness, crime, homelessness, and high cost of living, just intensified my emotional state and motivation.

Drastically, my life and income would change after retiring. That thought plagued me daily. So, I had to act sooner than later, rethinking when to retire. Aging, I was mostly concerned about keeping a roof over my head, my health, and my physical safety here in America. Although my retirement plans were about two years away, I had my sights set on moving to France earlier, before the U.S. elections in November 2024.

Before the pandemic, an ever-present and nagging feeling kept urging me to decide about where to live in France and when to move. It was a decision I needed behind me and out of my head. My concerns are valid. The fact that once I retired, I would not be able to afford to live anywhere in the United States on my social security retirement alone, weighed heavily on my mind. I like living alone.

Can't imagine being forced to live in Los Angeles and then need a roommate just to split the cost of rent and utilities. I am not into having roommates like some college kid, I need my own space and peace. Numerous seniors are in this same financial boat when they retire. Many seniors were not privileged or had good jobs that included 401K savings, brokerage accounts or big pensions when they retired.

Plus, savings do not last very long if you rely on them to live on. I did not want to struggle financially in Los Angeles. Instead find a better way to live somewhere else comfortably on less and also be able to write in peace. France fits my financial scheme nicely and offers me a better and much quieter lifestyle.

Being able to write full-time was high on my list of retirement activities. I just needed the right environment in which to do it. Most days in Los Angeles, I could not write without distractions because there was too much noise, loud music, and police activity around my apartment. Lots of crime and gang activity.

Initially, I thought that Paris was where I wanted to live. I love Paris. I am very familiar with that city. However, I no longer wanted to live in another big noisy city like Los Angeles. Paris is expensive. Los Angeles is expensive. I'm not interested in trading one big expensive city for another big expensive city to live in retirement. Also, I was looking for a little solitude because I wanted to slow down my life's pace and enjoy the remainder of my life more peacefully and leisurely.

A less congested, slower paced, quieter, flatter, and much more affordable for living with a higher quality of life. Am I asking for too much by wanting to feel safe and secure, to be comfortable, and partake in inexpensive activities while I live within my meager means going forward. I also wanted to travel more by train. Subsequently, I began focusing on a few smaller French cities that would very much satisfy my retirement needs for a slower paced life, safer, and quieter environment. More importantly, I was also seeking relaxation and peace of mind. Peace is extremely important to me at my age.

Some of the smaller cities offered a similar culture as Paris, walkability, great restaurants, an expat community, fun activities, green spaces, wine, and most importantly no subways, just excellent above the ground public transportation like trams and buses. All necessary and important aspects of a life that I perceived as being mentally and physically healthier. Major factors to consider and check off my 'must have' list as I planned my six-city scouting trip.

Once I knew where I was going to put down roots in France, then I could realistically start planning my move. First, I thoroughly researched the six cities I chose off the map to visit. It is important to get a real sense of a city's vibe, its access to transportation, its walkability, the available activities of interest, the crime statistics, local culture, affordability, housing costs, infrastructure, and the friendliness of the locals. A city where I would feel safe and at home immediately.

A French city where I could get by on my limited French and finances. In addition, I wanted to have access to a diverse English-speaking expat community which is essential when you land in a new country for cultivating new friendships, having a supportive network, and obtaining helpful information about the city in which I choose to live.

I've seen expat posts telling people not to rely on expat communities in France because you want to immerse yourself in French culture. Sure, you do, but that advice is not practical for someone who first arrives in a country, speaks little French if any, is without any ties, friends or family living there. You will need the support of people who live in that city and speak your language as well as French to help when you run into issues or need help locating services.

Expats have knowledge about the place and if needed can help you navigate and adapt to your new city. So many expats have lived in France for decades and they do speak French fluently. So don't listen to the naysayers. Had I listened to people who could not understand or see my vision, I'd still be living in Chicago.

Relocating to another country isn't easy, it takes a lot of research, planning, and adjustment. As a retiree moving to France is easier than someone still of working age, thinking they can find a job in France. Working in France isn't an option because French companies must hire French natives first to fill vacant job roles. Also, the ability to speak French fluently is necessary to get a job in France to work for French companies. Those companies have to show that you qualify more than a French person, or that they have exhausted their pool of qualified French candidates.

Foreign companies operating in France must offer non-EU candidates a job before they enter France. You'll need an employment contract. Plus, entering France on a visitor Visa, you are not allowed to work. However, if you are setting up your own company, then you will need to apply for a different Visa, one for entrepreneurs. There are various Visa types for other professions too. This is why research is very important rather than assuming you can move to France and find a job easily. You can't, especially coming from the USA.

For my many reasons, I researched and in advance specifically chose these six cities across five regions to visit and explore over three weeks: Bordeaux, Biarritz, Toulouse, Nice, Lyon, and Paris. I knew it was going to be a challenging trip due to the logistics and time frame. Nevertheless, I was up for what would become a very hectic, fun, and fast-paced French adventure in the fall of 2023.

I chose to go in September, the shoulder season, because the temperatures are usually milder, the crowds are fewer, and the prices are lower. Even with my limited French, I would still mingle mostly with the locals and learn as much as I could about each city and a few of the neighborhoods while visiting. This way I could get a sense of what each city offered. What I liked or didn't like about each one. Then choose the most ideal one from this list.

On paper, specifically these six cities appeared to tick the "what I wanted" boxes for me. Biarritz is a city in the Basque Country on the Spanish border. I've always wanted to visit there but not necessarily to live in Biarritz. Since this city was along the route I had carved out logistically, why not? Maybe it would surprise me.

Paris was on the list only because I wanted to give it another shot. Ultimately, I knew that I no longer wanted to live in big noisy Paris. But it's Paris! How could I not go there when visiting France? Plus, I had to fly in and out of Paris, so it had to be on the list.

My travel planning is all about logistics and safety. So, I always buy travel insurance for my peace of mind. Now that I'm older, it is a must to have travel insurance when traveling. France has great medical care so that wasn't a concern. Due to my age anything can happen medically, accidents or illnesses would be a costly out of pocket expense without travel medical insurance, especially if I needed a hospital stay. What if I had a serious injury, died or needed to be transported back to the USA by medevac?

That care and flight to a hospital in the States would cost over $100K out of pocket. Without travel insurance, I'd be in a world of trouble medically and financially. Medicare and my US and VA Medical Insurance does not cover international medical care. Plus, I would need added insurance coverage for airline delays and cancellations too.

I have always recommended buying travel insurance, especially when traveling internationally, it is well worth the small cost you pay to have it, even if you never have to use it to file a claim. Peace of mind is priceless. "What ifs" do happen. You can't predict if you're going to get sick or have an accident abroad.

Too many people either are not thinking about buying travel insurance or just disregard the need for it. Some have suffered the financial consequences of not having this type of insurance when they've traveled out of the country. As a travel agent, I always recommended it to my clients and told them why, and they all purchased travel insurance.

My sister was happy that she bought travel insurance for our trip to Mexico, where she became ill and had to be rushed to a hospital by ambulance. Without travel insurance, she would have been financially responsible for paying those emergency out-of-pocket medical costs in Mexico. Travel insurance covered those costs. Since that trip, my sister has never traveled without travel insurance. She thanked me for suggesting we get travel insurance. Additionally, she received excellent care in that very clean and efficient Puerto Vallarta hospital.

Although some credit cards like Master Card and American Express provide some medical coverage when travelling; I would not rely on those cards completely to cover major medical costs overseas. Some private U.S. Medical Insurance, Medicare, and Medicaid cannot be used outside of the country.

American Express credit cards are not widely accepted in Europe unless you're staying at an expensive upscale hotel or gourmet fine dining. Many merchants do not accept Amex due to the merchant fees incurred. Most people don't even check their private medical insurance policies or credit card benefits before traveling, others fail to purchase travel insurance, which is a big costly and regrettable mistake.

Also, those 'one size fits all' travel insurance policies offered by the airlines and cruise lines are limited in scope and coverage. Okay for a short domestic trip between States, but not practical coverage for international travel. Since those policies most likely will not cover any existing medical issues, repatriation, or costs beyond 25K.

Best to buy the full coverage travel insurance from an insurance company like Allianz offering different policy options for your specific needs, length of travel, and age. It's just the smart thing to do if you want peace of mind away from home. For my scouting trip, I purchased travel insurance from Allianz, which cost $227 for my policy.

CHAPTER THREE

Not A Simple Plan

I began my trip planning in February 2023 after my divorce was final and I changed all my accounts into my maiden name. Whenever planning a trip, my first step is to create a budget and make a travel "to do" check list in Excel. No need to check my passport's validity or Global Entry since I renewed both in January 2023 with my change of name. It's a good idea to know when your passport expires and renew it early. Many airlines and countries will not allow you entry if your passport has less than six months validity before it expires.

Since this trip to France is less than 90 days long, I won't need a Visa. I'll be traveling as a tourist using my U.S. Passport for entry into France and returning to the U.S. Additionally, I'll have to enroll in the State Department's STEP program. Its purpose is so the US Embassy can notify me via text with information and instructions if there's a crisis or other issues like civil unrest, protests, or plagues abroad or in France. Before leaving, I did register for STEP. Then while in France I received an alert about protests.

I'll also let my bank know I'll be traveling out of the country. I'm aware that banks now use GEO Location tracking, but still, that could be anybody using my cards.

Speaking of credit cards, on my list of questions was which credit cards to take? Although American Express isn't widely accepted throughout Europe, I took it anyway along with my Visa and Mastercard; I took my bank Visa debit card as a backup. Visa credit cards are accepted everywhere. I didn't purchase any Euros in advance, since I don't like carrying lots of cash.

Next, I planned my day-to-day itinerary first by securing my accommodations. It's easier to cancel a hotel reservation than a flight if your plans change. For this trip, I reserved lodging for each city I'm visiting. Will I stay in hotels, Airbnb's, or a combination of both? How long should I stay in each city? Will I take the train or rent a car to go from city to city? If I rented a car, I'd need an International Driver's License (IDL) (good for one year) from 'Triple A' (Automobile Club of America) just in case I'd get stopped by the police or have an accident.

This license is a translation of your state's driver's license printed in several languages. It isn't needed to rent a car but it is recommended for driving through France and Europe in case of an accident or if you're pulled over by the police. It can happen.

I take recommendations seriously. I'll purchase this IDL just in case I decide to rent a car. It doesn't hurt to have it. It's good for a year from the date purchased. The cost is very low, approximately $30 which includes the four photos the Auto Club takes, after using one photo on the card. You are then given the other three photos.

Next, what tours should I book and attractions should I see?

Additionally, I'll locate the Tourism Offices for each city I plan to visit. Then I'll research tours and activities. Perhaps book some city sightseeing tours, like hop on/hop off, gourmet walking, wine tastings, and/or bike tours. These types of tours help familiarize you with the city.

I am most interested in day trips available by bus or train to other nearby cities as well? I want to make the most of this trip and see as much as I can while in France. Although I won't be visiting any museums, just other historical sites instead. I want to feel an immersion as I visit these regions and learn about these six cities.

Looking at this itinerary, I question whether I can accomplish everything I want to do in only three-weeks. Knowing I have a very short time to get this scouting done, I would have to make it work. Since I'm still working a 9-to-5 job, I'll be taking some time off, two weeks actual vacation with an additional week of remote work.

Feeling confident that the six cities I choose to visit can be accomplished within that time, although I am excluding Biarritz and Paris as living choices, it means only four cities are really the main candidates on this trip.

After sorting out my accommodations for each city, I begin researching and then arranging my transportation for flights, trains, car rentals, and ground transportation. I wanted to get as many of these tasks done online and checked off my list as soon as possible. So, after checking the current roundtrip Airline fares on Hopper, I add an alert on my phone. I'm hoping the prices will go down in a few weeks.

Currently, the round-trip nonstop fares are around 1,300 to 1,500 dollars on the major airlines flying nonstop from LA to Paris.

I will purchase my airline tickets directly from either American Airlines/British Airlines or another One World Alliance partner on their websites because I get airline points when I use my American Airlines Credit Card.

Additionally, I would be taking Colonel with me, he's my little 6-pound Chihuahua Service Dog. He'll need a lot done to leave the country, such as Vet visits, vaccines, a health certificate, the required International ISO microchip (in addition to the one he already has) for travel abroad, and supporting paperwork for his service dog status. I'll have to fill out and submit two Department of Transportation (DOT) forms and the American Airlines forms for his Service Dog ID which are supposed to be submitted to these agencies 48 hours in advance or sooner.

Also, he must be included on the airline's online form when I'm booking my flights. Each airline has similar requirements for service dogs or pets flying in the cabin or cargo. Plus, before leaving I must make sure I have my months' worth of medications; so, a doctor's appointment for an exam and refills (my usual three months' supply) with a printout of my prescription to take in my carryon. I'll have to carry my Covid Vaccines records too.

Additionally, I researched online eSims services like Airolo for WiFi, texts, and data while traveling in France. My phone uses eSims. Airolo is an Asian company, so not sure about their eSims for France. I also checked Verizon's monthly international travel plan. Usually, whenever I visited Mexico for a week, the Caribbean or Central America I would use Verizon's $10 per day WIFI and Data plan for tooling around town. But this trip would be very different and much longer.

So, for a monthly plan, I'm hoping to find a more cost-effective mobile travel plan. In addition, I want to buy a new Samsung Galaxy 5 Flip phone before leaving on this trip. I'll be purchasing a new Sony digital camera for shooting videos as well as still shots for my trip as a backup camera to my phone. I'm taking my iPad-mini which also has a camera. My laptop is also coming with me for working remotely. And I'll need new prescriptions for glasses and to replace the sunglasses I lost.

As I arranged and booked each component for this trip, I would check items off my "Trip to Do list." Creating to-do lists saves you from a lot of wasted time and aggravation. The packing was relatively easy, I knew I would check a larger suitcase for clothes and shoes, my carryon tote bag for essentials I'll need in-flight, and Colonel's dog carrier.

In my carryon tote bag, goes my laptop, cables, digital camera, electronics, and toiletries; plus, the Euro plug adapters and one small portable travel voltage converter (200-2000 watts). Also added a small packing cube with a change of clothes. I needed to bring both my Samsung earbuds and Bose headphones for noise cancelling on the plane.

Lastly, I prepared two slim plastic notebooks holding Colonel's paperwork, the other with my backup travel itinerary, and confirmations. I must have hard copy paper backups of everything relevant that's on my phone. A zip lock bag of kibble and an empty water bottle to fill for Colonel in flight. Plus, I travel with a small CO_2 detector but that can go into my checked baggage.

I wanted to order two Samsung Smart Tags to track my carryon and checked bag that I added to the list. The first company I placed a Smart Tags order with took too long to fill it. Due to the shipping issues at the time, their shipments faced long delays. So, I received a refund and then ordered those tags from another online store which shipped out those two smart tags right away.

Best packing advice I can offer, use packing cubes. I stand by packing cubes after discovering how great they are for organizing, compressing, and compartmentalizing my clothes and accessories; I also used two small ones for packing Colonel's clothes and his accessories inside my luggage too. You'll be surprised how much you can pack by using these space savers. I have used packing cubes on every trip since 2013. His service dog harness, lease, and small blanket will go inside his new carrier with him.

Colonel has two collapsible plastic bowls for his food and water tucked away inside a pouch using Velcro. I attached the pouch onto the inside back door of his carrier. His zip lock bag of snacks is tucked inside a small side pocket on the carrier. I'll toss my luggage scale (a stress buster and must have travel gadget) into my carryon to be exact for the USA (pounds) and European (kilos) airline luggage weight requirements, each weight is measured differently.

I started this very detailed solo planning early in February of 2023 with the last reservations booked in August. We depart on September 1, 2023, with all my dates set, I could begin arranging my tour bookings left to complete. Also, I have the essential and necessary travel Apps on my phone which I will be using on this journey. Most reservations can be made on those Apps. Over the years I have accumulated many travel Apps for airlines, hotels, trains, ground transportation, ride share, baggage storage, toilet locations (flush), and day tour providers.

All these Apps are relevant, useful, easy to access, and crucial for checking my reservations, while the bar-coded confirmations can be scanned to access tickets for flights, trains, and tours. Bar codes printed on electronic tickets and vouchers are making travel quicker, easier, and more convenient. Well, sort of when the internet and WIFI are working, and your phone is fully charged. Only then is electronic ticketing great. Still, I'm old school cautious, and paranoid without any paper hard copy backups. I prefer having a paper copy of my itinerary and for all my booked confirmations printed-out.

Often while traveling mobile technology may fail when it's not working or shuts down, maybe due to spotty or no WiFi, dead phone battery, losing charger cables or discovering that there is no place to charge a phone are possible issues causing us agony. I have experienced a few of these hiccups plus when the Internet was purposely shut down in one country during an entire trip.

We often take our mobile devices for granted and fail to consider that things can unexpectedly go wrong when we're traveling. Being prepared for the unpredicted by having my travel documents as hard copies too also helps avoid or at least lessens such aggravation while traveling.

Since I had never used Airbnb accommodations before for myself, I decided to give it a shot on this trip. As a former travel agent, I was reluctant to use Airbnb because of its bad rap in the industry for not actually managing the properties they listed, or vetting the property owners or providing any source of liability insurance protection for the rental customers. In addition, the quality of accommodations was not the same across the board. Not every host/owner is a virtuous one, so it was like a needle in a haystack often scary situation reported by some travelers who booked listings.

Moreover, the many crazy issues revealed and widely reported about renters being videotaped and spied upon inside some rentals. Early on there didn't seem to be any property inspections on the part of Airbnb or any government regulations about these growing issues concerning some sketchy owners they allowed on that platform. But I observed over time how the company's executives stepped up to the plate after receiving numerous customer complaints and a few lawsuits concerning some issues mentioned. Operations on that platform appear to be more professional and more customer focused nowadays. It seemed safer and was easier to book the apartments.

After booking and using Airbnb, I was satisfied with the platform's ease of use, the reviews left, my experience, the clean accommodations, and the responsive owners with whom I worked. Therefore, I can recommend using this short-term housing solution for global travel. I just can't guarantee anyone's specific experience. Airbnb provides good customer service, verified owners. Also, all the housing information about the place rented that you'll need such as the host's info, contact, instructions, any house rules, and payment.

Additionally, you will receive a confirmation number and rental receipts all accessible by email, on your phone, desktop, tablet, or laptop. You can even download a PDF for Visa purposes to show you have the required housing necessary for a long stay Visa. Booking these apartments were easier than I first thought.

First, I carefully searched through each city's listings on this apartment sharing platform, viewed the photographs, read the apartments' descriptions, and read the past reviews left by prior renters to find an accommodation suitable for myself and my canine companion. According to Airbnb if you have a service animal you don't have to mention it. So, I didn't but I should have let the owners know I'd be traveling with a canine, my small service dog.

In France, apartment owners are "not supposed" to turn you away just because you have a dog, but many do anyway. Deciding to book an Airbnb apartment for three of the cities: Bordeaux, Toulouse, and Nice for the first half of my trip was a good choice. My reason for staying in short term rental apartments, because I wanted to blend in districts, and feel like a local so I could get a real feel for the neighborhoods and community as well as the city.

In Bordeaux, I researched the area and the quiet neighborhood where I wanted to stay, opting not to be in the busy city center. Still, close enough that I could walk or take public transportation to get into the center of this city quickly. After scrolling through the pages of Airbnb, I chose a cute one-bedroom apartment on the second floor in a more modern building with an elevator and stairs in Les Chartrons, costing €661 for 5 nights.

Google Street view enabled me to see this neighborhood and the building. Photos from the host showed this apartment's clean interior, open layout, and contemporary furnishings which was invaluable. It was exactly the type of accommodations I had envisioned for my five nights; six-day Bordeaux stay.

Plus, the apartment had a furnished terrace facing the street where I could sit outside to read, drink coffee or have a meal while soaking up the autumn sunshine. The bedroom had an ensuite with a huge bathtub-shower combo, sink, and dresser. A separate water closet (the toilet) was just off the living room. There were a very comfortable sofa and chair, and a large TV with Netflix included.

The kitchen area had a nice Island table with four bar stools, a washer, big fridge, oven, and microwave. Although no built-in stove top burners for cooking, a hotplate was available. From the pictures, it looked very modern, clean, and tidy. I was sold immediately.

On Airbnb for this property, I got in touch with the Bordeaux host/owner Mikael about my arrival date and the days I needed to book during the first week in September. We locked in my week, I prepaid him in full through Airbnb to reserve it, and received my confirmation and the payment receipt. This owner was very accommodating and easy to work with on this booking. He reassured me that I'd be able to pick up the keys upon my arrival. My first lodging was booked. I checked it off on my list and was super excited. It's happening.

Then it was onto finding accommodations for my next two cities, Toulouse and Nice. In Toulouse, I found a cute little one-bedroom apartment on the ground floor not far from the city's center, which cost €284 for three nights. It too had a modern vibe and was equipped with a kitchen, and a separate bathroom. Small living room with a TV, sofa, and table. I contacted the owner on Airbnb to lock in my three-day stay.

This host, Lili, was delightful to deal with and said she'd send me the information for the lockbox to access the apartment's keys closer to my check-in date. I also paid in advance for that three-night booking and received a receipt from Airbnb. Another lodging item checked off my list. Note that I used credit cards to book every aspect of this trip. Read the cancellation policy.

It took a while longer to find the right apartment for my five-night stay in Nice, costing $898.40. This one was on the second floor of an older building with no elevator. But it had a portable air conditioner in the separate one bedroom and a separate bathroom that included a toilet, sink, and shower. It was spacious with an open concept combined living room and a fully equipped kitchen. I could prepare meals in this apartment if I wanted, like the other two apartments I had booked on Airbnb.

This apartment was only 10 minutes from the train station in Nice, so it was an easy walk into the city center. In fact, all the apartments I chose were near shops, restaurants, bars, and shopping. After booking those three apartments, I was content with all my Airbnb choices. I appreciate Google maps for being able to view distances between locations, like from the train stations to the apartments, and the routes for walking and giving me a better sense of where I am and where I will need to go. Street view is very helpful too. I was able to view those neighborhoods.

Next on to the hotels for Paris, Lyon, and Biarritz. Although I had not considered living in Biarritz, I really wanted to visit that city. Since it was close to Bordeaux and along my planned southern route, I booked one night in Biarritz. My plan was to spend a day exploring that coastal upscale city before making my way to Toulouse the next day.

I found a small boutique hotel, Escale Oceania Biarritz, that was about a 10-minute walk to the beach and to old Biarritz, costing $134 per night. Since my trip in 2023 this hotel's name was changed to Hotel Akena Biarritz - Grande Plage and from the photos it looks like the interior and rooms had an innovative modern updated design. It was a perfect accommodation for my short stay.

After confirming this Biarritz hotel, I realized that I made a mistake by booking it through Expedia instead of the hotel directly. It's a blunder to have both websites open on my browser at the same time. Going back and forth between Expedia and the Hotel's website to compare pricing and other relevant information about the hotel. Fortunately, I only booked this room for one night on that platform.

I'm not a big fan of third-party online agency booking sites because these sites are merely "middle-men" for other third-party consumer to consumer or business to consumer booking services, not a traditional travel agency. If something goes wrong with my booking, then it would take time for me to sort through the chain of providers to have my issue resolved. Rather than calling a travel agent, hotel, or airline to handle the problem. Booking mishaps do happen, a reason why I prefer dealing directly with suppliers like airlines, cruise lines, and hotels that I can more easily and quickly hold responsible.

Certainly, I want to avoid travel booking issues while on vacation. So, I don't usually recommend using third party travel companies for hotels or flights. I choose to go directly to the supplier source. Especially since I'm not looking for unfamiliar budget hotels or cheap flights with very long layovers. I use third party sites like Hopper or Expedia simply to check on the prices of flights or hotels, not for booking my travel. Occasionally, I have used booking dot com with success.

Booking accommodations in Lyon was easier with so many

accessible Accor Ibis hotels throughout France. These are the chain's budget hotels on the same scale as a Holiday Inn Express, Courtyard, or Hampton Inn. I booked two nights directly with Ibis Lyon Gare La Part-Dieu near the train station. Paid in advance, $130 per night. I could walk from and to that train station without needing to call a taxi or ride share service. Usually booking hotels near train stations are not the most desirable locations, due to high crime and congestion. I felt staying at this one for two days would not be an issue.

With three-star hotels what matters most to me is cleanliness, a comfortable bed, and good customer service. I'm not looking for fancy, just a nice and bug free room for stashing my stuff and sleeping when I travel. If it has a restaurant or breakfast café then that's an added bonus as well. Note that three-star hotels are not the same as the ones in the USA. They are a bit better.

Well, my visit to Lyon turned out to be more complicated than I had expected, which you'll see in my description of this trip in Chapter Nine. Furthermore, in each chapter I describe in detail the costs of all my travel for meals, transportation, lodging, tours, and other expenses I paid on this trip. Later, I would be happy with my decision to divide my lodging between hotels and Airbnb's due to the hectic pace of this trip. Ultimately, towards the end of my journey, I would most welcome the relaxation and pampering that staying at hotels offer weary travelers.

My last hotel booking was for Paris, I chose the Hôtel De La Porte Dorée, which cost €1,010 for 5 nights. I found this quaint boutique hotel in the quiet 12th arrondissement from a Google search. It's owned by an American woman whom I met after arriving. Choosing a roomy deluxe one bedroom from photographs of rooms on its website.

The hotel has a tiny narrow elevator and a small restaurant that serves breakfast only. It is close to a metro stop and on a walkable street with very easy access to transportation, restaurants, bakeries, and other shops. This hotel seems ideal for my needs and should be easy for getting around Paris with a subway stop just steps away.

There was also fast food like a Subway, MacDonald's, and a Burger King on the corner (Google Street view) not that I'll want American fast food while in France but you never know. A beautiful park is across the boulevard which is nice for running or walking a dog. I booked my five-night stay on the hotel's website, got my confirmation, and then checked this one off my list too. I felt this hotel would be ideal for my Paris stay, it was quaint and looked well maintained and modern from the pictures on its website.

Finally, with all my accommodations booked for this trip I moved on to my transportation needs. My best travel planning tip is to use Google's Street View to see the area or neighborhood where the accommodations you want to book are located and the walking distances from the train stations or to other places. Usually, I will take a virtual tour of the streets and area around my lodgings and the train stations.

Will I feel safe staying in those locations? Should I choose a different area? What are the crime statistics of the area, which you can Google? Important information to acquire when traveling alone. Most cities are the same, so when traveling just exercising caution and being aware of your surroundings is the most common rule for safety. Ironically, I usually now feel safer while traveling in other countries than I do in the USA.

Next, I booked my transportation and tours which I will provide the details about later in this book. My airfare costs over $2,000 including those high taxes. Sometimes the taxes cost more than the ticket. Train tickets from city to city and the tours' costs are mounting. All costs are discussed in the chapters about each of those cities visited. International travel is expensive so you want to get it right.

After all my bookings were secured and my itinerary set, I sent a copy of this travel itinerary and a copy of my passport to my daughter by email. She's my emergency contact and listed on my mobile phone as ICE (in case of emergency) after her name in my favorites is at the top of that list along followed by a few other friends and family members, which makes it easy for anyone to contact her or them if I have an incident anywhere in the world. She and I will keep in touch via text and facetime throughout my trip.

The last things on my list I had to do was have a medical checkup and have my prescriptions refilled. The Vet visits for Colonel would happen closer to our departure date, so I made his appointments too. He may need a sedative for the flight. In the meantime, I bought him natural calming tablets for animal anxiety just in case.

Verifying his current vaccines and then getting the other vaccines he needed cost $31.75; his exam and nail trimming cost a whopping $96.50. He also needed an ISO international microchip, cost $80; a USDA health certificate to travel, cost $268, plus a $38 processing fee. American Vets are very expensive. I also wanted to get his teeth cleaned before this trip but when I quoted over $800 for that procedure, I decided to wait on his dental work.

There was quite a lot of paperwork to fill out and sign for Colonel just to accompany me on this journey. US Animal health certificates are on APHIS forms filled out and issued by a USDA accredited veterinarian and then endorsed by APHIS (Animal & Plant Health Inspection Service) under the USDA. Not all Vets have this USDA accreditation.

I had to find a new Vet who was USDA accredited to obtain Colonel's health certificate to travel. The health certificate is valid for only 10 days after being endorsed and issued by the USDA. Therefore, a dog or cat's exam needs to be scheduled before those 10 days start ticking up to your departure date. This trip took a lot of timing and logistics planning. Much work.

My Vet suggested that I purchased a prepaid shipping label with the mailing envelope from either FedEx or UPS for an additional cost of $35.00. That overnight label had to be addressed to me (recipient) and from me (sender), not from the USDA to make sure I received it before departing, then give that label to the Vet on the day of my dog's exam. Vets know when to send the certificate to the USDA.

Once endorsed, the USDA then sends me the overnight express envelope containing the health certificate. This return procedure usually takes within 1-3 business days after the USDA receives the document from the Vet. This precise process guarantees that the Health Certificate reaches the recipient in time. Ultimately, you will receive the certificate before your departure, your vet will help with the timing.

I make several copies of his health certificate to carry with me and as a pdf on my phone. You can see how overwhelming this task could become if you aren't organized and using a check list and a calendar, along with an established itinerary.

I also downloaded and filled out the Service Dog forms for the DOT (Department of Transportation) (no fee). Then I applied for an Airline service dog ID by filling out the airline application online to submit directly to American Airlines and Air Tahiti Nui when I booked my tickets. I had to submit proof that he was indeed a Service dog. Service Dogs fly free so no airline fee for Colonel.

Fortunately, this visit to France did not require me to get a Visa, no expense incurred there since I was going as a tourist for less than three months. I just needed my Passport to enter France and return to the United States. Global Entry helps you avoid the long immigration lines coming back into the U.S.A.

In late August, I purchased my new Samsung Android phone and a Samsung Galaxy S5 Smart watch that was a no cost bonus, but upgraded the watch to a Galaxy Flip6, so I paid for it. Also bought and downloaded to my mobile phone a 30-day eSim from Airolo for €10.

Then realized I had jumped the gun on that purchase after having an issue with my newly purchased android phone from Verizon. I could not install the eSim. After contacting Verizon, I learned that my new phone was still locked and would be for 60 days. So, I could not use the eSim I had just purchased. Airolo kindly extended me a €10 credit to use later. Now what?

To resolve my eSim issue I had to contact Verizon and purchase their more costly monthly international travel plan for $100. Nevertheless, it was worth the money and more cost effective than paying $10 per day for WiFi, text, and data for three weeks. My escalating trip costs and my efforts to remain within my $6,000 budget was tricky. I always have a budget in mind that I can track before and during travel. Most times I can stay within my budget.

I published my first Facebook post about beginning this scouting trip on August 31, 2023, the day prior to my April 1st departure. So excited about sharing my journey on Facebook with family and friends who became my virtual travel companions.

After arriving in France, I posted daily about each city I visited, my experiences and adventures on this journey until it ended. Due to the positive feedback which I received from my countless friends and family on Facebook about my French adventure postings, and their suggestions about writing a book influenced me to write this book about my scouting trip with added back story details.

The last chapter of this book recounts in summary my visit and exploration of those six cities and what I learned and took away from each one. Then choosing the desired city where I could quietly live the remainder of my life in retirement. The Epilogue recounts what happens next.

Celestine Cooley

Thursday, August 31, 2023 | Departure Eve

Bonjour, Mes amies et famille! In a few hours, I'll be on my way to FRANCE. So excited! I have devoted much of these three Covid-19 pandemic years to learning French, the language that I love but can't speak well yet. Still feeling a bit confident to try anyway.

My three-week scouting trip is to find the city in which to live when I retire. We, Colonel and I, are flying non-stop from Los Angeles to Paris before boarding a train to Bordeaux, the first city on my list to explore. Can't wait to share this journey. It should be a fun adventure, full of new cultural gems and discoveries.

I'll spend a few hours in Paris upon landing to meet up with my close high school girlfriend, Rozlynn Dozier, who is also traveling around Europe. My little Airbnb in Bordeaux is so cute. I've booked three apartments and three hotels to stay at on this journey. Can't wait to begin my trip. It is going to be a fast paced and fun adventure by train.

At LAX, Colonel and I board the airplane before the first and business class passengers. He has his official service dog ID from American Airlines and Air Tahiti Nui. Flying with an animal means a mountain of paperwork and vet visits for his exam, shots, and a health certificate.

Once in France, I have several day-trips planned to visit other cities outside of the six cities I've chosen to explore. Excited! Downloaded my boarding pass last night and had all my hard copy travel documents in a folder ready to go. After months of planning, being organized is key to having a stress-free, sane, and successful trip. By the time I booked this flight the prices had gone up substantially, so I chose the least expensive non-stop flight to Paris on Air Tahiti Nui, an Alaska/American Airlines OneWorld partner. My return is a connecting flight on American Airlines.

Visiting six cities in the Southwest, South, and Central regions of France should be an eye-opening experience. Older now, I'm seeking an affordable, safe, slow paced, walkable city with good public transportation too, and a more peaceful urban environment.

Looking for a better quality of life. It should have a rich culture, fun activities, excellent food, great wine, good healthcare, and a supportive expat community. I don't plan to buy a car. Walking to nearby shops, bakeries, banks, pharmacies, restaurants, markets, doctors, vets, and hopping on convenient public transportation is preferable.

Even though I have many activities planned for this exploratory journey, I hope to pace myself, not push myself, rest, and take it easy as well. Ultimately, I prefer walking around a city's neighborhoods to explore and discover its many different environments and hidden treasures. Often, I'll hop onto public transportation and ride to nowhere in particular just to see where the bus or subway will take me.

We're departing tomorrow, Friday, September 1, 2023. I'll arrive in Paris the next day on Saturday morning. Time to sleep, if I can. Bonne Journeé!

Celestine Cooley

CHAPTER FOUR

Exploring Six Cities

Friday, 1 Sept 2023 | Day of Departure

I took Colonel for a quick walk before my uber arrived at 8 am, going to the Flyaway Bus Terminal in Van Nuys, California, just a few minutes' ride from my apartment. Easily purchased my one-way bus ticket that cost $9.00 online the week before. I'll purchase my return bus ticket when I return to LA.

The airport bus is my preferred transportation to LAX rather than driving or taking a shuttle, taxi, or Uber. I have taken this LAX bus for many years since living in the San Fernando Valley, suburbs north of Los Angeles. This LAX Flyaway bus leaves the terminal every 15 minutes for the airport. The terminal has long term parking too but I don't need it. Taking the airport bus is a stress-free and aggravation free, a positive way to begin any journey. Our bags are stored in outside compartments under the bus.

Onboard next to our roomy seats are USB ports for charging our mobile devices and a nice moveable foot rest under the forward seat. This bus is convenient and economical. Usually, the entire ride to the airport is very comfortable, quiet, and relaxing; taking about 30 to 45 minutes via the 405 Freeway's diamond lane. Arriving safely, we are dropped off in front of our designated departure terminals.

Although, I left home with a three-hour window, that time was quickly devoured by transitioning from Uber to the Bus. Then standing and waiting in the airport's long check-in line to check my big 27" suitcase, and presenting all the service dog paperwork to the agent before going to TSA's security check point.

Of course, walking through LAX's lengthy terminal towards my gate took some time too. Finally, I'm standing in the regular line to clear security all because the TSA Pre-Check is not printed on my boarding pass. It should have been, I have Global Entry and Pre-Check is a part of this service.

After getting through TSA's Security check, Colonel and I now have about 45-minutes to wait until boarding our flight. Which means boarding is in 15 minutes. Most flights board 30 minutes before departure. Quickly, I settled down in a seat near the gate and surveyed the area. From the number of passengers waiting with me, our plane looks sold out.

Those waitlisted would be waiting for another flight unless someone doesn't mind giving up their seat to leave later. Most passengers on my Air Tahiti Nui flight were French. I released Colonel from his carrier to stretch his legs for a while. The plane would be boarding soon.

Due to the time crunch, we could not visit the Centurion Lounge which was too far away from our gate. We did stop at the nearby dog rest area, but Colonel only sniffed around that area rejecting pee spots. So, he'll have to wait until we arrive in Paris to relieve himself. Although I put a pee pad in his carrier, I know he won't pee on it there. Before boarding, I contacted the TSA agency online to find out what happened to my TSA Pre-Check. My Global Entry status meant Pre-Check should have been automatic. A few hours later that issue was resolved.

The snafu had to do with my last name change I made on my Global Entry account and Passport earlier this year. Names cannot be an issue when you are traveling. Your full legal name, the one on all accounts and documents regularly used must also be the same name used on all government documents (IRS, social security, Drivers Licenses, etc.), no nicknames or initials either or else this will cause issues or delays at airports. These changes about legal name status came about after 9/11 for security reasons and to establish our legal identities (we are legitimately who we say we are) when flying to and from the United States.

My mid-morning, 11:30 am flight on Air Tahiti Nui was nonstop from Los Angeles-LAX to CDG-Paris, no layovers and it left on time. I prefer nonstop flights, if available on my travel routes. I'm not big on changing planes and waiting for several hours to board another plane. Certainly, I want to get where I'm going as soon as possible without delays. This ten-and-a-half-hour flight is expected to arrive in Paris tomorrow morning at 9:30 am.

All aboard, we're on our way. Colonel is secured in his carrier tucked under the seat in front of me. This French airline's floral design was reminiscent of an island setting. My first flight on this airline. We had such delightful, helpful, and kind flight attendants capturing that French Polynesian spirit. My premium economy seat is very comfortable with plenty of legroom. I stowed my carryon in a bin above me after grabbing my Bose headphones from it to cancel out the ambient airplane sounds.

Of course, Colonel was a big hit on the plane. He slept most of the way, waking to have water and a few nibbles of kibble before retreating to slumberland once again. I tried taking cat naps but I'm unable to fully fall asleep inflight. Instead, I watched a few movies, listened to an audiobook, ate the meals served, drank plenty of water (too much), and held Colonel in my lap a few times during the flight. He prefers to sleep in his carrier while traveling. Luckily, he didn't need any tranquilizers which I received from his Vet in addition to the natural calming tab I bought.

Right now, I'm feeling extremely happy, relaxed, and comfortable in my window seat, viewing cumulus clouds floating by like puffy cotton balls suspended in the sky. I can't believe how much noise my headphones and ear buds cancel on this plane. Makes for a more pleasant and calmer flight.

Celestine Cooley

Saturday, 2 Sept 2023 | Arrival in France ~ Paris

Day 1 - The challenges of long-haul travel. First, Colonel did very well on our flight. He even looked out the window, saw the clouds, and seemed unfazed by them. On the plane, he said hello (Bonjour) to many French children, receiving lots of pets and many giggles before going back into his carrier. The mostly French crew and passengers were all impressed by his good behavior. The flight attendants were very engaging, talking to him, giving him water, snacks, and much attention. It was an easy and uneventful flight, the best kind.

I'm not keen on public toilets. Foolishly, I neglected to visit the plane's restroom before it landed at Charles de Gaulle airport. Big mistake! So, my first major issue after exiting the plane in Paris and before picking up my checked bag was to find a restroom. At first, I couldn't find a soul to direct me to one immediately. After approaching a young couple and asking them in French if they knew,

"Où est la toilette, s'il vous plaît?" *(Where are the toilets, please?)*

They gave me a curious look, then indicated that they didn't speak French. They are from Spain, so I asked in Spanish,

"Donde este el banjo, por favor?" *(Where are the bathrooms, please?)*

They smiled and said in Spanish,

"¿Tú hablas español?" *(You speak Spanish?)*

Gleefully, I responded,

"Un poquito!" *(A little!)*

Unfortunately for me they didn't know the locations of the toilets either. Now walking away to continue my mission, I thanked them anyway saying,

"Gracias! Adiós!"

Finally, after rambling around in circles searching aimlessly, I spotted an airport employee, who pointed me in the right direction. Merci! We had to go downstairs. Good thing I only had to deal with my carryon bag and Colonel's carrier with him inside it now. I'm concerned, it's near that final moment where I really had to go and I'm uncertain whether I'll make it to the toilet in time.

When I arrived inside the restroom, I needed one euro to access the toilet stall. Of course, I don't have any euros yet. I explained as best I could in French to the female attendant my current dire state. She nodded and was kind enough to let me go in anyway. Extremely grateful and wished I could have tipped her for giving me a pass.

Navigating airports is never easy and especially in a foreign language. Plus, you must watch out for nefarious people lurking around airports and train stations fishing for victims, to either pick your pockets or con you out of money in some way. A lady with a clipboard approached me; I know about this scam. She asked in French if I would take the time to fill out a survey. Why on earth would I want to fill out any type of survey in France? I rigidly declined, "No, Merci!" It was a hard NO.

Then I told her in English to step away from me. She could see by my expression that I wasn't having any of her nonsense, so she walked away. This is a distraction technique used to steal your bags or pick your pockets or whatever they intend to do. These criminals work in teams, so you don't know who's doing what in a crowded area. Now, I'm on red alert and paying closer attention to everyone around me as I make my way through the masses. I so detest crowds and swindlers.

After waiting to grab my luggage from baggage claim, I see my metal case. Soon I'm roaming off to find the train. But before catching the train, urgently needing cash, I locate a currency exchange bureau to get €30. Normally, I would find a bank's ATM to use instead of this service due to their very high fees.

But instead of using an ATM, I'm feeling this is a safer way to get money for now. I have used ATMs around the world. Here I exchange $30 US dollars (cash) and receive €15 which includes the exchange rate and this company's fees. Big rip off! Ridiculous!

I could have ordered euros from my US bank. Instead, I wanted to learn how to access euros in France, the right way but not this way. So, throughout this trip, if I needed cash, I would simply use my bank debit or credit card at ATMs and decline the conversion fee. So many darn fees.

Next, I found my way to the billet (ticket) bureau (office) to buy a train ticket using a credit card, which cost €12. The ticket line was very long. I did not dare attempt to use the ticket kiosk this time. This train ticket I wanted to purchase in person, not online because I had questions about getting a transit pass for Paris later.

After securing my paper train ticket, it took a moment to find my train. So happy the ticket agent spoke some English, and answered my question about the cost for the weekly transit pass. Getting out of CDG seems so complicated at first. Following the

French signage with pictures helped me locate the commuter train station inside the airport. Uncomplicated, it was a straight shot from Terminal 2 to catch the RER commuter train into the city of Paris. It's now just noon.

Carrying my little dog inside his carrier, I board the jam-packed train, holding on tightly to his carrier, my suitcase, and the carryon tote bag over my shoulder. I'm wearing my windbreaker. My compact fanny pack is securely anchored around my waist under my shirt so no chance of losing it or getting pick-pocketed. This train is warm and stuffy. Quickly, I find a seat and get comfortable for our 30-minute ride into Paris. Keeping track of my bags to ensure none are left behind when I exited the train is another task to remember.

I received a text from AMEX that some criminal in the airport, perhaps near that ticket counter or currency exchange, had cloned my Amex Card then tried to purchase a very expensive $4,500 plane ticket on a French Charter. AMEX caught the obvious fraud attempt and declined the purchase. Career criminals are narcissistic sociopathic animals, the rest of us are merely unsuspecting prey to their stings. You work hard yet others try to take what you have acquired. Disgusting!

On the other hand, I always feel that my guardian angel 'out there somewhere' watches over me. Still, being vigilant about my surroundings anywhere I go in the world, a conscious effort to remain safe while traveling, especially solo. Staying as safe as possible and protecting ourselves is up to us. It's a different world today.

It's always a good idea to carry the emergency contact numbers for the countries and cities I'm visiting. Calling the police and filing a report may become part of my agenda unexpectantly. That text alert from AMEX reminded me to tuck my unprotected credit card case into my RFID blocking pouch where they should have been in the first place. Usually, I'm fearless when I travel, but do realize that my safety is in my own hands.

Riding the RER train from Terminal 2 at Charles de Gaulle airport into Paris' Gare du Nord (train station) took just 35 minutes. I arrived in the 18th arrondissement at 12:30 pm. This neighborhood isn't the safest at night. But one still worth the visit during the day to see the sights, the Basilica, shops, restaurants, and to experience the diverse cultures of this lively community. It has a colorful urban vibe with a certain grittiness; once populated by artists and writers, now it accommodates college students and immigrant residents.

Since it was midday, I had no concerns about my safety. Still, as an older woman traveling alone, I can't relax my guard. Finding the right exits out of most train stations is an exercise in patience. Once outside, Colonel still can't find an ideal place to pee or do his business. Instead, he's just circling and sniffing areas around this building. We must grab a taxi, so he is out of luck again for now.

"On y va!" *(Let's go!)*, I say to him as I push my bag and lead him towards a line of waiting G7 taxi cabs in front of the train station. After texting my girlfriend, Roz, that we cannot meet today due to my limited time, the traffic, and the impossible logistics of me getting to her location and then to my train in time. Maybe we can try to hook up later.

I was eager to get to the next Paris train station across town, Gare Montparnasse (in the 14th district) by one o'clock to catch the 1:39 pm TGV OUIGO high-speed train to Bordeaux. It's scheduled to arrive there around 4:01 pm. Booked my ticket on the Trainline

App, costing €39.16 one way. At last, I'm off to my first city destination where my illustrious journey and new adventures will begin. I smile, take in a big deep breath, and then slowly release the air. I'm in heaven right now. I made it to France.

I see an empty taxi and motion to the driver. Colonel goes back into his carrier for the ride. Hopping into the cab now around 12:40 pm, time is ticking. Paris in the 18th district was very crowded this time of day. I thought tourist season was behind me, guess not.

My Algerian taxi driver gives me a sweet insightful mini-tour of Paris pointing out famous places along our route to my next train station. This city is riddled with construction due to the upcoming Olympic Games. So, traffic is a mess. My driver speaks English and is funny, chatty, charming, and very animated. When we arrive at this train station, it's extremely crowded too. The driver pulls my two bags from inside his trunk. I pay him and include a 5-euro tip, then say,

"Merci beaucoup pour le tour de Ville." *(Thanks a lot for the city tour.)*

Before we go inside, I release the little dog from his carrier but still he's not peeing, I have no idea why not. He's held it in for hours. Just hope he's okay. Should I be worried? This dog is too much!

CHAPTER FIVE

Exploring Bordeaux

Saturday, 2 Sept 2023 | Afternoon Train

We made it across the city from Gare du Nord to the 14th arrondissement in about 30 minutes, which was fast considering the morning traffic. Inside the Montparnasse station, Colonel is still out of his carrier to stretch and walk through this building. Looking around I'm puzzled, questioning which way to go to find my train, then to find which platform it's leaving from for Bordeaux.

The station is noisy with many people crisscrossing paths and rushing around in different directions. Getting familiar with train stations and train schedules is going to be a constant part of this trip. Since I am traveling by train from city to city it should become routine and easier to figure out over time.

I see a crowd of people standing together and looking up at a board that shows the train departures and arrivals. On this board I spot my train and the track number it's on. Now I'm looking around for signs that will lead me to those tracks. I take the escalator down.

Six French Cities

My ticket is on my phone; my phone is charged. Just must scan the QR Code at the gate to validate it and go through its turnstile. Modern technology, love it. I would learn that every train station is different in the way they look and operate.

Naturally, I also have a paper copy of my ticket available in my carryon as a potential backup, just in case. Downloading SNCF Connect, the French Train company's App proved helpful in this ticket booking process. Also found and used two other train ticketing Apps, Trainline and Omio to buy train tickets in advance. Additionally, I check Rome2Rio for transportation: planes, trains, cars, or buses, their routing, distances, and scheduled times, which is usually synchronized with one of those other transport services.

Again, using third party suppliers can be hit or miss but I'm willing to try these two for train travel. I even looked at Rail Europe for booking tickets but decided these three companies are best for local and regional train travel around France. For EU travel outside France, and through the EU (European Union) then Rail Europe would suffice because it also shows the trains for other countries.

During this trip, I grew familiar with using the train departures and arrivals display board, learning how to read them quickly. Now finding the right platform for my train number 7653, took some time to sort out. As you walk along the platforms, the masses thin out as passengers disappear inside the various train cars. I boarded train Car 6; my second-class window seat number 611 is on the lower-level right of the aisle. I intentionally booked all lower-level seating, so I wouldn't have to climb stairs with these three bags.

I had to leave my big suitcase and tote bag in the luggage rack near the doorway. Luckily, I can keep an eye on both bags from my seat. Coming from the US, I'm conditioned to not be separated from my belongings. It was nice having a window seat so I could watch the countryside whiz by on route to Bordeaux, which is only a two-hour ride from Paris. I would be spending five nights (six days) exploring this lovely city on the Garonne River in the Nouvelle-Aquitaine region of Southwest France.

Most of the passengers on this train are French, so I had short and limited conversations. During the trip, the train made several stops in other cities on the route. I relaxed while watching the changing landscapes give way to the beautiful countryside aligned with farms, villages, and vineyards.

We arrived in Bordeaux safely around 3:45 pm. I took a taxi from the Gare St. Jean train station to a small market (grocery store) to pick up the apartment keys. I gave the store clerk a code that Mikael sent to me. He retrieved the three keys on a ring and handed them to me.

Then we walked about four blocks to the apartment rolling my bags on very narrow and uneven cobblestoned sidewalks. Did I mention how heavy my bags are…ugh! Anyway, I've managed to roll my 27" fully packed hard metal suitcase (by IT), my medium over stuffed carryon duffle bag (designed by Jessica Simpson), and Colonel's very sturdy and well-constructed dog carrier (Mr. Peanut) over cobblestoned streets for several blocks. Lucky, my suitcase has spinning wheels to lessen the struggle. But it's still a struggle.

This luggage circus juggling act would become a familiar theme in and out of every city we visited. There really is no reason to carry so much stuff for three weeks. Walking along I pulled out my phone to check the address.

Today, I really appreciated having Google Maps on my phone to steer me correctly to the apartment. Usually, Google and I disagree and argue about which way to go due to my ill sense of direction, reluctance, and doubt. Finally, after traveling for 15 hours by bus, plane, train, and taxi, Colonel found a potty spot near the Bordeaux apartment. I was relieved for him. Such a trooper. He lasted longer than me without a potty break. Amazing!

The Airbnb apartment building lobby is very bright and clean; we take the decent sized elevator with my bags to the second floor. The secured door was like getting into Fort Knox using three keys to unlock three locks.

Instantly, I feel safe here in this charming little apartment and in this quiet neighborhood. When I was getting off the elevator, I met a neighbor lady tenant from down the hall who began speaking to me very fast in French. She mentioned something about someone moving from her place. He looked like a college student. I nodded and smiled.

I responded, "Je parle un peu Français." (I speak a little French.)

Speaking with a lot of gestures and head nodding on my part. We laughed! Bon Journeé! Then I settled inside, first by unpacking and hanging up a few clothes that I would wear during the week. My phone and watch need charging after a full day of traveling. So, I pulled out my multi-charger and the French adapter, plugged it into the electric French socket.

While my mobile devices are charging, I set up the WiFi on my laptop. Then I set up my mini home office in the kitchen on the island table so I can work remotely all next week. After which I relaxed on the sofa to watch part of a French TV series (in French) on Netflix. My host has set me up on his personal Netflix account which displayed my name Celestine. Most of the shows are in English. Thoughtful!

The owner, Mikael, and I exchanged several text messages back and forth before I arrived, so I felt very comfortable about staying here before and after booking this place. Did I mention how clean it is here? It smells good too. This apartment is only a few blocks from the Tram and bus stops; near a few shops, markets, and cafes too. So, I can walk to nearby places or hop on the Tram to go into the City Center.

So far, I really like the people and the vibe here in Bordeaux. You can tell right away in a city if it's going to be a good stay or not. This one isn't congested with oodles of people everywhere. Colonel and I relaxed for a few hours. Late evening, I ventured out to grab a bite to eat before calling it a night. Tired, in need of good sound sleep.

Tomorrow is Sunday, my adventure begins by exploring this beautiful city on foot. Maybe even take a day trip somewhere special. Right now, content, I'm spread out and relaxed on this sofa watching TV with Colonel asleep snuggled next to me. Bon Nuit!

Six French Cities

Saturday, 2 Sept 2023 | Bordeaux ~ Evening

The first day of my French journey was rather smooth. Nothing went wrong, well except for my unusual toilette dilemma. After arriving in Bordeaux this afternoon, then picking up the apartment keys, unpacking, and relaxing, I'm in need of some nourishment, a hearty meal. So, at 8 pm, adopting the French dinner routine to eat after 7 pm when most restaurants open for supper dining, I charge off to find food.

I'm looking forward to experiencing the French food scene. Off the elevator, it's now dark and pin drop quiet outside, the amber street lights illuminate a peaceful stillness. I feel at peace. Of course, I'm in a new city and have no clue as to which direction to begin walking. By chance, I stopped a kid on a motor bike in front of my building to ask about eateries. I'm going to test my fractured unrhythmic French, as I think carefully how to construct a sentence and to say each word,

"Bonjour, Où est ...un resto...manger...près ici." (Where is (pause) a restaurant (pause) to eat (pause) near here?)

Well, he looked at me, smiled, and then wittily said in English,

"I don't speak French, just Arabic and English."

I laughed and responded,

"I don't speak French either."

He chuckled and asked,

"Where are you from?"

"America, Los Angeles," I replied.

Then he says, "I love America."

Me: "Everyone loves America."

Him: "I want to go to America."

Me: "I want to leave America."

We snickered at my response. Then I asked where he was from.

He: "I come from Sudan."

Me: "Nice!" "I have visited Northeast Africa, Ethiopia."

He seemed impressed. We spoke some more about his country and the African continent before I said,

"Okay, back to eating."

With a laugh and even bigger smile, he pointed me in the right direction, telling me to go downtown (for this neighborhood) but not into the City Center.

We said our goodbyes. I thanked him for his guidance and walked off with Colonel on his lease to find food. I love having these local encounters with people I meet randomly, which continues happening throughout the night. Several blocks away I find a few restaurants with tables outside in a little plaza near Rue Camille Godard.

Instead, I wanted to explore more so I turned the corner and found CENT 33, an award-winning upscale French restaurant on Rue Jardin de Public. I'm still in the Chartrons neighborhood where I'm staying and starting to adore. France is in many ways unapologetic and inexpressibly magical day or night.

A couple which I learned where a father (60s) and daughter (30s) (Americans) and his dog (a white Westie) were sitting at an outside table. Standing adjacent to them, I am trying to read the French menu on the window when the father remarks,

"I recommend that you eat here."

Looking over and down at him in wonderment,

I responded curiously, "You do, why?"

Father: "The food and ambience are both excellent with a great staff."

Me: "Okay, well, guess I can't go wrong with a worthy recommendation. Thank you."

Then jokingly he asked,

"How come you speak such good English?"

Me: "Because I'm from America."

Father: "Let me guess, California, Texas..."

I interrupted him and said,

"California."

Coincidentally, his daughter was visiting from San Jose, California. A waiter came out from inside the restaurant and greeted me.

"Bonjour!" I replied.

Then I inquired about dining for one person.

"*Avez-vous une table pour une personne?*" *(Do you have a table for one person?)*

Waiter: "*Avez-vous une réservation?*" *(Do you have a reservation?)*

Me: "No, but I can make one for another time, Merci!"

English came out automatically; this happens whenever I can't remember what words to use in French. To myself, I'm thinking how exhausting it is to speak French or even try when you're just learning. Thank goodness the waiter spoke English but with a cute French accent.

Waiter: "Wait here, let me ask if we have an opening."

I nodded as he disappears inside then quickly returns to announce,

"We have one table outside."

He points to the end table on the sidewalk under an awning. Opposite the father and daughter on the other end of the patio.

Me: "I'll take it, Merci beaucoup!"

He seats me and first asks about my selection of wine. I was anxious for a glass. My first in France on this trip.

Me: "What do you recommend?"

Waiter: "Do you want a bottle or glass?"

Me: "A glass, please!" *(I know my capacity and it's late.)*

He suggests a white. Also, he asked if I'd like water,

"Oui," I chose mineral d'eau.

Soon the female sommelier arrives with a bottle of wine *(Sauvignon Blanc)* and a greeting; she shows me,

Sommelier: "This wine is produced on the right bank of Bordeaux," she notes.

She is speaking perfect English. I asked what country she was from.

"Originally, from Japan but I have lived all over,"

she said while pouring some wine in the glass for me to sample. A sniff and small swirl, the wine was smooth, smoky with a hint of grapefruit and had a lot of body. I meant to take a picture of the bottle to remember it, but I forgot. Too much talking.

Did I mention how much I love wine and enjoy being in wine country anywhere in the world but especially here in Bordeaux. I would soon learn just how much wine was produced in France and realize that I would never get to know every single bottle.

The waiter returned with my water and a small block of wood stamped with a barcode. A menu solution adopted during the Covid Pandemic to avoid touching menus.

Waiter: "Scan with your camera to see the menu."

"Okay," I responded.

The first scan gave me a menu with over-the-top pricing. I asked the waiter about this pricey menu. Apparently, it was an older menu so I need to download the new menu link. With my waiter's help, I found the correct menu which offered two choices, a six-course, and an eight-course meal.

Suddenly, looking at the *"much more than I usually pay for dinner"* pricing, when a *"you deserve this"* feeling draped over me. Afterall, I am preparing for a big move. I've survived my lengthy journey to realize it, and now feel overdue a celebratory meal for my years of longing and my efforts to get here.

Granted this was one of those chic gourmet restaurants serving micro morsels *(tiny portions)* and not my first, I have an opinion about this type of dining, but will save it for another time. Tonight, I am going to contradict myself about eating tiny portions that cost enough cash to feed several families.

Anyway, I chose the six-courses fearing eight courses would be too much food. Then laughed about the absurdness. My waiter explained the food and ingredients for each course. Farm to table organically sourced.

Well, that dining experience turned into a three-hour affair. About 30 minutes after being seated, a heavy downpour of rain arrived. It was refreshing, listening to the rhythmic sound of rain hitting the pavement.

This scene provided for a pleasant outside experience while sitting under this awning to stay dry. The weather was still warm and humid but not unbearable. I forgot to bring his carrier. Colonel is standing under my chair. He acts like a little rain will melt him or something. This repas *(meal)* was delightfully tasty, every course's morsel unique. The rain showers did not last long. I was enjoying this food and the tranquil atmosphere very much. Any more relaxed and I would have fallen asleep.

Midway through my meal the owner, Chef Fabien Beaufour, came out and approached my table to see how I was doing. He asked what I thought about my meal. I gave him two thumbs up and a five-star review, which I left on Google reviews. I truly enjoyed his creativity with the fresh ingredients and how their flavors blended so well together. I am a big foodie; I've eaten different types of foods at many restaurants in cities and countries worldwide.

I'll usually leave a restaurant review. Naturally, as a food lover I will try most anything, but I do have limits about trying some food traditions which I won't mention. Here I was surprisingly full after having this well-prepared gourmet course, the portions were just right. Just enough to satisfy my hunger without making me feel bloated.

It seems funny now because I first thought small portions can't be enough to eat when you're hungry. Then later, I was comically begging the waiters to stop bringing me food. I swear they served me more than just six courses. Although the portions are minuscule, you do receive a lot of favorable food. I was pleasingly surprised and impressed by this restaurant's delightful menu. When I commented about the small portions making me feel full, my main waiter laughed and said,

"Although small portions, you get many different types of good foods."

I agreed. There was even a pre-dessert before the dessert after the cheese platter. When the father and daughter were leaving, the father, I don't remember his name, it was late evening, I was full and exhausted. He walked over to my table and extended his hand for a shake. A two-handed shake, saying how nice it was to meet me.

We exchanged Bon Nuits and goodbyes. He lives in Bordeaux.

Some other restaurant patrons *(French and Americans)* upon leaving, also greeted me and asked about my dining experience. They commented on Colonel's good behavior. He was lying down patiently next to me. They had been watching him from inside. A few people just walking down the street came over to say hello and asked me a few questions about the food I ordered.

Then said, "Bon Appétit!"

A little later, my dog and I closed the joint. It was near 11 pm when I paid my bill using my Amex Platinum card, costing €125, and worth every hard-earned penny. I gave the waiter(s) an American tip of €20 just because he/they were so gracious and their service was superb. Tipping is uncommon and usually not the norm in France. Therefore, my small 16% tip was considered unusually huge.

This restaurant recommendation by a stranger was a great one. I thoroughly enjoyed my dining experience here and will be sure to pass on my recommendation of this restaurant to other people I meet. You may be able to see the menu of my six-course meal on the restaurant's site at www.cent33.com. I created a resources guide from this trip. Also, you can read my Google restaurant review of Cent33.

Now, attempting to return to the apartment, I'm lost and don't remember which way to go. Usually, I forget all about the GPS on my mobile phone like I did tonight. Colonel guided me back to the apartment because I was all turned around. Somehow, he knew the way back. How do dogs do that? Without him, tonight I would have been wandering around this neighborhood for who knows how long.

Colonel was tired and not in the mood to mess around with my silliness and lack of direction. It seems strange to feel safe walking these three blocks back to the apartment in a strange city late at night. Call me crazy, but before coming to Bordeaux I did read up on this neighborhood, which I'll mention more about later.

As I aged, I became less secure about being out walking in Los Angeles at night. I stopped walking Colonel around 7pm in the summer and 4pm in the winter months. It was no longer the safe city I once knew. I didn't feel okay about being out late at night, like when I was younger. I took a video of the falling rain. Bon Soir.

Six French Cities

Sunday, 3 Sept 2023 | Bordeaux ~ Morning

Day 2 - Good morning, Bordeaux! I set my alarm for 7 am and woke up to a beautiful view of the rooftops and a dazzling amber sky outside my bedroom window. Sunrise! Can I tell you how rested and relaxed I am right now. So happy to have a break from all the hustle, bustle, and madness that is L.A. Feels like a big weight has lifted off my shoulders. No stress! A little more tranquility. This trip was the therapy I needed. Taking it easy today, it's Sunday so most businesses and some restaurants are closed.

Unfortunately, on this trip I did not know about the huge outdoor Sunday Market in Chartrons near the river. But I found other leisurely activities to do today. The French spend time with their families on Sundays, which means shopkeepers too. I had planned to go to Arcachon *(the beach)* on the Atlantic coast this morning but I think I'll save that trip for Wednesday. I did venture out this morning with Colonel for his walk and a little grocery shopping at the nearby Carrefour market.

After last night's exceptional meal, I want to be a little more frugal and practical with my spending and eating out on this trip. I brought a few snacks, salad mix, dog food, water, yogurt, and some breakfast items. I found a bakery and bought a croissant. Now, we are just relaxing in the apartment. I peruse through a small Bordeaux guide book and think about stopping by the Tourism office later today.

Again, on the way back from grocery shopping I had to ask

some Frenchmen how to get back to my street. One thing I can say is that the French are very accommodating and helpful. And I've spoken to a variety of French people in English and in French. The French women my age are very engaging. The men, immediately helpful, when I looked a little lost. I approached two men standing next to a car. I said,

Bonjour! Then asked,

"Pouvez-vous m'aider, s'il vous plaît?" *(Can you help me, please!)*

They responded, "Bonjour" with big smiles and some aid.
I asked about locating an apartment address,

"Ou est ce rue...?" *(Where is this street?)*

I give them the address. Said I'm looking for a friend.

"Mon ami." *(My friend).*

I've found saying, *"Bonjour!"* opens friendly conversations. Of course, I could easily look up directions on Google maps using my phone's GPS, but I'm trying to use French phrases that I know more because many of the people I encountered were extremely helpful in my language learning process.

Plus, the French seem more than happy to assist with my pronunciation of French words too. Good practice! These days it seems that everyone everywhere in the world will quickly whip out their phones to use Google maps for directions. Those two guys were no exception; they pulled up the street on their phone to put us on the right path.

Again, Colonel kept trying to take me back to the apartment and I kept insisting we go in the other direction. He was right, I was wrong as usual. I should just trust my dog with his keen sense of smell and allow him to lead the way.

Six French Cities

I have an exceptional Airbnb host. He has this place stocked with all the right stuff, condiments, coffee, and snacks. Kudos Mikael! This morning, I took daytime pictures of my comfortable little second floor apartment. This building has an elevator *(Thank God!),* and stairs which are not my thing anymore because of my Asthma.

But these stairs are doable, not winding stone steps. My heavy luggage is an issue because I must lug it from place to place, going up and down stairs will be a challenge. I didn't really think much about that part at the time I was packing. Who does?

Somehow, I must make my carryon lighter at least for carrying over my shoulder. My hardshell suitcase weighs 44 pounds and is on wheels and much easier to maneuver but not to lift. The carryon duffle bag with three zippered compartments weighs 22 lbs. But 15 pounds would be much better. Ugh! I'll deal with that issue later by taking the electronics I don't need to carry around out of my carryon and pack them into the big suitcase.

Right now, I plan to go down to the Garonne River and City Center, then walk more around this neighborhood to get a stronger sense of where I am. My bike tour is tomorrow morning, the meeting place is conveniently close by in this neighborhood, just a five-minute walk. I must figure out how to turn my scarf into a body sling for carrying Colonel strapped to me for the bike ride or see if they have baskets.

So far, I am enjoying the walking part of this trip. Walking on these narrow cobblestoned streets with their slender sidewalks takes getting used to because unlike concrete or asphalt none are evenly paved. Good walking shoes are necessary to wear like my practical thick soled sneakers that make my feet very happy while out on these long treks through this city. No sore feet or blisters for me because I'll have a lot of territory to cover on foot over these three weeks.

People walk and bike a lot in this city with many bike lanes and pedestrian only streets. The city offers bike rentals and scooter rentals (with helmets). It's nice to see all the parents riding bikes with their kids on the streets of Bordeaux. The kids here start riding bikes very young, under five on two-wheelers without training wheels.

Last night I noticed quite a few families carefreely riding their bikes in the streets through the rain while singing with their children. Like a small pep rally parade full of happy kids on wheels with their moms and dads and sometimes grandparents tagging along on their bikes.

You don't see that kind of family bike riding activity anywhere in America, especially riding bikes together. Life here feels a lot less hectic and more fun; this lifestyle certainly will be much easier to manage in retirement. I'll take more pictures by the waterfront. Looks like it's going to be a bright bright sunny day. I can hear that song playing in my mind.

Sunday, 3 Sept 2023 | Bordeaux ~ Afternoon

Bordeaux's City Center is just two or three tram stops away from this apartment. I spotted a BNP bank ATM across from the Tram. I need some cash so I use my debit card to withdraw a few hundred euros. Then we are off on the Tram to the city center. On my self-guided walking tour, I see sights such as the Mirror d'eau, several plazas, the Bell Tower renovation *(scaffolding around it)* in St. Michel and other city sights on my way from and back to the apartment on the tram.

Remembering things to do, I stopped by the Tourist Office in Quinconces Square to pick up a free city map. Here you can find all types of resources for various tours, other attractions, and city passes for museums and public transportation. It's the first place you should visit in a new city if you are not on a group tour but have planned a trip yourself. The Tourist office staff can answer most of your questions about a city and dish out helpful tips.

Tomorrow, after my city bike tour, if I'm up to it, I'll take a stroll down Rue St. Catherine, it's Europe's longest retail shopping street. Also, we may visit some other nearby neighborhoods and surrounding suburbs by tram, only if I have the time and more importantly, the energy.

More tales and plenty of picture taking of Bordeaux this week. I'm thinking that this city would be a calmer and quieter place to live. I'm digging it a lot and how easy it is to get around on foot or by tram. I love the tranquil vibe here which I felt as soon as I walked out of the train station yesterday.

What an exhilarating late afternoon we had. Delighted to have received my first French Bise (kiss) from a French person. But that comes later in this story. Don't believe what you hear about the French. I can tell you this, they are not rude but are very direct.

They are private and not very engaging with strangers for the most part but once you become friends, it's for life. They have manners and expect the same from others. Oh yeah, and they like to complain about everything and will debate about anything but no one gets hurt. I respect their culture. Another thing, they are not loud talkers like us Americans.

However, you can crack their code with the right attitude, disposition, a little cultural knowledge, and remembering to say, "Bonjour!" Between my positive attitude on life, my silliness, my calm demeanor, a willingness to accept rejection, and my secret weapon (Colonel), are very helpful traits to have in a foreign land.

Plus, being polite and trying to speak French really gives you an edge to break the ice with the French people. They love helping to correct you too, so let them. I welcome their assistance especially for French pronunciation of the words. There are so many French words and phrases still to learn and understand, many words I have a difficult time pronouncing. French language learning is an ongoing process and will be for quite a while.

First figuring out how to immerse myself into French culture seamlessly helped by leaving my American ideals back in California. I didn't come to France to compare it to the U.S or hope to change anything. Nope; I like France just the way it is. All I wanted to do was blend in, absorb the culture, and simply go with the flow while having new and wonderful experiences. I'm feeling like a local as I ventured off into the City Center of Bordeaux. Having a dog draws people to you, those with and without dogs. I had countless conversations in French and English about Colonel. More of my broken French (Franglish). Being in France aids in my ability to hear more French conversations each day, not that I fully understand any of these conversations yet. Still, I listen and I learn.

The French love dogs. However, many owners still don't pick up their dog's poop, so you will see it on the sidewalks or on the streets placed like strategic mind fields you'll have to dodge. It's okay, like in Los Angeles, you get used to seeing poop everywhere. I picked up Colonel's poop. It's my responsibility as a dog owner. Plus, I'd feel too guilty leaving it lying around for someone to step in which I feel is rather inconsiderate of others.

Many of my warm encounters with all people anywhere is attributed to Colonel. These unexpected conversations are fun, lively, and friendly even if I don't always understand what's being said to me. No random nastiness either. I like this immersive experience very much. Just feels pure, natural, and necessary. Usually, the locals without saying a word teach us a lot about their city and country.

We walked a lot; I didn't look at my watch today for the number of steps taken. At first, I disliked this new Samsung watch because I thought the battery had a short lifespan. But it has a longer life span than I realized and it charges quickly when I remember to charge it every night. Plus, tracking my steps and other health features, such as sleep score, heart rate, and oxygen levels offer fantastic bits of information to have on hand.

Doctors don't recognize these smart watch health features as being medically sound or accurate. Afterall, it's only an electronic gadget worn on your wrist but I think they underestimate the overall health value of these gadgets. I find my watch to be useful. If I fall hard, my watch sends an alert to my daughter. Plus, I can see my calendar, text messages, the weather, Apps, get notifications, see two time zones at once for France and my home town, if desired. Also, like Dick Tracy, I can answer my smart phone on my watch. What? I love technology and my new Samsung Galaxy 6 Smart Watch. For this gadget girl, it does everything I can imagine and more.

After taking a bus from the apartment, about a ten-minute ride we explored two areas of Quay du Chartrons, then walked along the boardwalk to a wharf area of shops and restaurants just north on the banks of the Garonne River; then strolled over to the Miroir d'eau just a few blocks south down that boardwalk. In the city center, we passed two lovely and intricately sculptured fountains; first at the Place des Quinconces which is a year-round outdoor venue for various fun fairs, sporting events, circuses, celebrations, and artistic events.

In this plaza stands the Monument aux Girondins, a magnificent bronze fountain and column in the center with a Statue of Liberty on top breaking its chains, emblematic of the French Revolution in Bordeaux. Then in the center of the Place de la Bourse across from Miroir d'eau stands the Fountain of the Three Graces (the three daughters of Zeus), a white marble pedestal supports th three bronze statues, built in the 1700s. I've taken many city center pictures and videos featuring this fountain.

I got lucky when the tram dropped me off at Quinconces station which has a steady flow of visitors because it is a multi-transport hub (trams B, C &D), a terminus for several buses, and bike share rentals. There is a small convenience store too but pricey. Here you can buy single transit tickets for the day, week, or month. I bought a block of ten tickets coded on thick paper stock from the billet machine; a kiosk located on the tram platforms at many stops. You must remember to validate your ticket on the machine outside or inside once you board the Tram or bus. There are a few restaurants around this plaza.

From this stop it's a short walk to the downtown area, the InterContinental Hotel, a big beautiful Grand Theater and Opera House, tons of restaurants, Rue St. Catherine shops, and other city sites. Our afternoon walk through the City Center was fun and invigorating. I very much enjoyed walking around clean and lovely Bordeaux. It was easy to locate places I wanted to visit. A stress-free experience too because no one bothers you. I felt free to be me here.

Walking and taking public transportation in a new city are good ways to acclimate yourself while you locate and discover landmarks, shops, restaurants, and streets of interest. This type of exploration is insightful and helpful for navigating through any city more successfully.

Also, the audio guided Hop on Hop off city bus tours are another fantastic way to become familiar with a foreign city. Booking a private guided tour to see the sites and to learn more about the history of a city is also recommended. I've learned so much about the cities I've visited on these types of tours and honestly just by walking and talking to locals I passed.

On the Chartrons Quay, it's almost 6 pm, it's before dinner so it's Apéro time at many restaurants (just drinks and light snacks) are served. Like our happy hour, but here drinks are served between 5 pm to 7 pm where the French often hang out to unwind from the work day or meet up with friends. And then may dine at a different restaurant later. I found a restaurant, MK, serving dinner before 7 pm.

Large restaurants in France that serve meals all day without a break (breakfast, lunch, and dinner) are called Brasseries. Then there are the Bistros, smaller casual restaurants, often inexpensive, more intimate serving hearty meals for lunch and dinner or just dinner. Cafés are casual eateries serving coffee, hot chocolate, tea, snacks, and pastries. Fine dining restaurants are elegant, expensive, expansive, or intimate, usually having dress codes and are open for dinner only.

The Wharf area caters to tourists evident by the line of the river cruise ships anchored nearby. This Brasserie looks like it's going to be a good dining spot, many tables already filled with drinks and meals being served. The wait staff, although busy, are very patient and accommodating. These servers are like a team of relay runners passing batons, scurrying about taking orders and delivering dishes. There is a great view of the river here too. The sun has not set yet, but will soon.

It is always a pleasant experience to sit outside which I prefer doing on a warm day. At this restaurant, I am watching boats cruising leisurely down the Garonne River where several river cruise ships like Amawaterways were anchored and lined up along the dock for the day. Scenic River Cruises and Viking River Cruises were here earlier but cruised off to their next destination.

This river is on the Mediterranean route taken by larger ocean cruise ships like Silver Seas going to Italy and Greece. Then the long boat river cruises traversing down several French and German waterways. There are plenty of people strolling along the riverfront too. It is a remarkably calm atmosphere even with the throngs of people walking and talking as they pass by apparently on their own meal quests too.

I ordered Duck Confit with Frites *(fries)* and a Coke. The duck was slightly salty *(sea salt)*. The fries are crunchy. I wish that this dish had come with a salad. I'm feeling vegetable deprived. I did pick up two bags of lettuce greens, cucumbers, and tomatoes at the little market for lunch tomorrow. Whatever oil they fried these Frites in was flavorful, not greasy, and didn't leave them soggy. Scrumptious!

The French Fry as we call it in America is just Frites *(fries)* in France. This double fried potato is believed to have originated during the 1600s in Belgium where French/Flemish, Dutch and German are spoken. The Spanish brought potatoes to Europe. French Chefs adopted and refined this potato frying method. Then Thomas Jefferson introduced the French fry to America from France with a recipe for pommes de terre frites a cru en petites *(deep-fried potatoes in small cuttings)* after he served as the American Minister to France from 1784 to 1789.

The waiters here are such gentlemen. I had two young cuties waiting on me. I took their pictures, of course. So, I started off speaking a little French, when Spanish tried to intrude. Finally, I gave up and spoke to them in English. Grateful that both waiters spoke English too. My limited language skills didn't stop me from saying "Bonjour, Merci, and s'il vous plait" though. I'm not giving up on French. Instead, I plan to stumble along using it until I can become better at having lengthy conversations in French.

Sitting at a table near the walkway, which I chose, tends to create an opening for conversations from locals who pass by me. I received many Bonjours and Bona Petites. See, the French are not rude at all. Sometimes, I'd initiate a conversation just to see if I'd get a response and a smile. It worked.

Other times locals would just say Bonjour and Bonne Soirée without any prompting from me. Colonel met a lot of dogs too. One can't be shy in a foreign country, you must push the envelope, step outside of your comfort zone, and be a little more engaging. Since I enjoy meeting, talking to, and getting to know people, it's easier for me to just be open and friendly.

After dinner I chilled with a glass of red wine, a Bordeaux Graves. Light body, smooth, with cherry and oak flavors. Getting better at tasting what's in the wine. What I like most about dining in France besides the food is that you can sit at a table for hours. No one hassles you or rushes you to leave. This time I only dined for two hours.

Also, a tip about tipping, you really don't have to tip waiters because they get a decent wage. But Americans have spoiled them by leaving large tips so now some servers pretty much expect something, I usually leave one or two euros. Recently I read an article about some Paris restaurants now asking for tips, or you may find gratuities, a certain percentage printed on the bottom of menus, so look out for that wording on menus in Paris.

My bill was €33; I left a tip of four euros. As I mentioned, 10%

or less is good unless you want to be generous and leave 15% or 20% like in the U.S. But normally a tip is not necessary. These waiters have been so good and attentive,

"Madam, can I get you anything else?"

"Madam, would you like more water?"

Consequently, I felt it was very necessary to leave this small tip due to the great service I received. The waiters were very polite. Wait time for service was quick at both restaurants. The service was excellent. The meal was delightful and the ambience could not have been better. I sat to watch the sun setting, a mosaic tapestry of light blue, amber, and steel blue colors painted the open sky. Beautiful! We left the restaurant just before the setting sun faded beyond the horizon.

Slowly enjoying the evening sites, we ventured to the City Center, taking the tram that runs along the river. You know many of the buildings here date back before the 14th century and were also built by Napoleon in the 19th century, an important period in world history.

I love history, antiques, and old buildings. In France, there is so much history and stunning architecture. Always look up at the top of buildings while walking through a larger city's streets in France. The architecture styles are divine; you will see so much intricate and beautiful detail carved into many structures.

The artists from other countries who came to France to paint were significantly influenced by the architecture, the landscapes, and the people so evidently portrayed in their lovely works of art. The writers who moved here from other countries were affected by the medieval ambience, unique architecture, charming villages, colorful character driven cities and the wines.

It's easy to be creative in France. Along with writing, art was another talent, an activity I dabbled in as a kid but never had a passion for it. I drew with pencils and charcoal a lot, colored with crayons of course, and enjoyed painting with watercolors.

So, I appreciate the 20th Century Masters and earlier artists, architects, and creative individuals. Mostly, I read and wrote poetry and short stories. I idealized other writers as I strived to become one.

Finally, off the tram and walking we reached Place du Borse and the Miroir D'eau (water mirror), a shallow reflecting pool, not really a pool. I took too many pictures. This man-made wonder was a site I wanted to see in person, it's so impressive. At night, the back lit buildings in the background reflect off the pool's water like an image seen on a pretty postcard.

We stayed until twilight, then headed back to the apartment. My second day here was full of good food and wine, wandering aimlessly around town, and having more delightful people encounters. As we walked back to wind down, the city was revving up for the evening. This is not a sleepy town. It's another college town so you will see tons of young people.

There are bars, pubs, jazz clubs, and discos for evening entertainment. The lit-up bars and restaurants are lined up across the street from the river; all are beginning to fill up with patrons of all ages. If you want to get a seat, you'll have to arrive at a restaurant just before 7 pm, unless you have a reservation. Between 10 pm to 12 pm many restaurants begin closing, bars are open late, some until 4 am. Too late for me, these days my stagecoach turns into a pumpkin around 10 pm.

You will also find plenty of movie theatres, sports stadiums, operas, concerts, museums, and performing arts events to attend here. No shortage of physical things to do either such as Yoga, Pilates, martial arts, gyms, dancing, the beach, bowling, and roller skating. Pickle Ball, Tennis, and golf aplenty.

There's even a casino, if you want to play the slots. Public indoor pools are everywhere. The parks are tremendous for picnicking, strolling or bike riding. There is plenty to do in Bordeaux, so you will never get bored living in this city.

I decided to take the tram as far as I could then walk the rest of the way to the apartment. Before boarding the tram across from the reflecting pool, I stopped two lovely young French women on the Tram's platform for directions back to Les Chartrons. Still a little lost in Bordeaux, but I am now starting to recognize landmarks when I see them.

The girls were sweet; one spoke only French. The other understood and spoke English, she gave me my first Bise, a kiss on both cheeks, at the end of our conversation. I thanked them in French and English for their assistance. I love this country so much, and this city feels like home. So far Bordeaux, the first city I have visited on this journey, is winning me over and is in first place in this city search.

Once off the tram, this time I used Google's GPS on my phone to guide me back to the apartment. We settled in for the night. I fed Colonel, and grabbed myself a drink of Orangina. I'm addicted to this fizzy orange flavored beverage. Soon Colonel is curled up in bed next to me. I'm still so excited to be here, I can't really fall asleep. Colonel on the other hand falls fast asleep. I study a little French using Duolingo. I vowed to continue to study this difficult language while on this trip. Still not sleepy. I listened to a few chapters of my audio book and then finished writing this post.

Now, it's nearly 4 am and I have a 10 am bike tour on this quickly approaching Monday morning. Ugh! My photos highlight a pleasant Sunday afternoon and evening in Bordeaux. People wonder what do the French wear every day? The French dress just like us, some older women dress more conservatively. Haven't seen any risqué outfits worn by younger women, nothing trashy. But I've only been here two days.

The French wear jeans, pants, nice tops and dresses, no short shorts that I've noticed. Nikes are popular athletic shoes worn on French feet. No flip flops. My apparel is casual and two summer dresses, a pair of sandals and a pair of flats. I prefer wearing my jeans, a light top, and my tennis shoes most days though. Finally, my eyes are getting heavy. Bon nuit!

Monday, Sept 4, 2023 | Bordeaux ~ Bike Tour

Day 3 – Up early and excited about today's 10 am activity, a three-hour bike tour around the city of Bordeaux – costing $37.72 – booked on Viator, a global website for city day tours. In my haste, I forgot to grab Colonel's blanket to put inside the bike's basket for his comfort. I may be sleepwalking because I did not get enough sleep.

The bike tour meeting location was a ten-minute walk. While walking to meet our group, I felt a warm feeling that this was going to be an amazing bike tour. Although I only had four hours of sleep, I felt good. Still, I have not ridden my bike since before Covid, I felt cocky and confident that I could survive this three-hour ride. Maybe.

Our three French guides were safety conscious, very amusing and knowledgeable about the city. Giving our English-speaking group in English on this tour. We rode across the city with glee, experiencing different neighborhoods, the old parts, and the newer developments. We cycled on both sides of the river. There is a lot of construction going on in Bordeaux. It's very modern in many ways, but not erasing that old-world magic; still many older buildings remain standing all around this city.

Looking down the numerous slender side streets, they feel trapped in time, many are occupied by businesses, apartments, shops, and restaurants. There is something very special about this city, it's diverse, warm, and so very inviting. Bordeaux takes you in its arms and holds you tightly, so you don't want it to let you go or you to leave.

The parks and green spaces are very lush and beautiful; some have gorgeous botanical gardens. The current Mayor of Bordeaux is an environmentalist which reflects in his modern eco-friendly city planning with many fresh and extensive green spaces. The trees and flowers were still in bloom, lots of green plants climbing up the sides of buildings like ivy. You could spend hours just sitting in the parks to enjoy the passive sounds of nature or even read a book. No one disturbs you here.

No one plays loud music nor are people talking loudly on cell phones or shouting at each other to invade your peaceful space and solace. Just nature and people walking, talking, biking, or sitting on the grass picnicking. Walking dogs, lots of dogs. Can you imagine a place where quiet is revered? It seems that people are respectful of each other and other people's space and peace here, I like that. It's a very slow paced and quiet city.

Even the neighborhood where I'm staying this week is very quiet at night. There are no crowds of people out on the sidewalks talking loudly, or noise emanating from apartments, or cars blasting music late at night. People out walking and riding bikes are talking in lower volumes than Americans often do.

Truly I can appreciate this type of peace and quiet. It's what I am searching for after years of living in a very loud and fast-moving city in America where you will hear a daily clash of high decibel sounds like cymbals crashing together. Noise wears you down. So, you become like a seeker of peace. I am seeking peace.

On this tour, the majority of the 12 participants are tourists, singles and couples from various countries, Ireland, England, Germany, Sweden, Canada, Australia, and America, all English Speaking, along with our three French guides. It was a lively and talkative group. We all related well. An Irish guy on our tour loaned his hat to Colonel for sitting on in the basket that's attached to my bike. The basket had holes catching his nails, the hat helped.

Often when leaving the apartment with this dog, a tote bag full of dog accessories, his carrier, and my purse, it becomes a big production for which I end up leaving something behind. This time, in a rush, I didn't take his carrier or a tote bag. Therefore, he's without water, food, or his blanket. It's a hot day. Me, totally sleep deprived and forgetful.

This bike tour in Bordeaux, which I highly recommend, provided so much insightful information about this city; the history of the Romans, the Dutch, the English, and Napolean, the Corsican, who built much of Bordeaux; the wine merchants and the slave trade that brought spices to France from the Caribbean. All contributed to the development of Bordeaux which rose from soggy marsh lands.

The French emancipated Slaves long before the Americans had but they are not very proud of that part of their history, yet they don't try to hide it or deny it much. It is a part of French history to be studied. Slavery has left an ugly scar on many countries; it was a sad reality.

Before all the buildings here were sand blasted to their current light sandy color, they were black due to the environment and carbon effects. The many ancient churches throughout the city were built without bell towers inside them. The reasoning was that the builders believed that the vibration from the ringing of the bells would cause the structure to collapse. That's why independent bell towers were built next to Les Eglises (the churches) in Bordeaux. The gothic style churches in this city are gorgeous inside and out carved with very intricate details, stained glass windows, and symbolic sculptures adorn each one.

The Dutch taught the Bordelaise how to remove the water from the land. A Dutch engineer, Conrad Gaussen, was hired and responsible for the dredging and draining. French history, from the 1st Century BC through WWII had always piqued my curiosity and interests. Napoleon Bonaparte had a major role in the way Paris and many other French cities are laid out and look today. The architecture is just splendid.

The buildings here are not as tall as those in Paris because of the marshy terrain. Most buildings only go up two, three or four stories. It is rare to see buildings here reach six stories but some older ones do in the city center. Newer multi-story high-rise apartments are seen on the outskirts of town surrounding the city but those are a rare sight to see in central Bordeaux.

Although, I did see a few newer apartment buildings squeezed in between older ones of the same height downtown and in neighborhoods. As the city grows and expands due to new construction and growth, it takes on a morphed 21st century look and feel, still old Bordeaux's allure and feel outshines the newer developments.

Early wine producers could only keep bottles of wine on their shelves for six months before it turned to vinegar. When Sulphur, a preservative, was added to wines, they were able to last for years, often decades without turning into vinegar. Organic winemakers are also making their marks in France by producing some of the best organic wines in the world.

Growing grapes takes the right soil, weather, and sun. Bordeaux has all the right traits needed for growing grapes and producing outstanding wines. Wine is cheaper to buy here too. The cheap wines are just as good as those more expensive ones. Forget about your Trade Joe's two buck Chucks back in the states. The less expensive wine here is supreme.

What I've noticed most about this city from walking and riding our bikes is how clean it is, except for the occasional dog poop I've mentioned. Also, I haven't seen many homeless people or any encampments yet. So, if there are multitudes of homeless people here, I don't know what the city has done with them.

I've always enjoyed architecture from growing up in Chicago and learning about Frank Lloyd Wright. When I was young, I thought the Water Tower looked like something from ancient times, kind of out of place with the taller more modern adjacent buildings nearby. Historic old buildings have their own stories to tell. I bet these buildings in Bordeaux could tell us a lot.

Somehow, I managed to endure, without passing out from exhaustion, this three-hour biking experience on only four hours of sleep. You know it takes much strength and endurance to ride that long on uneven pavement, dirt, gravel, and grass. I am more accustomed to riding my bike over smooth concrete and asphalt. Still, I managed to keep up with everyone until near the end of our tour. We rode across Pont Neuf (new bridge) to reach the right side of the river to explore Bastide and visit Darwin, the street artist venue. We spent about 15 or 20 minutes exploring and stopping for drinks and food at the cafes.

When we reached modern hydraulic Pont Jacques Chaban Delmas, the newer suspension bridge, near Cite du Vin, which starts on a slight incline, we peddled across it to Rive Gauche. Well, they all peddled across this bridge way ahead of me, while I walked my bike half way across that bridge because I could not pedal up the bridge's incline, while everyone else rode on. By the time I reached the center of this very expansive bridge over the Garonne, my group was at the bottom of this bridge waiting for me. Now, back on my bike I'm able to just coast down until I reach them. Literally, it was all I could do, I had run out of steam, out of pedal power, and I have no shame.

Hoping that tomorrow my body is not sore or achy. I plan to ship my personal bike here too when I move. Although fatigued from the ride, I enjoyed this very educational and fun activity. It was a very insightful tour where I learned so much more about the history of this city and the wine trade. Each time I've traveled solo, with a group, or with my sister, some sort of tour(s) was on the itinerary. Touring cities and participating in activities while visiting is an excellent way to learn more about them. Plus, you meet other interesting people on these tours.

On this bike tour, we had a great group of friendly people from different parts of the world and all were fun and very engaging. It's always very inspiring to meet other like-minded travelers and hear about their travels and trip experiences too. Tomorrow I'm taking a day trip to explore a village.

Six French Cities

Tuesday, Sept 5, 2023 | Trip to St. Emilion

Day 4 – We took the tram to Gare St. Jean train station, only eight stops from where we boarded. This morning is our day trip to the medieval village of St. Emillion. Our train leaves at 9:41 am and arrives at 10:12 am, just a 31-minute ride through the countryside. My 2nd class one-way ticket on the SNCF TER train costs €10.40, which I purchased on the Omio App in August. This is another famous wine producing region and a UNESCO World Heritage site as is the entire city of Bordeaux.

Additionally, online I reserved two one-hour wine tours at 11:00 am and at 2:30 pm. My plan includes having lunch here and later exploring this village. Today, I brought Colonel's dog carrier so he can sleep while I'm touring. He acts as if I'm tormenting him when we're out on these day-long tours which disrupts his sleep routine, so he's a little cranky.

Therefore, I want to make this journey for him as comfortable as possible. The carrier with him in it is a lot heavier. Still, having his carrier on our excursions is better than him being just on lease all day without his carrier. When he is comfortable, I can enjoy my outings, especially visiting this village.

We arrived at the small train station in what seemed like out in the middle of nowhere. Off the train, I'm standing on the small platform and looking around. It's quite a desolate location and there were no taxis waiting to whisk us away. Naturally, I had no clue as to how to get into the town from here. When I booked my train ticket, I assumed there would be taxis waiting at the station. This station was small, having just a platform without an operating building or any customer service to get information. I noticed other people from my train walking toward the village. I couldn't even see the town, just a long dusty dirt road possibly leading to it. Great!

Seriously, no way would I be hauling this dog around in his carrier for a long-distance dirt road walk. Even at just six pounds, he's no lightweight when inside it. I let him out to pee and walk awhile before putting him back inside. Then I spotted a six-passenger shuttle golf cart in the nearby parking lot. I walked up to the waiting driver and I asked if he spoke English and if he could take me into town. He did speak English and agreed to drive me into the picturesque village of St. Emilion.

I asked, "how much?"

"€16," he said.

I paid him in cash. He worked for a tour company and had just dropped off some clients at the train station. Lucky for me because I was not looking forward to a long walk to reach the village.

My ride request was unusual because he only drives small private tour groups around St. Emilion throughout the day. I asked when his next tour started, then if he'd have time to drive me to my first wine tour and tasting at 11 am. He agreed to take me for another €16. I don't mind paying for his shuttle service. It's convenient for me. This is a very hilly village.

Some Chateaux can be reached on foot, but others you need a car or shuttle to reach them. I didn't want to walk through these dirt-filled vineyards with this dog in his carrier. Going up and down hills on mostly dirt and graveled roads was not at all appealing.

Granted Colonel could walk too, still, he'll need to be inside this carrier off and on. Vacations should be relaxing. Why isn't there a shuttle service at the train station to at least take folks into town and bring them back to the train station? I didn't even think about calling an Uber.

Once in town it was now 10:20 am, I only had 40 minutes before my 11 am wine tour and tasting started. My shuttle driver dropped me off in a square with a few surrounding restaurants looking like a still shot from a Hollywood movie. The driver would return to get me in 30 minutes. I found a restaurant, La Bouchon, where I ordered a Petit Déjeuner Express off their menu. My €6 breakfast consisted of a cup of coffee and a croissant. These are tourist rates.

In Bordeaux, a neighborhood croissant from a boulangerie would cost €1.20 and coffee would cost about €2.20, half the price of this place. I sat outside to 'people watch' and gobble down my breakfast. Gave Colonel some water and offered him Kibble. I did not take a picture of this meal because I was pressed for time but got a shot of the restaurant and menu.

My first tour was at Chateau La Croizille, a family-owned vineyard. I booked this 11 am tour online through Viator for $17.75. It was a bumpy ride on this golf cart shuttle going down dirt roads that circled and climbed the rather steep hillside to the Chateau.

Walking this route would have been challenging for me, but many people were hiking up and down those rugged hills through the vineyards. I was more than grateful for the ride as I took a video along this rough journey. In this setting, the uniform grape vines were full of sun kissed grapes looking like a short miniature forest.

At this Chateau, our group of ten did not get to tour the exterior vineyards to see the grapevines, instead we toured the interior of the Chateau where the wine was fermented and produced. The knowledgeable young male guide gave his insightful presentation in English and in French about the Chateau and winemaking. He showed us barrels and vats and how they were used. Explaining fermentation and the wine making process. At the end of the tour, we sampled three bottles of their more recently produced wines. I bought six bottles of the one I preferred and had them shipped back to my home in Los Angeles. Those six bottles of wine cost €235 including Vat (taxes) and shipping.

For decades, I have enjoyed tasting and drinking different types of wines in California and other countries. This red wine blend was smooth, with a low acidity, nice aroma, and pleasant enough as an everyday table wine. However, I'm still a wine novice so no expert rundown of flavors or quality. Also, I am not a fan of high acidic wines. This in-depth wine tour lasted about an hour. In the future, my plans include taking a French wine class. A French cooking class, and a French language course after I move to France.

By now it's a little after 12 noon, I was ready for lunch and to head back into town. My shuttle driver appeared in the parking lot to take me down the hill on this short 10-minute drive back to the village. Finding my way back into town on foot would have taken much longer especially with my lack of direction. I don't mind paying the price for ease and convenience. It was a happy win-win for all parties.

When the driver dropped me off in the same square, I paid him then asked if he could take me to my next wine tour at 2:30 pm.

"Yes, no problem, it's between his tours," he replied.

He'd pick me up at 2:15 pm at the same spot. Back in town, I wanted to find a different restaurant, but not sure what I wanted to eat. So, we just walked around, Colonel is now walking on his lease. I'll feed him once we settle at a table. A small modest café, La Bonheur, appeared to my right. It was on an elevated landing with outside seating and one long communal table. It's a small outside patio, only three tables. My kind of unassuming dining option. I gestured to a waiter pointing at a seat. Grabbed a chair on the end of the long empty table. In France, it's better to ask a server about outdoor seating first before just flopping down at a table. Usually, you must wait to be seated.

This table was empty until an Italian family of five, husband, wife, daughter, sister-in-law, and brother joined me. They were warm, friendly, and spoke good English. We had a light-hearted chat about visiting France and this special little village. Both husband and wife were very funny and so engaging. We laughed a lot. I enjoyed meeting them. Their young daughter loved Colonel; they kept each other company. This family is on holiday touring around the South and Southwest of France. I had many international people encounters like this one on my journey.

I went inside the cafe to order my meal, selecting a chicken sandwich on a baguette with fries and a Coke. More than enough to satisfy my noon time craving. In France, frites (fries) are on the menu of nearly every restaurant. Atypical of me but I ate loads of fries throughout this trip. During all the chumminess, I forgot to take pictures of myself with this lovely family. So caught up in our lively and animated conversations before dashing off to my next wine Tour.

After lunch I had about 45 minutes to take a pleasant walk around this hilly village. At my age, hills like stairs inhibit my full enjoyment for walking. My lung capacity is less now than in my youth thanks to allergies and asthma. But I will climb hills and stairs anyway because sometimes I must climb them. My bionic knees, both total knee replacements, help rather than hinder my ability to walk. These days, I just want to take it easy. However, these medical issues have not kept me from enjoying life and activities. I'm just mindful of my limitations, not overdoing it, and focused on taking good care of myself. And my inhaler is always handy.

In France, like many European countries, while visiting these cities, you feel as if you've been transported back in time to the Middle Ages or beyond. Navigating these very hilly and narrow cobblestoned streets, I noticed the jagged alignment of ancient buildings along the way housing shops, restaurants, and apartments each unique in architecture and design. In this setting the only thing out of place are the people dressed in 21st Century attire.

I always imagined what it would be like to walk through a 15th century French Village, so I very much enjoyed exploring St. Emilion, which did not disappoint my expectations one bit. I look forward to returning here again in the future. There is so much more to see and do in this village and region. More wine tastings, and food to sample of course.

On my invigorating village walk, I ran into the Italian Family again when I stopped at the famous Canales shop, Le Veritable Macaron De St. Emilion, to sample this traditional pastry. This is one of the shops I hoped to visit. The Italian family was entering as I was leaving.

The wife said, "Hey, are you following us?" and laughed.

We hugged again. This pastry shop is where the first Canales were created by mistake and became a big sensation among the Bordelais. The locals love Canales. I bought two small ones from this shop. The taste and texture take getting used to so I am not an immediate fan. But it's always worth trying something new instead of passing up such an opportunity.

Around 2 pm, I found my way back to the square to wait for the Shuttle driver. He arrived. Then let me know that he had a tour around the time that my tour ended. Therefore, he could take me to my next tour but would not be able to pick me up. Then he added,

"You can walk back to the village with other people because it isn't very far away."

"No problem, and thank you very much for helping me." I responded.

Then, after he dropped me off at the winery, I paid him and wished him a Bonne Journeé. I so appreciated that Philip agreed to cart me around back and forth to my tastings in his golf cart. For his service, I paid him a total of €64 for those four trips, expensive but so needed. I would not have made it to and from my first wine tour without his help.

These wineries are scattered throughout this appellation, some high up on top of hills. Plus, the distances between them are not short. I wasn't prepared for all the trekking involved throughout this old-world village.

My Second Tour was at the Saint Georges Cote Pavie, Grand

Cru Classe – cost $18.86, which I booked on Viator. Most French wineries are family owned. Here we toured the vineyards outside, learned about the grapes growing on the vines, the winemaker, and the production process. We toured throughout the interior of the Chateau where the grapes are fermented in oak barrels and the wine produced. Then we sampled three bottles of red wine, another blend. I bought one bottle of their Cote Pave Grand Cru 2014 (the second one we sampled). I paid either €22 or €24 for it. I find the entire winemaking process very fascinating. It's a lot of work and takes manpower to produce wine.

During this afternoon wine tour, I met Kate who is from London and her boyfriend Perry. Colonel liked her right away. Kate has two cats. She wants me and Colonel to come to London to visit them. We exchanged phone numbers. I said I would (and we have kept in touch by text messages ever since). So sweet! I had so many lovely "by chance" meetings, fun experiences, and many insightful conversations with other tourists about traveling, on being in France, our similarities, interests, and traveling with dogs. I chose the right time of year to make this trip.

After the tour, we all walked back down the hill into town together. This walk wasn't bad at all. In fact, it was an easier walk than I had expected. With time to spare before catching our train back to Bordeaux, I took another stroll around this hilly town.

Colonel is on his lease walking, sniffing, and enjoying the scents. Of course, when it's time to return to Bordeaux, I have no idea in which direction to go to reach the train station. I needed a map on this journey. Naturally, I'm not thinking about Google Maps. Luckily, I ran into Kate and Perry who were sitting on grass in a small shaded plaza relaxing. I approached them to ask for directions to the train station and how far it was from here.

Perry says, "It's about a 15-minute walk from here."

"Oh no!" I reply, "Is there a cab or Uber I can call?"

Kate responds, "We called Uber and are waiting for it to arrive. You can ride to the train station with us."

I said joyfully, "That would be great. I'll pay for it or we can split the cost."

Perry quickly added, "No, we got it."

The Uber driver arrived soon and dropped us off at the station. We then waited on a bench together for the 5:15 pm train back to Bordeaux. Giving us 30 minutes to talk and get to know each other more before the train arrived. Slowly more people began arriving on foot from the village to catch this train.

On the train we sat across the aisle from one another in our assigned 2nd class seats. Still talking back and forth for a while. Colonel was on my lap now, just chilling as I looked out of the window to see several villages and vineyards rushing by like in a scene from a movie.

A conductor checked our tickets on our phones. Traveling by train in France is a wonderful way to get from city to city. I enjoyed it immensely. You'll see many backpackers, families, friends, couples, and solo travelers onboard.

We were back at the apartment a little after 6 pm and settled in for the evening. I prepared a petite tub of wet food for my little boss dog. After eating, he was ready for a nap. Then I popped a small frozen cheese and ham pizza into the oven that I had bought earlier. Made a mini-salad and poured a glass of Orangina, a very refreshing and bubbly orange flavored beverage. It's been a long day for both of us. I was very happy to have made that day trip to visit historic St. Emilion. It's one of many must-see village side trips when you visit Bordeaux.

My first French wine country tour and tasting experience here was so enjoyable, looking forward to more similar tours in the future. Day trips to another city, town or village are pleasing little adventures to work into your agenda. The French countryside is beautiful. I prefer living on the outskirts of a city but not too far away from the center. Bordeaux has an awesome transit system of Trams and Buses that run regularly and carry friendly, helpful people. A car isn't really needed in the city. It's a flat city, no subways, no stairs. Yippee!

Now I am familiar with taking the C tram from the City Center back to the apartment. And knowing my way around this neighborhood by recognizing the streets and buildings. Seeing and speaking to friendly locals regularly who make me feel at home. Now, I must hop on my computer for some remote work. Colonel has already jumped onto the bed. He's asleep. Á Bientôt!

Six French Cities

Wednesday, Sept 6, 2023 | Bordeaux

Day 5 - Yesterday (Tuesday) I had a tasty lunch in St. Emillion, a village outside Bordeaux but in the same southwest region. It's an appellation known for its over 800 vineyards. I had two wine tours and tastings, and then strolled around this hilly village for a few hours before catching the train back to Bordeaux. I took a few pictures with my phone camera but the majority are in my digital camera. Now it is just figuring out how to transfer these pictures to my laptop, the old way didn't seem to work.

This is my last night in Bordeaux. Sad to leave but eager to see what the next city has in store, excited to continue my journey, the next city will be revealed tomorrow. Hint: Tapas.

I got a late start today due to packing, cleaning, and doing laundry. Today was a long day spent out exploring Bordeaux and back at the apartment by 5:00 pm. This afternoon around 2:00 pm, we went to Cite du Vin to see the permanent exposition and taste wine. The entry cost €22 for adults. Arriving early, I missed the crowd and long lines. So, I bought my ticket inside the museum. Dogs are not allowed in this museum but Colonel was allowed inside due to his service dog credentials.

He went through a security check to verify that he was indeed a service dog and was cleared. He was also in his carrier, which I like taking to lessen the hassle of dealing with people who don't understand his status; plus, to keep him confined from people who may have dog allergies. I try to be as considerate as possible with him because he is always with me everywhere I go. Due to so many people who lack an understanding about disabilities and the ADA, service dog status is complicated; papers and certificates are not needed to prove a service dog's status in the US but I carry them anyway for the uneducated.

This wine museum located on the banks of the Garonne River is a six sensory experience. The permanent expedition provides a history of winemaking in Bordeaux and all around the world. There are so many grape varieties. Grapes grow in two bands - North and South. Learning why grapes go into vats first then into barrels. And why grapes are no longer crushed by stomping feet. How elevation, weather, soil, and sun affect the quality of a wine.

The higher the slopes the better the quality. Blending grapes, fermentation, maturation; also, how winemakers create new wines and the time it takes to develop them. To me the wine making process is captivating. How old are the barrels that hold the wines and how many years are they kept? The dates on bottles are the years when the grapes were picked. So much relevant information.

I was there for a little over 2 hours, then had to make a mad dash back to the apartment to begin work. Will have some Zoom meetings too this week. Since I'm dealing with a time zone difference, I can only stay up so long to work (5pm-12am) for morning Zoom meetings. Evenings in France are morning work days in Los Angeles.

I'm working remotely this week only. Caught up on reading and responding to all my emails, text messages, scheduling appointments and meetings for the boss, and our staff meetings. I have a staff zoom meeting to attend with the three Chiodo brothers who created the Killer Klowns from Outer Space movie. Our weekly 5 pm staff meeting is too late for me to attend due to our time differences. While here in Bordeaux I did attend our weekly 10 am (LA time) Zoom meetings with the show runners, Alfred and Miles and for Wednesday, the TV series on Netflix.

I took beaucoup photos at the wine museum. Also, showing what a wash day without a clothes dryer looks like in France. It took me a while to figure out how to use the French washing machine. Conveniently, the owner has stocked a box of detergent pods on a shelf. I've also found ice cubes in the fridge packaged in a blue disposable plastic bag shaped like cubes. I filled the bag with tap water, froze it, and later had ice cubes with my soft drinks.

This city was more vibrant today, since the French residents have returned from their month-long August vacations, parents are back to work and the kids are back to school on Monday. It's nice to see the city in full swing with the French locals everywhere. More energy but still pretty laid back in this town. Nights here are peaceful. The city of Bordeaux has a population of 265,328 residents. Students 56,000. The entire region (Nouvelle-Aquitaine) holds 1.6 million people currently. Still less than the 9.6 million living in Los Angeles.

Bordeaux does not feel overcrowded; there is a noticeable difference. I looked up rents online for one-bedroom apartments in Bordeaux, which start from €600-€1200. This is a college town too, so prices are ideal for students and retirees. You can even rent a two-bedroom house for less than €1000 per month in the suburbs. And these are not shabby rundown places nor are they far away from the city. Most old rentals are newly renovated or in newer buildings. So housing is extremely affordable in this city.

But like most cities it depends on which area you wish to live in. Downtown, around the city center, the prices are much higher. Within the outlying towns and suburbs, the prices are lower. Still, I find the cost of living much lower here in good neighborhoods. The prices at the grocery stores were less or comparable to the U.S. for some items. The cheapest wines I saw were about €2.35.

Of course, there are more expensive wines too. The mid-range bottles of Bordeaux wines are about €6-8; they are so very good. I tried a few 3-euro bottles which were better than Trader Joe's two buck Chuck. Healthcare is so inexpensive, I wonder why the U.S. does not adopt Universal Healthcare, our taxes would help pay for the cost.

It would be easier for me to live here because the rents in France are regulated and with small increases each year. I plan to come back to France next year hopefully to see the Loire Valley Region and Burgundy to the East. Tomorrow, I leave Bordeaux for another city, a quick trip, an overnight experience with a unique culture. Right now, work awaits me. My long fun-filled break is over. Au revoir!

CHAPTER SIX

Discovering Biarritz

Thursday, Sept 7, 2023 | Train to Biarritz

Day 6 – Last night I texted the Bordeaux apartment owner to let him know when I would be checking out in the morning, and to also thank him. I hope to return to Bordeaux someday. I left a review on Airbnb about these accommodations. Later, Mikael also left a great review about me.

He texted me later that day to say how surprised and pleased he was to find that I left the apartment extremely clean. No one has ever cleaned it like that, he said. Well, I was taught that if you find it clean, you leave it clean. Plus, I would never leave my mess, I like clean and tidy. Furthermore, I truly appreciated being able to stay in his adorable place for six days.

I noticed there were no leaf blowers in my Bordeaux neighborhood, so I was glad. Perhaps the gardeners use them in the suburbs. The leaf blowing gardeners appeared early every doggone day in my suburban Los Angeles neighborhood. Since getting older my noise tolerance has lessened. I've grown accustomed to kids screaming, they're kids. However, I have no tolerance towards adults making loud unnecessary noises day and night. I strive to find peace and quiet in my retirement. I know this peace I seek does still exist. Just not in my neighborhood or anywhere in L.A anymore. I sure do miss the innocence and calmness of 70's L.A.

Currently, I'm on an early morning train heading to Basque Country and the City of Biarritz on the Spanish border. It's just over two hours to get there from Bordeaux. Here the locals speak both French and Spanish. After watching a segment of Rick Steve visiting Biarritz, I knew I had to experience it too. It took a while to get to my train car due to the deboarding of the French Rugby team. We had to wait, finally I broke through to scurry down this platform and find my coach number. It seemed a mile away. I needed a cart or a shuttle to help me get way down there with my bags.

Spotty WiFi on this train, while writing this post, I keep losing the text. So, now I'm writing these posts on Google Docs to preserve them instead of typing directly into Facebook. It hurts to lose a lot of content you've just typed. The Big Rugby Championship is happening now in Bordeaux and all over France this month. Fans are everywhere, even aboard this train.

I booked an Uber from the train station in Biarritz to the hotel. Again, as usual not knowing exactly where I'm going. I think half the fun is getting lost in a new city, a labyrinth of ancient streets weaving towards who knows what or where until you are there. My three-star boutique hotel, Escale Oceania, which I booked on Expedia for $130 per night, is just a two-block walk (10 minutes) to Le Grande Plage (large beach) in a ritzy neighborhood.

Before booking this hotel, I checked its location on Google maps and street view. I want to be within walking distance to the beach. As of 2024, this hotel has new ownership and the name changed to Hotel Akena Biarritz. Also, I checked out its amenities not that I'll need many for a one-night stay. At check-in, the receptionist asked if I'd like breakfast at their restaurant in the morning for €16.

My response, "Oui. Merci!"

They serve breakfast between 7:00-10:00 am. Usually I would skip this amenity and find a local restaurant nearby instead. But I'll be leaving this hotel early tomorrow and would like to have a quick hearty and hot meal beforehand. After checking in and dropping my bags off in the room, I took Colonel for a walk. Our strolls usually take several hours to just check out a neighborhood and surroundings.

Again, I chose a great hotel location. We walked down to the beach where Colonel greeted a few dogs. Lots of people were stretched out on the sand, sunning and swimming in the ocean. I passed by a famous five-star hotel, Grand Palace. Then I looked on Google to find the direction to old town Biarritz. Just two more blocks away. Trés facile (very easy).

The closer you stay to the places you want to see then traveling is less hectic. Because you're not wasting time trying to get across town through crazy traffic. I like being able to walk to some sites, cafes, and attractions when possible, or at least being close enough to public transportation so I can take in foreign cities easier. Logistics and planning efficiently makes for a smoother and less stressful travel experience. Although sometimes planning a trip can be overwhelming. It's still worth the time and effort.

It's easy to see that Biarritz is where a lot of wealthy folks come to relax on holiday. There's also a casino near the beach. At first, passing by the Casino, I hesitated, then kept walking instead. I love Casinos, they were my great escape when I was married. Still the costs for eating out, ordering wine, and booking a room here in

Biarritz won't break your bank if you are on a budget. Staying a few blocks from the beach costs less. I dismissed the idea of staying at a hotel on the beach. Lovely as they were, their rates for one night were between $250-375, not bad but I'd rather spend that on eating, shopping, and having other tourist experiences for one day. This city would make a nice two-day getaway for anyone visiting Paris or Southwest France for a seaside escape and taste of Spain.

In the old town, I found a Tapas Bar, Cafe du Commerce, at 4 pm but it was too early and closed. Instead, I walked a block down the street to a different restaurant. At Bar Jean Biarritz, I'm in a seafood mood. I ordered the fried Sardines, fish soup, frites, and a soothing glass of white wine. That was a very interesting and delicious meal. It's these atypical dining experiences that I seek out and enjoy the most. Excellent food and service. My young waiter was very handsome and sweet. He spoke English too.

Now, I'm back at the hotel and working right now. I enjoyed that quick self-guided walk through the city center. It was a short walk because I had to get back to the hotel to hop on my computer by 6 pm France time / 9 am L.A. time to work. This is my last day to work remotely. Therefore, I could not partake in any nightlife activities in Bordeaux like going to a jazz club or even dining out for a late dinner after 6:00 pm this week. But my mornings and afternoons were full of fun and insightful activities.

Next week, without the work obligations I'll be able to participate in some nightlife in my next four cities. Pretty happy that I have time to just relax in the mid to late afternoons. While traveling, I like getting up early and being out around 8 am to start exploring a destination. Then around 4-5 pm I'm ready to return to my accommodations and wind down. I'll relax for a few hours then go out for a bite and a glass of wine in the evening around 7or 8 pm. Colonel needs his beauty sleep nap times too. So, these breaks help to keep us both from being cranky old so and so's.

I truly enjoy traveling solo. While on the train to Biarritz, I had a nice chat with a woman named Maren from Holland. She and her son were on their way to Portugal. We talked about people, attitudes, and traveling. When we arrived in Biarritz, she invited me to sit and wait with them at a little cafe outside the train station.

But I couldn't as my Uber was 2 minutes out. She was so affable and genuine. Outside the station, I chatted with a nice Australian family from our train. The father, a gentleman, helped put my heavy suitcase in the Uber's trunk. We all wished each other well and to have a good and fun trip. I've had very nice encounters like these while traveling in France. So far so good. I've taken a ton of photographs and videos. Feeling like Ansel Adams capturing still shots of landscapes and cityscapes except all of them in color.

Celestine Cooley

CHAPTER SEVEN

Exploring Toulouse

Friday, Sept 8, 2023 | Train to Toulouse

Day 7 – Got up early, we're leaving Biarritz. Glad I made this overnight trip; it was very relaxing. Now I'm off to Toulouse by train, costing €47 one-way on SNCF Connect. This is a four-hour train trip. Toulouse is another city that I'm considering for my retirement move to France in two years.

There are other cities north in the Loire Valley that I'd like to visit next year such as Tours, Angers, Orleans, and Nantes. I want to give all these cities a chance against Bordeaux. See if they can also live up to my 'must haves' list of wants and needs.

The other three cities of interest are smaller than Paris in size and population. They offer similar things by way of lifestyle, quality of life, cost of living, Vets, and great healthcare. My social security and retirement accounts aren't taxed by the French government. I've done lots of research and have contacts on the ground in France to help with my transition and with other matters if needed. I'm learning a lot on my own from my research. I am a hands-on type of person, who appreciates the autodidactic process.

For this move, I don't know where I'll land yet, or whether I'll buy or rent, stay in the city, live in a village, suburb, or the countryside. Those decisions will be made after I've explored the regions to choose a city. Turning an idea into an action doesn't take much effort, it is a matter of taking the needed steps to make it happen.

It only takes ambition, desire, and determination. I have a lot of all three. I've never been afraid to explore and just "go for it." I'm too curious and too adventurous not to take a chance. Once I have decided on doing something, I'm committed, and I'll do it.

That very first trip across the Atlantic was a true learning experience. Being a novice foreign traveler, I hadn't made any hotel reservations in London, Paris, or Cannes. Miraculously, we were able to book hotels in those cities upon arrival. We were lucky to run into so many helpful people, so our trip transition from city to city was seamless despite my lack of travel knowledge. Our street smarts helped us survive that trip because we met plenty of sketchy male characters along the way.

At that time, I knew nothing at all about travel planning. I thought all you had to do was read a travel guide, buy a plane ticket, and off you go. Hotels you could book once you arrived. Well, yes and no. Learned a lot about travel on that trip. Later I went to travel school at night to become a travel agent. Thus, I am no longer naive about travel planning. Since that first trip, I've gained tons of travel experience and knowledge about the proper ways to plan a trip, along with many life lessons over the years to make informed decisions about visiting foreign destinations.

I had breakfast in the hotel's cafe at 8 am after walking Colonel. It's now 9 am and time to check out of my Biarritz hotel, then contact Uber, and grab the train. Taxis are great, but it is also nice to have Uber drivers in most places around the world. At the Biarritz train station, 1 just met an American couple now living in Utah. The husband is from North Carolina originally, his wife from Connecticut. They looked a little lost so I showed them which track we needed to be on for our trains and where the elevator was located. I feel like a train station expert now. HA! They spent three days in Bordeaux, then Biarritz, and now are going back to Paris. You meet such nice and interesting people while traveling. They too liked Bordeaux a lot.

I should have been a journalist; I like asking questions, getting answers, and listening to people's stories. Not afraid to chat with traveling strangers anywhere I go, especially if they are willing to reciprocate. Elevators and escalators, I want to hug the inventors. I know we need to use steps for the exercise and reaching some places, but not when pushing and lifting heavy luggage around airports and train stations. Americans look for more convenient ways to get around, if possible, and to avoid climbing up and down stairs. Europeans are more accustomed to stairs and inclines like hilly ancient streets. I don't practice climbing stairs or trotting up hills.

Listening to the French speak everyday helps me to better comprehend this beautiful language. I'm beginning to understand spoken French a little more from hearing the language often. I really need real world immersion if I am ever going to learn this language well. Plus, I use Deepl and Google Translate to look up words and phrases I don't know when reading signs, menus, and speaking French. I also have a French/English dictionary App on my phone.

I need all the help I can get with this language when attempting to communicate in French. It will take me a great deal of time before I master this language. I'm trying though. Plus, I carry a pocket-sized French phrase book for reference. It's so helpful. We are never too old to learn anything, especially languages if we desire. It just takes a want to do it, a little time, some patience, effort, and a whole lot of determination. Voila!

What a nice train ride through the countryside on our way to Toulouse. My apartment check-in time is 5 pm. Since I arrived in Toulouse early around 2:30 pm, I booked a nearby luggage storage service at a hotel in advance. Conveniently this storage place in a hotel across the street from the Toulouse train station. That way I can see some of the city nearby, grab a bite, and walk Colonel without lugging my bags around for a few hours. I used an App called Bounce. Cost €13 for a few hours, which I think is the day rate. I'll see how it goes, what I think of this service, and if my locked bags are truly safe there while being stored. When I return to pick up my bags, I will then walk or take an Uber to the apartment, just 10 mins away.

Another thing about European trains, not enough luggage storage. So, you must keep an eye on your bags wherever you manage to put them, usually near an exit doorway. Then there's the mad dash to find your train car (coach), car number, and your seat inside before the train takes off. All the signage at airports and in train stations can be bewildering and confusing but with a little fortitude you can figure it all out. Once on board the train, you can't beat the ambience, relaxation, and beautiful scenery viewed along the way.

I love traveling and want to spend the rest of my life traveling by land, air, train, and maybe by sea. I am not too keen on boats and water, although every trip I've taken has involved me getting aboard a boat of some kind, big and small. Once I retire, relocate, and get settled in France then I plan to travel around Europe, Southeast Asia, and wherever else my impulse takes me and my little dog. Being single and carefree with time to travel is a gift. Right now, on this journey I am just so happy and hopeful!

Just before our train pulled into the station, I received a text from Lili, my Airbnb host, to let me know that the apartment was ready. Well, I did not have to wait several hours before checking in after all. I responded to her text, then had to cancel the luggage storage reservation. Bounce offers free cancellations. We arrived in Toulouse on time at 2:30 pm.

Slowly, I moved along towards the exit with the other passengers to grab my bags and disembark. This train station was huge but I found the exit and made my way to a taxi. I asked how far, showing the driver the address on my phone. The taxi driver pointing toward a long street said,

"It's a short walk that way, just a few blocks. You don't need a ride."

He steers me in the right direction going straight down a street adjacent to the train station. Colonel is walking on his lease as I push my three bags together along this wider smooth non-cobbled sidewalk. The apartment was an easy and short nine-minute walk. Inside the building's interior hall, it's dimly lit, I found the code locked mailbox holding the apartment's keys.

Unlocked the box and retrieved the keys. Next, I'm trying to figure out which apartment was the right one from several on this ground level. Once I found the right apartment, which took several minutes, the entryway was too dark to see the lock. I have no idea how to turn on the lights. There were two steps leading down to the doorway for this small basement apartment making it very difficult for me to find the lock. It's frustrating. I just want to get inside and get settled. Later, I remembered I had a small flashlight in my carryon.

This apartment, located inside an older building with a gated courtyard and parking in the back, isn't as nice as the newer apartment I stayed at in Bordeaux. Once I managed to get the key inside the lock and entered this basement apartment, a musky odor greets me the moment I step inside. I am not a fan of basements or unpleasant odors.

The place is clean. The only ventilation that I notice will come from one small window in the kitchen looking out to a back parking area. In front of this window is a set of stairs leading up to the first floor. No elevator. Well, I'm certainly not going to leave that window open for any length of time. That's not at all safe.

Colonel doesn't like this abode so much. He hesitated upon entering the place. Then it took him a while to settle comfortably once inside. Dogs just know. We feel somewhat safe here but not so warm and cozy. Glad this apartment is only booked for three nights.

Airbnb's can be a hit or a miss I'm learning. Not all the properties fall under the same building code standards of habitability. This one would not have passed the building code tests for a rental in Los Angeles. There was no window in the bedroom or bathroom, so both were very stuffy (can't be legal). You could feel the moisture and humidity. Later I bought a can of deodorized fragrant spray like Febreze to mask the odor. It could be worse, I guess.

We settled into this basement dwelling nonetheless happy to have a place to land. I set up the WiFi, no Netflix available, just French TV Channels. Read the house rules and unpacked a few clothes for three-days. It is a cute space but needs lots of work to make it truly feel safe and properly ventilated inside. I did find the ventilation unit in a cupboard, it's so loud. I can tell that moisture builds up in this apartment, a breeding ground for toxic mole. The dim overhead lighting helps illuminate the place just enough because it's too dark otherwise.

The small open concept kitchen next to the entrance was connected to the small living room. A similar high table and bar stools set in the dining tiny area is practical for the space. The bigger sized bathroom with a sink, toilet, and shower is in a separate room off the living room; while the separate windowless bedroom was quaint.

There is a portable pedestal fan, which will hopefully help circulate the air. I don't know how this place was ever approved as a living space. But it will have to do on this trip. Still, it is nice enough for sleeping and relaxing during my short stay.

Tomorrow, I'll start this visit with a city tour on an open-air Hop on Hop off bus. It should be an educational experience exploring the different areas of Toulouse by bus. While walking to the apartment, noticeably Toulouse is not as clean as Bordeaux. We passed a few homeless souls camped out on sidewalks and in doorways. There is a different vibe here, like a low-key intensity. Even the students seem different, rowdier perhaps because of the Rugby tournament. The environment's pace seems to be faster too. Lots of young people move by quickly. I noticed vigorous activities in the pubs and bars at night.

Toulouse was not at all what I expected. It took a moment for me to get into the vibe of this city. We ventured out twice on walks this first night and found protein. At a nearby steakhouse restaurant called Hippopotamus for dinner, I had a burger, fries, €18 and a blond beer, €4. Then for dessert added a Chocolate Mousse, €7 and an expresso, €3.

This city is lively with lots of diversity. Noisy around the bars of course. I'm staying in an area where many North and East Africans have businesses and reside. Everyone I've met or passed by has been Bonjour friendly. I'm in the city center so I expect it to be hectic.

After dinner, Colonel walks back on lease for his last pee before we call it a night. We need to reenergize for tomorrow, although I'm not feeling tired. Tomorrow will be a full day of activities, so we are in for the evening. I watched a French TV series then joined Colonel for a restful sleep. Bon nuit!

Celestine Cooley

Saturday, September 9, 2023 | Toulouse ~ Day

Day 8- It was windy this morning. I could not get the coffee maker working before leaving the apartment, then texted the host when I returned. I was excited to begin the day by touring the city on an open-air bus for this audio guided city tour at 10 am, which was a perfect time for this exploration.

I booked this 1-hour city tour, online with 'Get Your Guide' in advance for $17.35. We only had a five-minute walk to the stop where the bus tour begins. It was sheer luck that the tour bus stop was so close to the apartment. The audio guide is pre-recorded which we listened to in our various languages using earphones.

Also, our driver spoke many languages and filled in the historical gaps along the tour. He had a good sense of humor so there was lots of laughter on this bus. I think humor is a requirement for this job. Many passengers got on and off throughout this tour.

As usual, I stayed put but made notes of the different sites along the way. Only a few times in other cities have I gotten off the bus at a specific stop and then hopped back on the bus later to continue the tour. It's a full day tour, so there is lots of time to hop on and off throughout the bus tour.

This historical city tour provided the information about Toulouse through the ages, pointing out the horrendous executions and beheadings of citizens for various infractions. I read the history of France last year and learned that during the very brutal medieval times, the Middle Ages, where beheadings were the norm until guillotines were banned in 1977, and capital punishment was banned in 1981. I was surprised that guillotines were still used in the 20th Century. France holds many surprises.

We drove along the Canal du Midi where Barges slowly float along the canals of France carrying from 6 to 8 passengers over several days. These private cruise tours are like river cruises but smaller and more intimate vessels traveling slowly down these narrow waterways.

Some people live on barges (house boats) along the Canal too. If interested you can learn more on the websites about the costs and scheduled sailings of these slow-paced and romantic European Waterways or French Waterways Barge Cruises.

The Canal du Midi was built in the 17th-century which connects to the Garonne River then links to the Mediterranean Sea. This stretch of waterways can be travelled by boat, bike or on foot. With the Canal du Midi close by and views of the Garonne River, this was a very enjoyable and nature filled bus tour.

Along the route, we passed the very impressive St. Stephens Cathedral with its tiled roof and 13 bells. We saw the performing arts theatre, museums, the Garonne River, mansions, and several beautiful parks. Toulouse is called the Pink City due to the architecture and pink terracotta bricks used to construct many of the buildings.

We passed through Centre Ville where our rented apartment is located on a busy street that crosses another busy street. I can walk a few minutes to stores, drug stores, cafes, restaurants, bars, and the large indoor Victor Hugo indoor Market from the apartment. This city has a subway (Metro) system and seemingly efficient bus service;

the main bus terminal is close by too. Always discovering something of interest or importance on our walks.

Unfortunately, I've seen homeless people here sitting or lying on the streets due to lack of work for the high immigrant population. Some seek donations from the masses passing by them. So many people around the world are displaced by mental health, substance abuse, or unemployment, and are forced into homelessness and living on the streets of major cities. It is a sad worldwide crisis.

Toulouse's center is bustling much like downtown L.A. or Manhattan, people are everywhere. Also, with several universities. It has a large student population; one out of five residents are students. A city filled with young people. France values education and provides excellent academics, so all the major cities have Universities with French and International students enrolled.

The entire bus tour took about one hour to drive us around the city, pointing out the popular sites and other places of interest. After the tour, I stopped at Carrefour, the small express market to pick up snacks and wet dog food. These little markets are everywhere. I bought water yesterday to put into the small frig. Colonel tolerates this foreign wet dog food. I'm trying to stock up on it for the duration of his trip.

Yes, I have a fourth tote bag that I'm carrying around which contains water, my camera, snacks, my windbreaker, and his sweatshirt (don't laugh). Original bag lady. It comes in handy for random stops at the market. Then we headed back to the apartment for a quick break and to meet our Airbnb host. I decided not to cook anything in this small kitchen.

My host arrived to show me how to use the coffee maker. Her name is Lili. She's French, in her mid-30s and very nice. Said she loves California, especially San Francisco where she visits on her layover trips to Tahiti where her father lives. I asked her about the musky odor. It's from the humidity but she's hired someone to investigate it and figure out what to do.

This apartment is okay; it just wasn't what I expected. And I should stop comparing it to the one in Bordeaux (unfair). But then again, this city isn't what I expected either. Could I live here, I don't know. I haven't seen other areas yet and I do want to give this city a chance. The population is over 450,000. Still a small number but it's double the size of Bordeaux.

After Lilli left, we ventured out to find food. Where I found a cute little nearby Brasserie, Le Tchin, for lunch that cost €18. The French are serious about their meal times. Lunch from 12-2 pm only. At 1:50 pm, the waiter removes the silver, glasses and table ware indicating that lunch was over.

I like that the waiters bring the card readers to you. We never have to relinquish our cards here and then watch as the wait staff disappear to the back with them like in the States. You pay at your table; the credit card never leaves your hand.

So, if I get hungry between 2-7 pm, there are other options, such as the small market selections of frozen foods, sandwiches, or fresh sandwiches from bakeries. There are fast food stands on the street inside shops for chicken, or Tunisian, Algerian, or other ethnic foods. Then there is McDonalds, no thanks, I'm in France. Apéro (happy hour) drinks are from 5-7 pm. Dinner is served from 7-11 pm usually.

Oh, and forget about finding any USB plugs to charge your phone in at restaurants. I didn't see any at the train stations either. I have a portable Mophie charger that I charged last night, so my phone doesn't die when I'm out. I took a few shots of my Saturday morning adventure and lunch in Toulouse. We enjoy being out and exploring these ancient cities.

After lunch, we spend the rest of the afternoon getting to know this area of Toulouse on our own by foot until early evening. I was happy I had that bus tour earlier, it was very satisfying because we visited parts of the city that I would not have discovered normally.

Toulouse has its merits. It is relatively flat and a good candidate for consideration. I did not try the public transportation here, the bus or subway because most of my activities here are reachable on foot. I very much enjoyed meeting people and having lively conversations in Toulouse.

Now I've learned much more about this city and its history too. I'll definitely come back for another visit. The only downside to this stop was my accommodations. Had the apartment been brighter and better ventilated, I think I would have enjoyed this city stay much more. Plus, being stuck in a basement isn't an ideal lodging for me. But the price was right. It is what it is, so it will have to do.

Perhaps, younger people would appreciate this type of living arrangement much more than a very picky senior. Although the place wasn't uninhabitable, still I am trying not to let this apartment's issues overshadow my opinion of this city. Regardless of that, Toulouse is a fun city to visit. Pleased that I chose to check it out on this scouting trip. It is pleasant and worth revisiting.

We walked slowly back to the apartment after our all-day excursion around the city's various neighborhoods close by. These explorations help me better understand the city, its vibe, if it meets my criteria, and whether I like it or not. Looking at the shops and restaurants, stopping to gaze at a menu or two. Finding flea markets on little streets and outside in plazas. It's all a wonderful experience because you never know what you may discover. It is so different here, I can't explain it, you just feel it.

That is why these scouting trips are so important. I want to make the right decision about where I will live in a particular city. Plus, I dislike the process of moving. Also, I like being close to other cities reachable by car or train to explore. Once settled and living here, I plan to travel further and wider.

Celestine Cooley

Saturday, September 9, 2023 | Toulouse ~ Evening

Around 7:30 pm, I was ready for dinner. Just a block away from the apartment I found boeuf (beef). I grabbed a table inside this busy bistro. My French dinner at "Meet the Meat " was sensational. My taste buds are still dancing from every bite of that meal. The flavors, Wow! I was craving beef and after perusing the menu I added duck foie gras.

This Plat (Entrée) came with the creamiest scalloped potatoes prepared in a very light scrumptious sauce. My salad included delicate and tender duck gizzards that were cooked to perfection. I know about the duck fat controversy but I'm in France experiencing their traditional cuisines is a must. Foie gras is a keeper in my opinion.

This meal was paired with what I considered to be a very good red house wine, smooth and mellow, costing €4. I declined dessert but had an espresso, plus 2 shots of a Tiramisu Liquor concoction much like a dessert. My waitress gave me two of those shot glasses after a neighbor diner didn't want his. These shots were on the house. Merci! The ambiance was lovely, the wait staff on their toes and so friendly. My dining experience, meal, and atmosphere were very pleasing. This is a local favorite. Tables were never empty.

Restaurant dining tips in France: the Menu is called (la Carte) which will be printed in French or English. On some English menus you may find the meals may cost slightly more than prices printed on the French menus. Appetizers are (entrées), Entrées are plates (plats), the bill (l 'addition), a receipt (le ticket), water (d'eau), and coffee (café) at a café (restaurant). Children's menus may say, pour Enfant.

It's okay to put your hands, elbows, and arms on the table as well as your bread, so opposite of our American dining etiquette. The French use a knife and fork for everything, even pizza. I followed suit. Also, don't expect to ask for or receive steaks cooked medium well or well done. Won't happen. French steaks come rare, medium rare, maybe medium.

The French fries, if done right, are crispy on the outside. Ketchup may or may not be on the table. Loud conversations are not well received, lower your voice, don't shout. Remember our manners we were taught as children, (like saying please and thank you) because etiquette and respect go a long way in France. We are guests in their country.

Usually, if you dine alone, you really aren't alone. You'll receive many greetings mostly, Bonjour and Bon Appetit from people inside and outside the restaurants. At the table to my right sat two (30-year-olds) British guys, we chatted a bit. To my left, at a table closer to me sat two very pleasant English-speaking young men (20s) from Indonesia. We discussed living and working in Toulouse. Why this city is so crowded: visitors here for the Rugby World Cup. Usually it isn't as crowded, more chilled; a good city in which to live. I can see why young people are drawn here.

We talked about travel, developing knowledge as we age. How we explore life in our twenties and learn more about ourselves, and soon begin to sort through friendships, knowing some we must let go when our interests and our goals change. We laughed a lot, talked about our jobs. They work in hospitality. One day they would like to visit the USA, where one of them has family living in Seattle.

"It's much easier to get a Visitor's Visa when you have family in the States," I told them. Encouraging a visit.

These varied conversations are healthy and insightful. While traveling we get to meet other people who are like us, with hopes, dreams, struggles, and goals, no matter their backgrounds or nationalities. The cultural aspects of traveling are insightful, inspirational, and transformative. Plus, the educational benefits of meeting the locals are priceless. I really appreciate these stirring local encounters meeting new people from around the world. If you can't immerse yourself into the culture, why go?

Alternatively, not everyone who travels has the same positive experiences. Some people while traveling are just doomed from the start, due to their expectations, inability to adapt, and lack positive attitudes about being abroad, equally adding to their frustration.

I spent a good three hours sitting at that table eating, drinking, talking, and watching people pass by outside. My purpose in life has always been to engage with people, to teach, make them laugh, to learn something new, and just have fun.

Laughter like music is a universal language that bridges gaps and brings people (family, friends, strangers) together in an uncommon way. Life and living are still about people even if you're a loner like me. So, enjoy your life's journeys as much as you can. Life is too short to waste. Bonsoir!

Six French Cities

Sunday, Sept 10, 2023 | Trip to Carcassonne

Day 9 - It's a warm Sunday morning. On my way to the medieval City of Carcassonne to visit the 12th century Castle (Chateau Comtal) and village. My day trip by motor coach with an audio guide in 3 languages costs $34.71 from 'Get Your Guide'. It should be a very interesting adventure, a 45-minute ride from Toulouse.

We leave here at 9:30 am to meet the tour (three min walk from my apartment) and will return to Toulouse at 5:45 pm. I am so centrally located that it makes getting anywhere on foot easier and quicker. Plus, the day tours I selected on this trip are insightful and affordable for the value you receive.

This big 40-passenger bus doesn't have anywhere to charge our phones. Great! I did not bring my battery pack for charging my phone. Why not? I packed it. So, I'll have to use my Sony digital camera for most of the pictures I take on this day-long journey. I have a backup battery for this camera with me in its case. Making a note to myself, carry your phone charger on day trips. I don't like it when I'm away from the apartment and my phone dies either. So, I must get in the habit of carrying my back up battery charger and carrying it in my tote.

Passing through the small village, we arrived at the hilltop Castle. It is a breathtaking experience. This massive structure is what you'd imagine a medieval castle to look like, thanks Hollywood. I saw it from miles away on the bus and later from the train just stretching across the landscape. We arrived before the huge crowds. Walking around inside the walled castle, originally built as a defensive fortress and then the center of government, you get a sense of what it would have been like centuries ago. Inside the castle there were some cosplayers dressed to match the middle age period. Demonstrating their swordsmanship skills opposite children volunteers also dressed in costume.

We stopped to watch belly dancers perform for a while, then strolled along the narrow-cobbled streets where shop merchants sold tourist souvenirs (meaning memories in French) and other trinkets. Here I picked up a few souvenirs for family and friends. A name engraved bracelet for my daughter and a few fridge magnets for myself.

At noon, slowly we made our way to a plaza dotted with restaurants. After perusing all the menus on different boards posted outside each one, I selected lunch at a Bistro. The combo plat of pork sausage, frites (fries), salad, brie, water, and a glass of Rosé satisfied my hunger. Plenty of bread (pain like British "pan") for one.

We met two French women sitting at the next table, one who had a little brown dog that looked a lot like Colonel. The ladies thought it was "incroyable" (incredible) how much they resembled each other. Both being male. Their dog was a little snippy and growled at Colonel who just ignored him. I shared a little pork sausage with their dog and with Colonel. I did speak the little French I know but it's not guaranteed that I will always understand the responses.

After lunch we strolled more inside and outside around the castle. Now, as the time dwindled, Colonel and I were both getting tired after hours of walking up and down inclines on uneven pavements. Outside the castle, I was ready to give my feet a rest and set the dog carrier down. Tourists were still arriving on buses and passing the makeshift vendor stands now lined up before the Castle's entranceway.

Moving toward the parking lot, I spotted Le Petit Train taking passengers on tours around the outside of the castle and down into the village for €7. I bought a ticket and boarded this audio guided tour with a handful of other tourists just to rest and pass the time away. We listened to the audio guide for a history of the castle and the village of Carcassonne below.

After this 15-minute city tour, I found a shady spot in an open graveled area with benches to sit and relax while taking it all in. Colonel was free to walk around off lease, sniff, and pee. He greeted a few people and then continued exploring the grounds and grass beyond the benches until he was ready to get back into his carrier.

There were many types of guided tours offered online for visiting Carcassonne. When traveling, I usually divide my time in a new city by taking guided tours by bus, walking or bike and then a self-guided walking tour. Listening beforehand to audiobooks on Audible about "The History of France" gave me a preliminary introduction and lesson into this country's historical highlights, delving into its many conquerors and rulers across centuries. All the battles fought, won, and lost and the prominent people who helped build France and shaped its laws, codes, and the famous phrase, Liberté, Égalité, and Fraternité (the motto of France).

I was swept up in its violent medieval history which was much more than I had bargained for upon hearing the tales of Kings fighting for power and the many beheadings as a result. It's very hard to wrap your head around those times which people lived through. I know that I'm living in the right time right now. No doubt I would have been beheaded early with my stubbornness and willfulness. Still a very interesting period in history.

Then the Romans' history throughout Europe and into France, which I remembered learning about when I studied Latin for two years in high school. Also, I did not realize how occupied France was during the German invasion in World War II, just incredible the degradation and torment that the French people in big cities and small villages were put through in their own country by the Germans for several years in the early 1940s.

Pretty amazing to revisit this history. It's like a recap of history lessons from my school days but much more insightful, in-depth, and intense now that I'm older and can appreciate it more. I love history, it reveals a lot about all of us, our present and our past. Southwest France reminds me of California, similar in weather and terrain. Mountains, wineries, forests, rivers, diversity, and the sea.

And very close to the Spanish border and Pyrenees. In Toulouse, near the south of France, the weather is much like Florida, hot, sticky, and humid. I felt no sea breezes. Temperatures should be cooling off this time of year but global warming is having an adverse effect on weather patterns worldwide. I managed to live through this heat without air conditioning though.

This day trip was worthwhile; I learned more history about this region. What a nifty way to wrap up my visit to the Occitanie region near southern France. I highly recommend a visit to Carcassonne, especially if you have any interests in giant castles, walled cities, and medieval times. I'd like to drop by Nimes and Avignon as well, but don't have enough time to visit those cities on this trip. Tomorrow, I'm off to my next city. I'll catch an earlier train from Toulouse for a longer ride and a change of trains. So far, this journey has been fun and enlightening. Where to next, Celeste?

My impression of Toulouse: it's lovely and nice enough. I felt safe walking the streets alone at night. If I was younger, it could be ideal for me to live here. It's a hip city populated with young people mostly students and many pubs you could crawl for weeks. Still, it's a bit busy and noisy outside. Happily, it's not at all noisy around my apartment late at night. Restaurants, bakeries, coffee shops, fast food, small supermarkets were everywhere within walking distance to this place, so very convenient. There is a metro and bus system in Toulouse, so public transportation is available. I didn't have a chance to take the bus or metro, next time I visit I will test both.

The Canal du Midi and the Garonne River pass through the city adding to its charm. I can see why some expats like living here. A leaf blower this morning but much quieter than the ones I hear in L.A. Unfortunately, Toulouse does have a growing homeless population, people sitting on the streets were begging. Didn't see any tents or signs of encampments. Disenfranchised people living on the streets, it's heartbreaking. Still Toulouse is a contender; I'll leave it on my list. I think I'll return for another visit.

It's time to board our bus back to Toulouse. Colonel's a trooper! He's run around for a bit and now he's ready to rest, going back into his carrier to lay down. Thrilled that I could bring him along on this journey so he can get accustomed to the sights, sounds, and smells of this country. He needs to know that we'll be living here one day. Á Bientôt!

Celestine Cooley

CHAPTER EIGHT

Exploring Nice

Monday, September 11, 2023 | Train to Nice

Day 10 – My travel alarm clock wakes me up at 6:30 am. Made coffee. I took a shower and got dressed. We are all packed and now off to take the train to our next French city. Pleased that the train station is only a ten-minute walk away because dealing with this luggage isn't easy. Having my hard metal suitcase's spinning wheels with smaller bags on top makes it easier to roll and maneuver on these cobblestoned sidewalks.

This morning, Colonel is out of his carrier and walking on lease so he can do his business before we arrive at the train station. It's warm in Toulouse. So far, I have felt very safe and comfortable traveling alone on this French journey. I never really envisioned making this scouting trip with anyone other than Colonel. Consequently, solo traveling is stress free and more enjoyable without other people's drama. I have found that day tours with small groups are okay for a few hours though. Still, I prefer walking alone to explore a city, discover little gems along the way, and have unmatched enjoyable experiences in a new place.

Our train leaves at 8:45 am going to Nice. There is a one-hour stopover in Marseille to change trains. Total travel time from Toulouse to Nice including the stopover is six hours and fifty-five minutes. It's going to be a long travel day. My 2nd class train ticket for this first leg (Toulouse to Marseille) cost €39 one way.

We should arrive at the Marseille train station around 12:33 pm (3 hours 45 minutes). Then wait for an hour to catch our next train at 1:28 pm for a 2-hour 29 minutes rail journey. We expect to arrive in Nice around 4:00 pm. And the 2nd class train ticket for this second leg (Marseille to Nice) cost €41 one way. I'm looking forward to visiting the South of France again.

Now standing in the middle of the station and gazing up at the train schedule along with everyone else who has just arrived at this station to catch trains. We resemble a bunch of bird watchers without binoculars. The Toulouse station is packed. We have about a 45-minute wait for our train.

Whenever I arrive at a train station, I'm never sure how much time I'll need or have before catching a train. Some stations are massive, on several levels, and navigating them takes time. Thus, I would rather arrive early and wait than to be too late, rushing through a station, and risk missing my train.

We grabbed a seat in the lobby. I let Colonel out of his carrier for a little while. Once I sat down, I was happy to have found the outlet for charging mobile devices. This plug needed a European adapter instead of a USB one, which I have in my carryon bag along with all the other phone cables and various plug adaptors for my

Android and Apple devices. Later, I will learn that phone charging stations or outlets are not available on all trains or even in all train stations throughout France. Made sure that my phone is fully charged this morning, so the charge should last until I arrive in Nice.

Finding the right track was easier this time but getting onto the right train car, well I was one digit off and had to hustle down the platform to get to the next car. These trains seem to leave at the scheduled times printed on the departure board and on the tickets. It's a very efficient transportation system and a great way to travel around France. I'm enjoying these trips by train.

Glad I decided to take trains on this trip rather than driving because 1) I needed to become accustomed to this French train system and 2) some driving times would have been too long for getting from city to city by car. Toll roads are expensive here. So, I actually saved a lot of money, time, and aggravation by choosing to travel from city to city by train.

However, I look forward to traveling more throughout France and Europe in the future by train, plane, and automobile. Those plans will be more realistic and not rushed because I will have more leisure time to spend visiting many other cities and countries of interest. This trip plan included spending three weeks traveling by train with stops in other cities along this route. I had dreamed of traveling like this by train from city to city for a very long time. It is the prelude to my future train, plane, and car travel on this side of the pond.

Nice is in the Provence-Alpes-Côte d'Azur. I've visited this South region of France and Nice before in the mid-80s. Back then I really fell in love with this warm Southern region. However, that visit was in the Spring when the weather was warm not hot, we even wore light jackets then. Plus, I was younger and could tolerate the heat. I'm now visiting in the early fall (end of summer). Nice is on the Mediterranean Sea. I'll be exploring other cities near Nice during my six days stay.

There are five stops along this route that include three cities (Montpellier, Avignon, and Aix-en-Provence) that I wanted to visit too but even by car the drive time and distance from and back to Toulouse was too long for a day trip. Driving around this country is more practical when you have scheduled more time for the trip, like months not weeks.

Plus, I'd want to give those beautiful cities more time than just a few hours in a day to explore. Time, something we never seem to have enough of in our daily lives is especially noticeable while traveling on a schedule. By taking day trips to other cities, I'm experiencing the added bonus of those short visits and making the most of my time on this scouting mission.

Celestine Cooley

Monday, September 11, 2023 ~ Late Afternoon

Day 10 -- Our layover in Marseille seemed quick. The station was crowded but I found our train platform with ease. No time for a quick spin around this city or to grab a bite to eat. First class is often upscale. Inside, the first-class cars the decor is very different, a bit posh, and contemporary; the passengers are usually business people and wealthy tourists. Rarely will you see families with small children traveling first class. First class usually comes with added amenities. It's a quieter setting where you can truly relax. I'm traveling second class on this leg of my trip.

We soon board our train and settle into our seats, mine next to the window. This time I managed to be one of the first to board our coach. So, I found available space to store my two bags. Hoping to get a nap on this train. Too focused on getting to the right track, I failed to grab a bite to eat before boarding, but I have water and a few snacks in my tote bag.

Currently, I'm very relaxed sitting here gazing through my window in a dream-like state. Watching as the lovely countryside landscapes coast by often trading places with farms and villages that materialize like pictures from the pages of an old photograph album. The serenity and down time for me is very welcomed.

Typically, I'm listening to music or an audio book on my phone to pass the time away. Not now, I can't stop viewing the flashes of this magnificent and changing scenery. These seats are very comfortable which add to my enjoyment. The back of the seat in front of me has a pull-down tray to rest my phone, laptop, or tablet on like on an airplane. On this train, I spotted the USB plugs (two) under the window to plug in and charge my phone.

The WIFI on this train is working seamlessly which is not always the case on some trains. I have not conversed with the other passengers on this early ride, many are asleep in their seats, using laptops, or reading books. No chatter or babies crying or ruffling through bags.

It's eerily silent onboard this train except for the infrequent sound of it rumbling down the tracks. Colonel is out of his carrier on the floor; he's on my lap and chilling like me. Of course, I haven't taken a nap. Too excited. Can't believe I'm nearly halfway through this three-week trip. It's been eye opening and a fun adventure.

We arrived in Nice around 4 pm. Moments before arriving, I received a text on WhatsApp from my Airbnb host that the apartment was ready and to meet her associate in front of the building. I responded. It has become a major production dealing with my two bags of luggage along with Colonel in his carrier but I manage. Not forgetting my extra over the shoulder cloth tote bag containing water and snacks.

I need more hands. Just getting this cache of bags onto or off the train is a slow and arduous process. My silver suitcase is so heavy, it takes a lot of effort for me to lift it on and off the train between that gap below the doorway and platform. But I somehow succeeded. Sometimes a kind soul will help me if I'm holding everyone up from entering or exiting the coach.

After that, I slowly found my way out of the train station and onto the street. Then hopefully we're off in the right direction to our destination. During this trip, I've relied on Google's maps on my phone to get me from point A to point B while walking anywhere. I'm so directionally challenged it's pathetic. Prior trips, I used a city map or some guide book. I seldom needed to use this GPS while walking in Los Angeles, mostly using it in my car while driving. Quite a different experience. But then I do know most of the streets of Los Angeles quite well unlike in a foreign city.

Still, I lack any sense of direction even when using a GPS. Thomas Guides were better in my opinion (never got lost). We follow Google's instructions on this walk from the train station to the center of town. I must walk up a hill to get to the street that will lead me to my destination. This GPS isn't that easy to figure out because my map is upside down as I follow the arrow. Turning my phone in that direction doesn't help.

The apartment is in a decent neighborhood, near the Notre Dame Church just off the main shopping street Avenue Jean Médecin near a tram stop. Many French cities have a Notre Dame Church in honor of Mary, mother of Jesus. Some are not as magnificent as the one in Paris, but lovely nonetheless. It is also close to Alliance Française, the language school. This apartment is in a very nice older building on a residential block. I think the nights here will be quiet, I am hoping.

Outside the apartment building, I was greeted by Neil, the host's boyfriend (now husband). He unlocked the door leading to and through a small courtyard. Then we walked over to another door to unlock. Inside was a small foyer with steps leading to the upstairs apartments. Ours was on the second-floor. I'm looking up these winding stone steps, thinking to myself, *'Oh boy, this staircase will be a challenge every day.'* Once upstairs and inside, Neil gives me the apartment tour and shows me how things worked, like the washer and bedroom air conditioner. Also, he helped me set up the WiFi on my phone and for the TV. It's nice to have Netflix. After the apartment tour familiarization, he gave me the keys.

While Neil was still there, my host, Rommelyn, facetimed me on WhatsApp to chat and to get to know me. We hit it off right away. She made sure I had what I needed in the apartment. I showed her Colonel and explained his service dog status. She was fine with him. Most people are surprised that I am traveling with my dog. She left me snacks and a bottle of Prosecco (Sparkling Italian White Wine) on the kitchen table. What a nice gesture again. This apartment is nicer than the one I left in Toulouse. Happy for the homey comfort feel this apartment provides.

At first, it was very difficult for me to get all three of my bags up these two flights of wide winding stone stairs. Neil couldn't help nor did I want him to help me. My bags are heavy and are my responsibility. Earlier, I had brought the two smaller bags up the stairs, first starting with Colonel in his carrier and my carryon. I lugged both up when we first entered the apartment.

At this moment, I wished that I had my wheeled carry on for this trip instead of this shoulder bag one. Too late. My larger and heavier suitcase I had left on the ground floor foyer until after I had the keys. I figured anyone attempting to take it would realize their mistake and not want to risk a hernia. Luckily, it was sitting inside the foyer behind a second locked door.

Finally, after that little exercise of getting my heavy silver suitcase up those flights of steps and inside the apartment, I was out of breath and ready for a nap. I promised myself that on my next trip, I would pack less and travel much lighter. I've learned my lesson. I don't like struggling with this big suitcase, it is so ridiculous. I didn't even need half the apparel I packed for this trip. My smaller green carryon suitcase would have been just fine. Although that one does not have the same kind of easy spin wheels as the silver suitcase. You really don't need a lot of clothes when you travel since you can wash clothes as you go, I learned.

This small one-bedroom apartment with modern decor is very appealing and big enough for two. The bedroom window faced a back courtyard so I knew I would sleep peacefully at night. We settled comfortably into this new environment and rested for two hours before venturing out to find food.

Unpacked a few items that I'd need each day, along with a few clothes to hang up. Then set up Colonel's food station with fresh water and some kibble. Made a mental note to buy a few bottles of water to stock in the fridge and get a few evening time snacks. Later while walking we would find a small market nearby and a restaurant for a quick bite.

Walking my dog three times a day was tiring, simply because of the stairs we had to climb. Colonel did not want to walk down or up these "scary" French stairs, nor did I. "I feel you buddy." I didn't mind carrying him down the stairs, it was carrying him up that was a problem for me. It took enough breath power on my part just to get myself up each flight. My lung capacity these days due to asthma isn't very good; plus, I was a casual cigarette smoker for many years a few decades ago. Glad I quit.

This apartment building does not have an elevator. So, we just had to suck it up and deal with the climb but mentally I cursed with every step I took going up. Coming down the stairs wasn't as bad. I should not complain because this step climbing exercise is needed to maintain good heart health and strengthen my leg muscles. Maybe over time this trek up these steps will become much easier. It didn't matter though because I wasn't going to allow stairs to inhibit me from going out regularly.

Before this climbing experience, I knew that I would absolutely need a ground floor apartment when I moved to France. Not relying on any elevators either. Other than dealing with stairs, Colonel like me has really adapted to visiting and temporarily living in France, especially our walks and traveling by train. Going from place to place does not faze him in the least. He has now proven how easy it is to travel with a dog internationally.

Colonel is very much accustomed to traveling with me on road trips by car on overnights or long weekend getaways around California and into Nevada. If he has a big comfy bed to lie in everyday, then he's cool and content wherever we go. He's well trained, very social, well behaved, and has a great temperament. A perfect low maintenance travel companion. I feel so lucky to have him in my life.

Around 7:15 pm, I rested, and now we ventured out on a walk to find the Italian restaurant, La Saëtone, that I had spotted on an earlier walk. Colonel was walking on lease now but I had his carrier so he could lay down inside it comfortably while in the restaurant.

We arrived at La Saëtone just before 7:30 pm, to be told by the waiter that there were no tables available until 8 pm. I understood because I had not made a reservation mostly since I don't feel confident speaking French to anyone on the phone yet.

"D'accord," I accepted and said, "I'll come back at eight."

He asked my name in French.

I responded, "Je m'appelle Celeste." In an American English accent.

He said in English, "That's an Italian name?"

"Yes, it's Latin." I replied.

"Okay, come back at 8 pm, your table will be ready." He added.

I thanked him. We continued walking. I didn't want to walk back to the apartment, so we explored that block hoping to find a place to hang out for half an hour. Then I spotted a petite pub, called Pub Santana, which was just a few kilometers down the block from the restaurant.

The waiter/bartender was standing outside talking to a patron drinking beer. I approached and pointed to an empty outside table. He nodded. I sat and ordered a glass of beer, brand 1664 for €3 then sat quietly while other patrons who gathered outside watched the Rugby World Cup match on a big screen TV hanging on a wall inside the petite pub.

Colonel was in his carrier and now taking a nap. Those 30 minutes passed rather sluggishly as I sipped my beer deliberately slow. Along with a few patrons, I watched the Rugby game and tried to figure out what was going on. Some players were large and reminded me of Sumo wrestlers. It is an interesting sport.

All the competitors on each team were rough and tough. The male viewers around me were typical sports fans, cheering and jeering after every move made on the field. It was like watching the Superbowl with the same gaming atmosphere and heightened enthusiasm. Still, I had no idea what was going on in this game.

Around 7:55 pm, I finished my beer and paid my tab. We ambled back down the street toward the restaurant. Sun is still out but it doesn't feel as hot now. The waiter was standing in the doorway and saw me coming. He called out to me with a smile,

"Bonsoir Celeste, your table is ready."

I smiled back at him and said, "Merci beaucoup!"

Feeling like the main character in a French movie as he escorted me inside to a small table for two near a side wall between two other tables. The restaurant had a warm ambience teaming with locals and tourists. These diners all seemed to be enjoying their meals and each other. La Saëtone is a family-owned restaurant established in 1985.

The waiter is the adult son *(30s)* of the couple who owns it. All of them are very pleasant and accommodating. I feel very welcomed and comfortable sitting here. I am starving for a full meal and ready to eat. The food's pleasant aroma emanated from the kitchen and enhanced my hunger. From its delightful atmosphere, I could understand why this appeared to be a local's favorite eatery in Nice.

This family and their comfort food made me feel right at home. The wife came over and greeted me by name; the husband was in the kitchen with the female cook. He soon came out of the kitchen to have a chat with me too. They all spoke French with a tiny bit of English. So of course, I gave my basic French a whirl in response.

I must remind French people that I do understand their spoken English. In fact, their English is very good, better than my French. Like me most French people who speak English are a little tentative about speaking a different language fearful of not getting it exactly right or of being judged and criticized. No judgement from me. So, we unconsciously encourage each other and manage to make our language differences work in these bigger cities. But I am told that in the small villages all the locals speak only French.

I ordered a glass of white wine (Sauvignon au Chardonnay) for €5. The wife gives me a basket of fresh sliced baguettes and a bottle of tap water. After perusing the extensive menu, I settled on the Fisherman's Cooking Pot *(Marmite du pêcheur cuite au four)* which consisted of shrimp, clams, mussels, salmon, and cod fillet in a red sauce or broth *(made with butter, semi creme, and vegetable bouillons)*; plus, a dish of white rice on the side. Cost for this plat, €19.70. The dinner prices here were average and affordable.

I have never had this meal before, so it was a pleasant surprise after tasting the first few bites. This dish was like a fish stew but tastier, not bland, or fishy. I liked it. Being a lover of seafood, I can appreciate it more when it is prepared to perfection. Their service was quick and impeccable. I watched how each family member made their rounds to chat and laugh with each of their dining customers.

Their roles were well defined, each moving around like well-oiled machines, serving, chatting, getting their jobs done effectively. Making everyone feel welcomed and relaxed. It was a very tranquil place to dine. This lovely little restaurant with it's warm and charming atmosphere deserves a return visit the next time that I'm in Nice. I look forward to trying more of their menu items.

For dessert, I ordered a Crème Brûlée, €7 and an Expresso, €3.50. Now, I do have a pet peeve when it comes to this dessert. Often disappointed because I expect my custards to be hot or warm when served to me. But usually when this dessert is served in restaurants, it's never the right or an even temperature. It comes completely cold or half cold-half warm.

It certainly isn't as enjoyable when it's cold. I realize that chefs prepare these custard desserts in advance then refrigerate them, but 15 seconds in a microwave would help. So, my Crème Brulé at this restaurant was half and half. Not a good ending to a fine meal. Although I liked the warm half, the cold half was not pleasing, a little shock to the palate. Nevertheless, I ate all my scrumptious Crème Brûlée.

After dinner and dessert, my belly is now satisfied and I'm ready to head back to the apartment to rest. I thanked my hosts *(all three)* and paid my bill, I gushed with a big enthusiasm, "Bonne Soirée, Au revoir!"

They all countered with, "Bonne Soirée, A Bientôt!"

Then smiling, I added, "I'll be back again. Probably on my next visit to Nice."

Not a bad start for my first dinner in Nice. Hoping to have more good meals and fun experiences while here. Now back at the apartment, it's a little after 10 pm, we settled in for the rest of the night. I stayed up watching TV for an hour before finally giving in to sleep. Crawling into bed next to a very knocked-out Colonel. Tomorrow I will need to have more energy reserved for exploring this seaside city. The next day, I wrote a Google review and provided pictures of the restaurant. The owners later thanked me on Google for my positive review. My pleasure!

Celestine Cooley

Tuesday, September 12, 2023 | Nice ~ Morning

Day 11 – We slept in until 9 am, both of us are fatigued from traveling. Therefore, we got a later start this morning than I had planned. Took my time rearranging my bags, making coffee, taking a shower, and then getting Colonel ready to roll. It was past noon when we left the apartment. Today, I wanted to explore Nice on my own. A self-guided tour on foot.

On the way to the beach and promenade, I stopped at a local cafe, La Popete D 'Ondine for a Salade Cobb and a peach iced tea, costing €17.50. Just a few blocks from the apartment, this small restaurant serves lunch, brunch, and tea. So delighted to find this little gem. Very good food. I could tell that it was a local's favorite lunch time hangout, crowded with every seat occupied by patrons enjoying the good service and good food.

The people I met in Nice were friendly. I chatted with the young French couple sitting at the table next to mine. She resembled Lily Collins (Emily in Paris). After they left, two young French women sat in those seats next. One was from Nice, the other from Bordeaux visiting her girlfriend. I remarked how much I enjoyed visiting Bordeaux and was looking forward to my five days stay in Nice. They were delighted that I was visiting this city and wished me a good trip.

On my walk after lunch, I found Old Nice by accident and was transported back in time. We strolled past many restaurants and shops that lined the slender streets of this historic area. Very picturesque. I took many photographs. Around 2 pm, I made my way to the water (Mediterranean Sea) to stroll along Promenade des Anglaise where I spotted the petite train to tour Castle Hill. Bought a ticket, cost €7 for the 3 pm departure. I am trying to pack as many activities into my days as possible without passing out from exhaustion. These small train tours provide visits to some popular tourist sites along with an audio history of the city. Also, a moment to rest, ride, and appreciate the city views.

Nice is a small city, so it is easy to navigate on foot. The city also has a good tram system. We walked a lot on this trip in France. Perused the available apartment postings on the windows of several immobiliers *(real estate agents)*. Just to get an idea of the apartment rental costs in the different neighborhoods, I did the same thing in Bordeaux and Toulouse. Nice was a bit more expensive but not by much. Taking these strolls through different areas helps me see where in a city I would want to settle.

This petite train was a short trip up a very high hill above the city taking us to where the once fortified Medieval Castle, Colline du Chateau stood. This was another insightful historic audio guided excursion. We had a ten-minute stop at the top to get out, walk around. I captured by camera the sprawling view of Nice below. Then a short walk to see the cemetery and some of the remaining ruins of the Castle which was demolished by French King Louis XIV in 1706. After seeing these sites, we were taken back down into the city.

Then Colonel and I walked around the New Town noticing the buildings, restaurants, people, and shops. Taking many pictures while exploring. Colonel is now off lease; we strolled slowly back to the apartment discovering various shops along the way. Finally arriving there by 5 pm. I must carry him up the stairs. Immediately, I plugged in my phone and camera battery to charge. Colonel went to sleep in the big bed. Then I relaxed in front of the TV to watch an episode of Jack Ryan on Prime Video. Around 6:30 pm, Colonel woke up looking for food. I fed him. By 7 pm, it was time for me to find food too. Usually in a new city, without a recommendation I will check Google for restaurants nearby to see what pops up and read the reviews.

Tonight, I didn't have to ask Google for suggestions since I found a lot of restaurants near our apartment on our walks. They were around the corner and down a few blocks, less than ten minutes away. This cluster of restaurants were lined up in a row next to one another on a small street leading to a larger boulevard.

Most seating was outside. I selected one, Le Biskara, serving steak haché, frites, and salad, €16,50. Chose white wine, €4.50, got bread, and water. The service was quick. After dining there, I later felt that I probably should have chosen the Mexican themed restaurant next door selling tacos and ceviche instead.

I have to say that I enjoyed eating at the restaurants in Bordeaux and Toulouse much more but then it was just my second day of dining here in Nice. Not all restaurants I dined at in Nice were as good but that was just from a limited selection and the amount of time I had to explore. I'm sure that Nice has very fine restaurants. This one was okay, nothing outstanding or even fresh, like heated frozen fries, a premade hamburger patty, and spring greens from a bag. The waiter was attentive and kind.

On the other hand, the wine with a light body, was smooth, and not acidic which I much appreciated. I chose the wine well. But this less than fresh food dinner and dining experience did not impress me. We sat outside. The outside tables were jammed too close together and were too close to the tables of the other restaurants on both sides of this one. This entire block was lined with about five restaurants on one side of the street. Across the street from the restaurants was some sort of large and long commercial building. That building was a Monoprix market.

We took our time to stroll back to the apartment, taking a different and longer route. Then back to the apartment by 8:15 pm. Both of us now relaxed on the sofa, I watched another episode of Jack Ryan before calling it a night. Tomorrow my Nice adventure continues, we're taking a day trip to Cannes and Grasse by train. I have never had to buy a train ticket for my dog to ride on any trains. Bon Nuit!

Celestine Cooley

Wednesday, September 13, 2023 | Nice ~ Cannes ~ Grasse

Day 12 - For this portion of my trip while in Nice, I didn't book any activities like day trips to other cities in advance like I had for Bordeaux and Toulouse. Instead for Nice I wanted to be more spontaneous. Although I researched things to do prior to my departure from Los Angeles, I just wanted to go with the flow to see how I felt on a particular day before deciding what to do.

Thus, waiting until after I had arrived in this city to plan those extra side trips. So, before I turn in for the evening, usually I'll book an activity using my phone such as train transportation and a day trip, site visit or city tour for that next day. Then I'll write my post about today's adventures. It's a routine I find easy to stick to.

I've decided not to book commuter buses or rental cars on this leg, just trains. I'll either book a round-trip train ticket in advance using my phone, or just get a one-way ticket from the ticket *(Billet)* machine but only if I'm not sure what time I'll want to return to Nice. Figuring out how to use the ticket machines wasn't difficult.

Getting electronic train tickets in advance is usually a better choice and easier than dealing with some ticket kiosks if you don't speak French. Mostly because you can book them in English and you'll have those tickets downloaded directly to your phone for easier access. I use several online ticket outlets, SNCF Connect, Trainline, and Omio. I have gotten into the habit of using travel apps too, essential to have when traveling.

However, it's a good idea to make sure your phone is fully

charged and you carry a power bank back up battery before venturing out for the day. As I mentioned some trains and smaller stations may not have anywhere to charge your mobile devices. You can't catch a train without a ticket. So, if that ticket is on your dead phone, you are screwed and will have to buy another ticket from the ticket office or ticket kiosk. And I don't know if getting a credit for the unused ticket is even possible. That would have to be researched by reading the ticket provider company's terms and conditions.

Usually, I'll print out hard copies of all my ticket confirmations that are organized inside a binder chronologically by date. I keep this flexible binder in my carryon bag along with Colonel's Service Dog binder. I do like having the paper backup. However, sometimes on the road I am unable to print out documents when printer access isn't available. In that case, I must rely on my phone to maintain all my confirmations and tickets. Keeping my phone charged is a must while traveling.

For booking my tours and activities, I really like using and rely on two phone Apps "Get Your Guide" and "Viator" which are good sources for day tours tickets. They have an infinite selection of affordable things to do in cities with decent cancellation and refund policies. It's very easy to use the tickets on your phone after purchasing them. Plus, you'll have your receipt and all the necessary information on hand. If you wish, you can download and print those tickets.

These online purchased tour tickets are usually good for skipping the line or VIP access. Alternatively, you could wait in line at the tour offices of the attractions to purchase tickets instead. It's an option. I don't like waiting or standing in long lines. But I do enjoy planning and arranging my own trips. If you plan to arrange your international trip yourself, these are a few helpful tips to make traveling easier. These tips are for "Do It Yourselfers" if you are not working with a travel advisor.

However, I highly recommend using a travel advisor to help plan more complex trips like this more intricate multi-week trip to France. Working on your travel plans with a travel agent makes it easier to organize your trip; which you will find to be more cost effective, stress-free, and seamless. Trip planning takes an enormous amount of time, energy, and effort, it can be overwhelming and mistakes are easy to make. So having professional travel assistance to advise, guide, and sort out the logistics and scheduling details will save you hours of grief and frustration.

Last night, I booked a round-trip train ticket to Monte Carlo, Monaco for Thursday at 9:50 am, a 20 min ride for €12, round trip. I plan to take a Hop On-Hop Off city bus tour there that I can catch near the train station in Monaco. If available, I recommend these bus tours in any city you visit or that has a similar type of guided tour. These tours provide an audio history of the city along the route. Additionally, I wanted to see the famous Casino Royale and try my luck. I'll continue this adventure in part two on Thursday. Tomorrow I'm off to Cannes and Grasse.

Another thing about doing laundry, most short-term apartment rentals have washing machines but not dryers. In case you need to dry your clothes rather than hanging them up on a drying rack there are laundromats in France. Although clothes dryers are available it seems the French don't use dryers much. I've read posts from expats on Facebook groups who purchased those combo washer/dryers like you'll find in high end RVs. Some conveyed their disappointment because those dryers took many hours to operate and weren't very effective in drying their garments.

I'll probably stop by Darby's, the electronic and appliance store to check out prices of washers. I don't mind hanging my washed clothes on a rack. Do remember seeing Darbys on one of our walks along the main shopping avenue Jean Medecin. If one gets a little homesick for big box stores, Costco, Ikea, and Albi are here in France.

Lots of Brand-named retail stores can be found here too like Zara, H&M, Apple, and Nike. Happy, I made the decision to book both Airbnb's and hotels for this trip. I really miss the convivence of room service when staying in an apartment. Both types of accommodations have their advantages though while traveling.

Getting to the Nice train station on foot was easier this morning because I took a straighter route. I am only taking the dog carrier and my fanny pack. Colonel has food, snacks, and water in his carrier. I booked a second-class one-way ticket, costing €8.00 for this 35-minute ride to Cannes.

Train travel in France isn't too crazy; you must give yourself enough time to get to the station and wait. At least 30-45 minutes before your departure time at minimum. It may sound silly, but you never know what issues you may face upon arrival at the train station. Although most trains leave on time, sometimes there are cancellations, delays, or changes.

Plus, don't hesitate to ask people at the station about the train you want to take, like the platform location or if you need help with the billet *(ticket machine)*. Often you will find people who speak

English and can help you. If not, use a language Apps like Deepl or Google Translate to convey your inquiry. Those Apps work well enough to get your message understood by French people or any other language you may be using.

The station was teaming with commuters. The long line I'm now standing in to show our tickets and to enter the platform area was moving slowly. Representatives from SNCF are standing at the gate with devices to scan your ticket's bar code before you can proceed through to the train track area.

"This Nice station is a mess," said the French woman standing in line next to me.

She was obviously replying to me after I complained aloud about, "What was taking so long for people to pass through the entry gate leading to the platform?"

Slowly, we were easing our way forward toward this gate with a cluster of passengers looking like a herd of cattle in a confined space. I dislike crowds jammed together like sardines in a can. We are too close together, it makes me feel uneasy. I am not a crowd person, since getting lost and separated from my mother at a Chicago parade for a few minutes. It felt like hours. Immediately, panic set in but I could do nothing but stand still like a statue and cry as hordes of people moved around me. I was five years old. Mommie found me.

Closer now, we are all holding our phones open to display our ticketed barcodes for scanning these tickets and going through the narrow gateway to the train platform. Then the fun search to find the right track to locate our train and then finding our assigned coaches. Time is ticking. A mad dash! I always feel like an Olympic

Sprinter when I come to these crowded train stations. Europeans are accustomed to taking trains, most Americans are not, so you slide into a panic mode when you notice how far you must walk to reach your coach. Usually a very long way. It's much easier getting to your train without hauling luggage.

These budget IOUI trains are intercity commuters so the station is extremely crowded this time of morning with people going to work. Finally, I made it to my train car after boarding the wrong one (First Class, very nice) which had no crowds and plenty of available seats. It's becoming a thing with me, in a hurry and hopping on the wrong coach. Then I had to scurry past seven train cars before reaching mine, which was the last one before the engine. That was a very long haul on foot with this dog.

Certainly, an adrenaline rush for me with less than 5-minutes to board. So happy I had no suitcases to lug around. This train leaves on time at 9:57 am. I can't believe the length of these train cars, which are very long. Often it takes some time to find the right train and then find your coach number.

On the platform I did see a posted diagram of our train showing all the car numbers which was very helpful. That earlier crowd of passengers stalled at the gate slowed me down. We took our seats and settled in for the short ride. This route travelled along the sea, so the morning views were breathtaking and calm.

I haven't been back to Cannes in decades. So, with fresh eyes I'll see how much it's changed since my first visit in 1985. Quick trip. The moment we pulled into the station I could feel the positive vibe. The humidity is lower in this city too. It's a pretty city, small, and doesn't seem as hectic. But I only stepped outside the station for a quick look around. Instead, I changed my mind about exploring Cannes and decided to take the next train to Grasse at 11:24 am, and bought a round-trip ticket for €11.04.

I'll spend a few hours in Grasse, have lunch, and then make my way to the perfume factory for a tour to learn how perfume is made. This train ride to Grasse goes up into or near the Alps. We keep ascending higher. Oh boy! The beautiful views are indescribable, stopping along the way in towns and villages. Very nice! A cooler temperature permeates this car. I'm wearing my blue windbreaker jacket. Colonel is asleep in his carrier. It's still too early for him to be active.

Finally, we've arrived after a 35-minute trip from Cannes. Looking at a posted public bus schedule at a stop outside the station, I took the city bus "C" to Centre Ville from the Grasse train station. I guessed that Centre Ville (the City Center) was where I wanted to go. It was a six-minute drive up more of this mountain. Off the bus, I saw an outdoor market where I purchased a belt and a coin purse for 10 € from a nice middle-aged male vendor. I needed that belt for my jeans. Since I often wear belts on my jeans and other slacks, I don't know why I forgot to pack at least one belt in my suitcase. Atypical of me.

I appreciate the much cleaner air at this higher elevation except when suddenly its freshness is disrupted by an occasional cigarette smoker ambling by us. In France I have noticed more people using those E-cigarettes or not smoking at all. The French like their cigarettes but seemingly there are a lot less smokers at cafes or walking around with cigarettes than there were 30 years ago. Like in many U.S. cities, smoking is banned in public places and inside buildings here too. Saw a few advertisements here about the ill health effects of smoking.

I passed the Perfume Museum and a few shops before stopping for Pasta Romana €12, a Coke, €3, and a glass of Rose, €4 at Bella Napoli, an Italian cafe which I spotted along my walk. I spent under 45 minutes at this restaurant before taking off to further explore this hilly city. By accident I found a little street that took me down into old Grasse. Then to the tourist office to ask for directions to the Fragonard Perfume Factory. We had a pleasant stroll through this area of shops and restaurants. This is a mountainous city, windy, so not a place where I would want to live and not on my list.

Tourist offices always offer good sources of information about a city. We found the tourist office on our walk and picked up a one sheet street map. Currently this small city isn't too crowded with tourists. So, walking down the narrow undulating streets without crowds was more enjoyable. I appreciate these slow strolls and peering into shop windows or popping inside to look at their wares.

Smelling the aromas of fresh baked bread and the cuisine from different cafes, getting a scoop of ice cream, and buying souvenirs to take back home. It is all a part of the travel experience and of making memories. People who don't travel can't even imagine what these experiences of being in a foreign city is like or how it transforms your perspective about other people and cultures.

I took the free perfume factory tour at Fragonard created and owned by the Fuchs family who named it after a famous Grasse painter. After touring the museum on my own, I joined a small group of about six other people to tour the factory and learn how perfume was made. After the tour, conveniently we ended up in the factory's gift shop where I bought some tiny bottles of perfume as gifts and a fragrant oil that we had sampled. Worth the experience and the price which was €125.

After spending five hours in Grasse, it was time to head back to Nice. Around 3:50 pm, I found a bus stop, the wrong one. Not sure, I asked someone about taking the bus back to the train station. A young teenage girl kindly escorted me to the right stop about 5-minutes away from where I was standing. I needed to catch Bus #5 which goes directly to the train station. I didn't think to use my transit App like Movit for the bus schedules. You can catch a taxi or Uber in this city. So that transit mode back to the station was also an option.

"Merci beaucoup, bonne Journeé!" I said to the young lady as she was leaving.

"De rien, Bonne Journée, Au revoir!" She responded.

I waited for the bus but not for very long. This bus ride was quick getting to the station and dropped us off in front of the train station. My train was leaving at 4:28 pm. Happily, I made it to the station in time to catch my train back to Cannes. There I would change trains for Nice. I'll have to visit Cannes and Antibes on my next trip to France. Neither of the charging plugs next to my seat on the train worked. However, inside the train station, I did find USB plugs for charging mobile devices but didn't use them on my return.

Soon, we are back in Nice, it's 5:39 pm. Colonel is tired, hungry, and grumpy. Although he had some kibble in Grasse, it wasn't enough. He wants to get back to the apartment so he can eat and go to bed for his usual nap. His daily routine. Back at the apartment, I'm exhausted from trekking like a goat up and down those hills in Grasse. Of course, like a kid I'll fight the sandman until 10 pm.

Tomorrow, I may sleep in until 8 am. Plus, I've gotten into the habit of writing my daily journals in Google Docs at the end of the day so I can paste and post them later into Facebook. I'm trying to stick to a daily schedule in order to accomplish all these tasks. Traveling at this pace has been taxing but I'm managing to keep up with it. Colonel seems to be holding up pretty well too.

I plan to have dinner in Nice later tonight. Right now, after feeding the hungry dog, I'm sitting on the sofa with my feet elevated. It's always nice to wind down after a long day out walking and exploring. After an hour of watching a French TV series I'll be ready to venture out for dinner. I don't know if Colonel will venture out with me or not. Probably not!

Celestine Cooley

Wednesday, September 13, 2023 | Nice ~ Evening

Day 12 - Around 7 pm, I put Colonel's lease on him to go out walking for dinner. I have his carrier too. It starts raining. We are walking from the apartment in our neighborhood in search of food. After circling a few blocks, I opted for a smash cheeseburger and a coke at BenBurger on the main boulevard. Eating in, not taking it out. I had enough to carry.

Colonel opted to go into his carrier so he could rest. I know he's sleepy and wants to settle down for the night. I don't know if this is a chain restaurant but the burgers were pretty good. I have eaten a ton of hamburgers in the South of France. After dinner, I'm hoping to find a Patisserie open to grab a few delicious treats before turning in for the night.

I planned to go to Menton and then Ventimiglia, Italy for the day on Friday. Thinking of getting a one-day car rental from the train station. Or just stay in Nice and take a big bus tour. I haven't really decided yet. No pastries found. So, it's back to the apartment to chill. Chow for now!

Six French Cities

Thursday, September 14, 2023 | Monaco

Day 13 – This morning, we are off to Monte Carlo, Monaco. Getting pretty used to this train station and how to read the departure schedules. I really adore train travel. Our train leaves at 9:50 am. It's a short ride just 21-minutes from Nice to Monaco.

We arrived at 10:11 am. I wasn't sure what time I wanted to return. So, I bought this one-way ticket which costs €4.40. Another quick and comfortable ride along the sea. Colonel is in my lap and looking out of the window, he's very content. This dog is too laid back and quiet for being a Chihuahua.

Sometimes when you don't know where you're going, you discover the unexpected. When I arrived in Monaco, I asked Google to take me to the Bus Tour location. I let Colonel out of his carrier on lease to stretch his legs and find a spot or two. I turned left toward the sea and headed down a steep street. Monaco is another city perched on the side of hills. It's two square kilometers in size and the second smallest State in all of Europe behind the Vatican.

At the bottom of this street, I turned right and walked about 10 feet. Google said turn left, and when I looked to the left, I could see the Marina filled with yachts way down below. From my vantage point, I'm wondering how high up we are? Suddenly, some steps appeared cascading down toward that street and the Marina. I felt a little vertigo looking down the length of these stairs. I didn't know if I could do it.

Exhaustedly, three young women were making their way to the

top of the last flight and landing near where I was standing. I asked if there was a non-stairs way to get down to the bottom. One answered my inquiry in a Slavic accent and pointing down the street to the left,

"Not really unless you want to walk a very long way around that way. The steps are the best way to reach the Marina."

I looked toward that "long way around" direction, shook my head and hesitated. What should I do? Give those deadly looking steps a try. They looked longer than the tall buildings next to them were high, at least ten stories. I swear! Not knowing what I would find on that 'long' walk way down there, I opted for the steps. I've never ever walked down so many steps. France, you're killing me with all these stairs.

However, the girls were right, this staircase was the quickest way to reach the street below and directly where I needed to go. Stairs should not make you want to cry, but on this trip, steps were plentiful, especially in all these perched medieval towns I've visited. Plus, the three (not two) flights of stairs I had to climb several times per day in the Nice apartment building. Jeez! This journey has turned into a real cardio workout trip.

To go down without falling, I released Colonel off lease so he could walk down on his own. I grabbed the left handrail and gave it a go. Fear came and went as I slowly descended those steep steps. Crazy, civil engineers. A quarter of the way down I met a young girl, Angelique, (an angel) from Prague was sitting on a step looking at her phone.

I stopped momentarily to rest and chat. She often visits her boyfriend who lives in Monaco. Noticing my reluctance to even be on these stairs, she got up, asked if she could help then grabbed the dog carrier to help me down. At the bottom, she guided me to the tour bus. We chatted all the way down. Angelique was a great distraction. Merci! She also pointed out a Glace shop for Italian Ice. I thanked her three times for helping me. Glad she spoke English.

Before hopping on the tour bus, I noticed a Steak n Shake across the street and laughed. I'll go there for lunch after the tour. That would make three hamburgers in a row since arriving in the south of France. A record for me.

This audio guided bus tour took about 45 mins, and cost $24.94 from Get Your Guide. Rather than hopping on and hopping off, I elected to stay on the bus throughout all its stops to people watch, listen to the city's history, and see all the sites along the route.

Although the bus stopped at the Casino, I couldn't see it, from where I was sitting on the bus's lower level. Naturally, I did not want to sit higher on the opened top deck. More stairs, too much heat, and blazing sun for me up there especially after so many steep climbs. I had no reason to climb those steps. Plus, I wasn't dressed up for the Casino. At this stage, I'm already tired and almost punch drunk, delirious like a boxer who's stayed in the ring too long.

After the tour, I popped into the Steak n Shake to order a cheeseburger, fries, and a chocolate shake to eat inside. A normal American hamburger fast food joint. It was filled with tourists and kids. If I had more time I would have found a proper restaurant to dine at in Monaco but this one was just fine. Reminded me of the Habit Hamburger or the Counter in San Fernando Valley back home. Not much I can say about a burger.

Monaco is a very small city (principality) with an unusual

layout that is somewhat circular near the sea. It is hilly. I could not live here walking up and down these steep streets reminiscent of hilly San Francisco. Even though I didn't walk a lot here except to go from and back to the train station. I saw enough of that city on the tour bus winding around, going up and down hills. So, I wasn't in the mood for hiking.

So many expensive exotic cars were driven through this town by neatly groomed men and women, the people walking around were wearing swanky evening attire at midday. Lots of tourists too. I am getting a Beverly Hills vibe. It's like a fancy resort town. Good for a visit and people watching. I could not imagine living here at all. Not much to do after you visit a few museums, the Japanese gardens, and the Casino.

Dining out at expensive restaurants or shopping on the little street I saw filled with the same designer stores as the ones on Rodeo Drive in Beverly Hills, well no, thank you! I can only imagine what it's like here during the Monaco Grand Prix, Formula Race through this city's narrow streets, around the marina, along with all the racing enthusiasts. I suspect there is more going on in this city like festivals and concerts but I didn't research events here or even stop by the tourism office.

Instead, I only spent four hours in Monaco to tour the city by bus and was ready to leave. Someone told me there was a short cut to the train station. Finding that shortcut meant less steps to climb and would put me right there at the station to catch my train back to Nice. My train was leaving at 4:49 pm, costing €4.40.

People you meet at the stations and on the trains are often characters. Four French passengers helped me with my French.

They were delighted that I knew some French, so I'd ask something in French and they'd ask me something in French. They also spoke English with French accents. It was fun engaging with them!

Why I'm not intimidated by this difficult language and keep trying to use it amazes me. I couldn't wait to get here to test my "little" language skills. At times, I still must translate from English to French in my head. Not the right way to do it. Sometimes the words come easy, but there are also complicated sentences to remember and verbs to conjugate. French is not easy to grasp. Comprehension takes time just to understand what is being said to you. The French speak very fast. Still doing my best to keep up with the basics of this language. No where near proficient. I must keep studying and learning every day.

Often, French people will start speaking to me like I'm French. Thrown off by the conversation, my quick response may be: "Je ne sais pas" *(I don't know),* or "Je ne comprend pas" *(I don't understand)* [the French often drop the "pas"] or I'll respond, "Parle plus lentement, s'il vous plaît," *(speak more slowly, please).*

Mostly, I get asked where I'm from, and either everyone has been or wants to go to California. "Il a mon chien" *(he's my dog)* "a boy" *(garcon),* or "fille" *(girl).* Quel age? *(How old?)* "Il a neuf ans," I answer. *(He's nine years old.)* These are the basic French phrases I use often. Hearing the repeated questions about my dog help s.

During this trip, I met quite a few American tourists who were not prepared for their visits to France. Many seemed to lack any understanding of French culture, manners, or etiquette. Some were unaware that saying, *"Bonjour!"* is very necessary when greeting French people or to get the services you want without any drama.

For instance, I met an older couple from California while waiting for the train to arrive at our platform. After establishing our American connection, I asked why they were not having any good restaurant experiences here especially with the waiters. When the husband asked for ketchup for his fries, he said,

"All hell broke out." Then added,

"The waiter was indignant and went nuts because I asked for ketchup and then butter."

"The French rarely butter their bread." I responded.
He looked at me a little confused.
I continued,

"Instead of ketchup, they may use mayonnaise for their fries like the British and probably most of Europe."

This man's wife was distraught over the whole incident. She was not having a good time on this trip. I have seen French people using ketchup too. Some restaurants do serve it. Some don't. Read the room. I've been lucky on this trip. No restaurant drama with any of the food or French servers. They always served me ketchup which I never asked for and seldom used.

Tourists should prepare for foreign travel by doing their homework. Taking the time to research a country's history, habits, culture, cuisine, and traditions before buying that plane ticket will provide a much better travel experience.

The wife was equally upset because no one spoke English.

I stated, "Well, you are in France."

"Saying Bonjour, goes a long way to get you what you want here," I added.

The French are different. Just being pleasant helps! We often think our American privilege extends across the ocean. Nope! This kind of experience happens when travelers fail to learn about the culture of the destination they plan to visit. I felt sad that this couple did not enjoy their visit to France. Also, it isn't a good idea to bring your American values along on an international trip. When in Rome! The train was pulling into the station; I wished them well as I headed down the platform to find my car.

Fatigued and so eager to get back to Nice to take a nap. In my haste I jumped on the wrong train. Well, it was going to Nice but I didn't have a ticket for this earlier train at 1:40 pm. Mine was for 2:20 pm. These tickets are not interchangeable, so if caught, I'd have to pay a big penalty and buy another ticket. I won't make this mistake again.

This earlier train was packed. A young girl gave me her seat. In Nice, at the apartment by 2:30 pm. Desperately, I needed to rest. Ordered carry out, washed a load of clothes, and put them on the drying rack. Chilled for the night. So exhausted, I didn't want to deal with those stairs to go out later for dinner. Bon Nuit!

Celestine Cooley

Friday, September 15, 2023 – Last Day in Nice

Day 14 - I slept in this morning until 9 am, exhausted from yesterday's day trip. Decided to stay put in Nice instead of visiting another perched city. My thighs are thanking me because they were slightly sore. After all of that walking up and down stairs and hills and stairs yesterday, I'm paying for it now.

Although I really wanted to visit more cities, I'll visit Menton, France and Ventimiglia, Italy at another time. This is my last night in Nice; a new city is waiting to be explored tomorrow. Going into my final week of this trip. Last night, I reorganized and repacked my bags in an attempt to lighten them a bit. Cleaned the apartment and took out the trash. Paid some bills online because I still have my life back in SoCal.

Around noon, Colonel woke up, he was ready to eat and go out. His timing is impeccable because I was ready to give Nice one last spin. He peed as we walked to the Tram stop a few blocks away. I purchased a plastic metro card for an additional €3 and then bought a day pass for €7 that loaded onto the rechargeable metro card. This card is used for all public transit, including the buses. I'll keep this plastic card to use for my next trip to Nice.

I noticed there are three tram lines in Nice run by Ligne d'Azur which are numbered, Ligne 1-Red, Ligne 2-Blue, and Ligne 3-Green. Line 2 goes to the airport and connects with lines 1 and 3. Good transit. The transit and tourist offices have Metro maps.

I decided to hop on the tram to see where it would take us.

Taking this Tram line from the Jean Médecin stop. I figured I could ride this tram to the end of the line, then return to the same tram station. I told Colonel we were going for a tram ride. I planned to ride this tram (red line 1) to the end of both lines, going in opposite directions. My curiosity prevailed. I'll often explore this way in a new city, if not by tram, then by bus or metro to the end of the lines. Taking buses and trams are better for this type of urban exploration in my opinion.

These roundtrip Tram rides are inexpensive and really expose the ever-changing settings and textures of the various neighborhoods passed through. Each 'end of the line' ride took about 35-45 minutes each way. It makes sense to see as much of a city as possible even when I have no clue where I am going. My curiosity guides me beyond the usual tourist areas into neighborhoods on the outskirts of town, where I get a different perspective of a city overall. When I have time, I will get off to explore these areas on foot as well.

On my next visit, I'll have to ride the other two lines (2 and 3). The South of France really wore me out. I very much enjoyed touring this city by tram and on foot, losing myself in neighborhoods and taking public transportation, because you never know where you'll end up or what you will discover. Some neighborhoods are a bit sketchy and perhaps less desirable. But I'm interested in seeing all sides of a city. What's interesting about riding through communities is that you can tell the changing economic status of the area and its residents.

In one direction leaving the city center, going North toward Henri Sappia, the landscape changes to a more inner-city vibe. We rode through various neighborhoods where I could see how the environment and the people getting on and off this tram changed. Going through the North section of Nice, you'll find the ethnic part of town where mostly immigrants live. Parents look weary and ill-content; their kids appear happy, full of energy, and laughter. There is a higher concentration of diversity in this community filled with high rise apartment buildings some displaying graffiti.

Each community here has an area name. Even the middle-class area I'm staying in has a name, Jean-Médecin. At the end of the line, we waited for the tram to go back into the city. Venturing off in the other direction going east on this Tram, passing through less diverse neighborhoods that were well maintained and much nicer. Taking Ligne 1-Red back in the other direction all the way to Hospital Pasteur.

After leaving the city center, I noticed the difference again. Heading south then east, people getting on this tram tend to dress in business casual attire, smiling parents and kids with backpacks all seem content. Less diversity though. The area looks like the suburbs on the outskirts of any city.

Older French apartment style buildings as well as tall newer buildings lined up like soldiers standing in formation. This ride took about 45 minutes total to the end and back. I like taking these mysterious rides to nowhere just to explore new areas by public transportation which gives one a better sense of a city's residential makeup.

Off the tram, we're walking through the city center again. After that little journey of urban discovery, I was ready for lunch. It's gonna take a while for me to get into this meal time routine. If you miss lunch between 12-2 pm, good luck finding a place serving food. You won't find any diners like Denny's in France. All you'll find is French Tacos, sandwiches, or pizza if you're lucky, and fast food like McDonald's. Other than that, it's a liquid lunch of beverages (beer, wine, cocktails, coffee, tea, or hot chocolate) until the next mealtime beginning at 7 pm. Around 4 pm is snack time.

So, of course I missed lunch again. I did find some pizza and a beer. I had a lemon tart meringue glace (artisan ice cream), one scoop (une boule de glace) in a cup. It was just enough with bits of tart crust mixed in to fulfill that ice cream craving. Yummy. When I'm living in France, I certainly won't be eating out every day. I'll prepare many of my meals at home like I do in the States.

After eating, we walked around old Nice again, which was like stepping into the 16th Century. Many of the buildings looked ancient. It seems natural to be walking around this city not riding in a car. I enjoy exploring new places, discovering hidden gems, and new sites, and not necessarily the popular landmarks.

I attempted to find the beach and Promenade de Anglaise once more without Google Maps but failed. For whatever reason, I could never find my way back to the sea. Being from Los Angeles, I loved driving out to the ocean. Around 4 pm, we headed back to the apartment to relax. I took the tram back to our neighborhood this time, then walked four blocks to the apartment. This area is full of stores with a pool of people streaming steadily through retail shops to obtain coveted merchandise.

Going up these apartment stairs just adds another layer of exhaustion to my already weary body. The cause of my fatigue is the pace of this trip, but I don't want to slow down or miss anything.

I'm having too much fun. We settle down for a few hours; Colonel eats then sleeps. I write a little, then watch some television. Always thinking about my life and what it will be like living in France. I pretty much know how it will be to live in this country from being on this adventure and checking out these cities.

Around 8 pm, we take the slightly spiraled stairs down to the ground floor. I'll never get used to these 'scary' French staircases, so steep, so narrow. I've seen interior staircases in France without railings, how is that even safe? We take our time walking toward the main boulevard in search of a dinner spot. Colonel seems rested and happy to be out exploring. His two-hour nap helped his disposition.

The noticeable dinner crowd was out and growing. So, we had plenty of company in our pursuit of a good restaurant. We found Le Cernac Restaurant, a small eatery in that area with the other restaurants in a row. I craved and ordered steak, fries, and salad, which cost €25. I also ordered a Pinot Noir, €4 and a glass of tap water. This meal hit the spot but there was nothing outstanding about it, I was just happy to have some protein.

The steak was cooked to my liking (medium well) and the fries were crispy. I haven't had a bad glass of wine since arriving in France. This was my last dinner in Nice! This city wasn't so bad after all despite the heat. Still, I have no real desire to live here although I enjoyed my visit. Should I keep it on the list? Every year, Nice has a jazz festival in July, which is a good reason for me to return.

Back at the apartment, I packed my now dry clothes and the rest of my loose belongings inside my bags. Cleaned the apartment and took out the day's trash. Texted my host regarding my departure time for checking out in the morning. She thanked me and welcomed me back anytime. Yeah, well, second floor, no elevator; thanks, but maybe no thanks. Although I liked staying in this apartment, I think it is more suited for younger people. I'll send her referrals. I wrote a review on Airbnb for all the apartments I rented for this trip. It seems that the owners also leave a review of us too.

Oh, I wanted to mention one thing about France that takes getting used to is the smells, not fresh baked bread or food or perfume but body odors. You will notice musky odors emanating from some people when you are out exploring. The musky scent is either light or heavy. I was hit with this same strong odor while traveling through Ethiopia a few years ago. Apparently, certain cultures don't use deodorant. This is an everyday occurrence which you can't avoid in a hot densely filled city with various odors and aromas. When traveling it is best to just relax, tolerate, and accept the differences. Travel can be life altering. Best to go with the flow, appreciate the just environment, culture, and the people respectfully.

Where to next, Celeste? A Bientôt!

CHAPTER NINE

Exploring Lyon

Saturday September 16, 2023 | Nice to Lyon

Day 15 - I am packed and ready to leave this city. It's early so it's not as hot and muggy yet. So long Nice, it was fun and now I'm off to my next new city adventure. We left the apartment at 8:45 am for our walk to what is now a very familiar route to the train station. Colonel is snug in his carrier. Inside this busy station, I approach the departure board.

My train's track number is not yet listed. Intermittently, while watching other passengers scurrying to their tracks, I keep looking up to check the board. Then as soon as my train's track number appears for our departing train, I gather my bags and stroll over to the gate to show my ticket and board our coach.

My sold-out (TGV INOUI), was a fully packed train leaving Nice at 9:57 am. My ticket was purchased earlier on the Omio App, costing €106. This train journey to Lyon via Marseille was supposed to take a total of five hours and seventeen minutes, including the one-hour stopover in Marseille. However, our arrival in Lyon wasn't at our scheduled time of 3:14 pm. Instead, due to many delays on route, we pulled into the Lyon station much later than expected. So, we were extremely tired and irritable when we finally arrived in Lyon.

Getting in and out of Nice by train isn't as easy as you might expect especially if incidents along the way cause delays. You must go through Marseille to change trains. What should have been a seamless trip from Nice to Lyon, this time it wasn't. It takes longer to travel from the South of France to go up North by train or car. I don't know how often I'd make that 6-hour trip each way from Nice to Paris by train. In this case, flying is more appealing.

At first after pulling out of the station, our train chugged along the route normally for about two hours. Then suddenly, between Nice and Marseille near the Toulon stop, our train paused due to an accident on the tracks up ahead. We had no idea what was going on until the conductor announced the delay over the PA system.

Now motionless like stranded refugees stuck between borders we sit impatiently on this stalled train. Every passenger onboard was desperately hoping for the tracks ahead to be cleared to continue our scheduled journey. But as time passed uncertainty grew shredding our optimism of arriving in Marseille on time to catch our connecting trains.

Unlike Amtrak, SNCF (the French train operator) isn't strategic enough to provide a few buses to take passengers on to their next destination or even to the next train station on this route around the accident. Why not? Ridiculous, I thought. I dislike waiting because it consumes your quality activity time while you're lingering and doing nothing productive. For a moment, I could only think about all the fun activities I'm missing during these wasted moments in limbo on a train. Can't get those moments back either.

The train, after stopping for long hauls, would then proceed a little but only to tease us with several more annoying false starts- moving forward slowly for a few minutes, then stopping again. These false starts continued three more times before the train finally froze on the tracks for the next three hours.

Stranded and feeling worse than I did while sitting in a plane on a runway for two hours, I knew that I would have to notify my hotel in Lyon about my late arrival. But I couldn't know at this juncture when I would be arriving. I'll notify the hotel about this delay once we finally arrive in Marseille.

When we first boarded this train in Nice, our eagerness to get where we were going showed on every passenger's face. But now, the other passengers and I could only express signs of bewilderment, disappointment, and frustration. Clearly, not one passenger in our train car looked content. Just confused and left wondering when our train would begin moving down the tracks again.

Attentively, we listened to each intermittent broadcast conveying updates over a PA system in French. With each new announcement, the foreign tourists and French people became more animated and annoyed. Sounds of disgust amplified through our car at first like a low rising hum that increased in volume.

Since this was my first ever train delay experience, I was irate and struggling emotionally not to react negatively. Instead, I tried to remain calm to patiently deal with this situation that was completely out of my control. But some of the other passengers could hardly contain themselves, not totally melting down but getting close.

A lot of the people in this car were grumbling about their consequences due to this delay, verbally expressing out loud their concerns and dissatisfaction about this stagnant situation to no one in particular. Some people were going on to Paris, thus for them an even longer trip than mine. It seemed that everyone would have to change trains in Marseille to proceed on to their ticketed destinations. Right now, we were a bunch of disgruntled customers stuck out in the middle of nowhere, going nowhere at all.

So, when someone tells you that train travel from Nice to Paris is easy, it isn't always the case. In fact, this train route takes over 6 hours to get from Nice to Paris. I much prefer the ease of going back and forth to Paris from Bordeaux or Lyon, which is only a two-hour train trip each way.

It would be much quicker to fly (1:35 minutes) from Nice to Paris round trip for about the same price. Don't get me wrong, I do enjoy traveling by train when it's moving and gets to my destination at the expected time or close to it. This delay was unexpected, so I guess in the future I should expect train delays like this are possible.

Had it not been for my seat companions with their light-hearted spirits and senses of humor, this ride would have been unbearably boring. Our quad seating consisted of two people (an older couple) seated together across the table facing me and the person seated next to me.

A young Scandinavian woman (early 30s) sat to my left on the aisle, she spoke English, but not French, and worked on her laptop throughout the trip. We casually chatted until we reached Marseille. She was a very sweet, kind, and helpful young woman.

She asked me, "Do you speak French?" "Do you know what the conductor said?"

I responded, "Well, I speak and understand a little French."

I paused to think about the announcement and then continued,

"Sounds like there was an accident on the tracks between here and Marseille but not sure what type of accident. We must sit and wait until it is clear to go."

The older French couple sitting (face to face) across from us were very animated and entertaining, speaking only French. The husband had a sense of humor and kept speaking to me in French about the train situation. He made funny facial expressions and flailing hand gestures.

Some Americans were two seats back from me and kept making phone calls and recounting to each recipient that answered their calls about the reason for our train's delay. There were many manic back-and-forth conversations but soon everyone simmered down. Our car was quiet for a while until the next announcement irritated the passengers again and set off a wave of complaints.

The four French people in the same row but across the aisle from me were seated in the same four-person configuration. They were more conservative and much quieter. When I took Colonel out of his carrier and onto my lap, all four noticed him and brightened up, becoming more engaging. We heard their vocal elation upon seeing him. One of the women began asking me questions about Colonel in French,

"Oh, Le petit chien, il a un garçon ou une fille? *(Oh, The little dog. Is it a boy or a girl?)*

I answered, "C'est un garçon et sa race est Chihuahua." *(It's a boy and his breed is Chihuahua.)*

The woman said, "Tres minion." *(Very cute.)*

Quel age? She inquired. *(How old is he?).*

So many questions so quickly besieged me, requiring me to answer in French. So, I kept speaking to them in my basic French.

Responding to her, "Il a neuf ans." *(He's nine years old).*

I am glad Colonel helped pull her out of her shell. Now other people around us have noticed him too, looking at him, making comments about his small size, and his good behavior. Unaffected by their attention, Colonel nuzzles his nose under my right arm to rest comfortably. I had been watching much of the landscape pass by before we stopped moving completely. Now accepting the lost time, I settled in my seat, pulled out my earbuds, and continued listening to an audiobook murder mystery.

Another hour passed, and another announcement, this one about food which prompted many passengers to get up and move around the train. They left their seats, disappeared, and then returned a few minutes later with cardboard lunch boxes filled with sandwiches, chips, and a beverage. Although I left my seat to find this food, I was unsuccessful.

After walking through several cars, I could not find the car giving out those lunch boxes. However, when I returned to my seat, I noticed that some people had two lunch boxes each. Fortunately, in my tote bag, I had stashed snacks and water for both Colonel and myself, so we were fine for a while. Although a sandwich would have been nicer.

When we finally arrived in Marseille around 4 pm, a fury of passengers from my train began fanning out in different directions and were frantically rushing around inside the station. I wasn't sure what to do or where to go to have my ticket reissued. I just knew I wasn't going to pay for a new ticket. This was an SNCF problem. I'm scanning the room when I see numerous people scurrying in one direction to get their tickets reissued. I spotted a long line at a counter where a woman from SNCF was passing out Lyon tickets to people from my train. You had to show your old connecting ticket for Lyon to get a new one.

With my phone ready and displaying my ticket, I managed to aggressively nudge my way through that crowd to receive my newly reissued ticket for Lyon too. Got it and moved away from the crowd with my luggage in tow. I looked around for the departure board and spotted it. Standing nearby was a British guy traveling with his mother. He mentioned that they were on the same train out of Nice as me. Then while on our train, he realized that they would miss their train to Lyon. So out of panic and desperation, he purchased new tickets to Lyon from his phone but they still missed that train by 2 minutes. That was a travel rookie decision I thought but responded differently.

I said, "You'll have to ask SNCF about a refund or credit." I then conveyed to him my stance on the ticket situation.

I said, "Due to so many delays with the train starting and stopping and waiting, I was unsure about our arrival time into Marseille. So, I didn't want to chance buying another ticket then miss my connection anyway. Plus, I wanted SNCF to reissue my ticket since the train was delayed and not missed. I certainly wasn't thinking about buying a new one."

Looking fatigued and defeated, he said,

"Yeah, that was smart."

I told him to "Have a good trip in spite of this situation."

Then I made my way to the departure board to find the track and locate my train. Fortunately, I was able to catch the 4:50 pm train to Lyon. Although I was disheartened by the delay of missing my earlier train, I knew it was totally out of my control. Just very happy to be off that last train finally.

Upon boarding my train to Lyon, I knew this journey was going to be another very long and tiresome 4-hour train ride from Marseille. I stored my luggage and found my seat. I settled down emotionally letting out a huge sigh of relief as the train began to inch down the tracks. At last, we were on our way, hopefully without any further delays. As the sun was setting, time seemed to slow down.

Exhausted and hungry, I tried to relax to enjoy the remainder of this journey and this day. At the station, during the frenzy and before leaving I did not have enough time to grab something to eat. Seated, I grabbed my earbuds from my carryon and inserted them into my ears to drown out my thoughts and listen to that audiobook on my phone. I closed my eyes but I did not fall asleep. Instead, I now felt a calmness slowly blanket my entire body at last. By now, Colonel was asleep in his carrier.

Celestine Cooley

Saturday, September 16, 2023 - Evening - Lyon

Day 15 - Finally, twelve hours after leaving Nice, we arrived in Lyon at 9:00 pm. So very disappointed from not having had the opportunity to see Lyon today on my first day in this city during daylight. Before that long delay, I thought I'd have at least half a day to spend exploring Lyon. Instead, a whole day was wasted because someone leaped in front of the train that travelled ahead of us. Despair is a heavy burden to carry.

As a seasoned traveler, I realized that our specific plans aren't always guaranteed because Murphy's Law *(anything that can happen, will happen)* lurks in the shadows while we're traveling just waiting to crash our party. You learn to go with the flow as best you can even if some situations are aggravating. At this point, I was just happy to be here now in Lyon, even if not at all-in-one piece physically or emotionally. Nonetheless, I was pleased that my hotel was only about five minutes from this train station.

I wasn't a happy camper. Even though my hotel was around the corner from the train station, maybe a five-minute walk, I did not look forward to walking or fighting with taxi drivers. I was too tired and it was too dark. That block looks too long to tote my luggage down; and I just spotted a rat larger than Colonel scurrying across the street.

Also, I was cranky and suffering from hunger pains. Not in the mood for any drama whatsoever. I just wanted to get to the hotel as quickly as possible. Approaching the taxi stand in front of the Gare (train station), I was determined to negotiate a ride to the hotel. These drivers don't like short fares but they do like money. The first driver I approached was older, in his 40s.

"Bonsoir," I said and then asked in English, "How far was my Ibis hotel from the Gare?"

He started with, "Just around the corner, 5 minutes."

I shot back, "Well, I don't want to walk in the dark, the hotel is not close enough for me to walk at night safely with my bags, I'll pay you."

Another older driver hearing my plea approached. So, I asked him about taking a taxi to my hotel. I told him that my train was delayed for hours, so my ride to Lyon was extra-long, and "Je suis fatigue." *(I am tired),* et "Je suis vieux." *(I am old) (that excuse works in a pinch.)* I just can't walk right now, I begged, almost in tears. He could see my sincerity and feel my exhaustion.

He said, "Okay!"

Then he instructed a younger driver to take me to the hotel. Although reluctant, the younger guy drove me to my hotel which seemed like only two minutes away by car. I was so happy that he conceded and I gave him a €12 tip for his trouble. This ride costs €7.30. Certainly, this cost was a rip-off but now, I did not care about cost just getting safely to the hotel. I handed him €20, and told him to keep the change,

"Pour toi." I stated.

His face lit up and he responded,

"Merci, madame!"

He helped lift my luggage from his truck and placed it near the hotel's entrance. A fare is a fare. If he makes no other money tonight, he got those euros. I bet that young guy was glad that he drove me around the corner to my hotel after all.

Before going inside to check into the hotel, I let Colonel out of his carrier and off lease so he could find a few spots. Right now, I'm feeling like the walking dead and so doggone hungry. Colonel was very hungry too. After checking in, I was happy to see that the hotel had an actual full-service restaurant unlike Holiday Inn Express. I dropped off all my bags in the room, gave Colonel some water and kibble which he gobbled down quickly as if it were his last supper. Then we scurried down stairs to the restaurant before it closed.

By now, it was 9:45 pm, and near closing. I was the last customer. So thankful, the waitress allowed me to order a hamburger classic with string beans and a coke. It was a double decker burger with cheese that I wasn't expecting. Usually, I don't eat double-deckers or this late at night but I was famished and needed nourishment.

Since I have lost weight on this trip, I don't mind this late dining time. Sometimes you're so tired that it is difficult to eat or think. I was just that tired and mowing through this meal like a slug through wet grass on a rainy day and simply ready to fold. I should've ordered my meal to go.

Around 10:30 pm, the wait staff began cleaning the tables and floors around me. I'm a very slow eater anyway and by then was only halfway through this meal. I really wanted to experience the traditional cuisine of Lyon, not another American hamburger. Lyon is known as the gastronomic center of France with numerous Michelin Stars awarded to restaurants and chefs here, maybe more than in Paris, I can't remember.

So out of sorts and brain dead now, I left the restaurant and forgot to pay my bill. My keen waitress caught up to me and asked,

"Would you like to charge this meal to your room?"

Embarrassed, I responded,

"Oui, absolument. Désolé, je suis très fatigué. Merci, Bonsoir!"

Then I gave her my room number, took Colonel out for his last pee for the night. Then grabbed the elevator up to our room. By now, I am a Zombie. Inside my room, it's now 11 pm, Colonel crawls under the covers. He's done! I want to take a shower but fearful I'll pass out. I put on my jammies, recharge my phone, lay down, and soon I'm out like a baby after a big burp. I'll explore Lyon tomorrow when my brain wakes up. Bon nuit!

Celestine Cooley

Sunday, September 17, 2023 - Morning – Lyon

Day 16 - I woke up after 9 am. 10 hours of sleep that I needed. My sore muscles and creaky joints salute me as I stretch before hopping out of bed. After my feet touched the floor, I popped a Tylenol Arthritis tab into my mouth for relief. No time to be moving around like a crippled old woman battling arthritis and losing the fight.

Because I'm stretching and moving so much, I don't often feel the aches and pains or other side effects associated with my age and osteoarthritis, which a hereditary often-crippling disease diagnosed decades ago. Happy to have pain relief when I need it, so Tylenol like Colonel is my traveling companion.

Luckily, I do not have osteoporosis, like a teenager my bones are still very dense and strong. I get plenty of calcium from my diet. Yoga helps keep me flexible. But if I sit for too long, like those hours I spent sitting on trains yesterday, my body retaliates. Aleve arthritis (not recommended by my doctor) offers me better relief than the Tylenol unless I take extra strength. I have both with me on this trip. Not playing around with any pain today. I don't want pain to slow me down or sideline my fun.

After a nice hot shower, I take my time to get ready to go out on this Lyon city adventure. Still sad that I did not have my two full days to explore this city. I persevered, deciding to walk less and ride more today. Outside the hotel and a short distance away is a bus stop, I asked a nice African lady who spoke English about where to take the bus to Vieux (old) Lyon. She gave me good directions. From her advice, I took a bus from that stop to Bellecourt, a large square where the tour begins. By now, it's 1:30 pm, and I spotted a pizza place for lunch before taking the bus tour. I'm not going to experience as much of Lyon as I had planned, especially dining out. So, unfortunately it won't be a fair assessment of this city.

My waiter was bubbly with a great attitude. You can always tell when someone enjoys their job. I ordered Salade Lyonnaise, the traditional salad with a poached egg, bacon and greens, and a coke to drink. It was tasty but heavy with walnuts and Balsamic vinegar which in France is lighter, slightly sweet, and less vinegary than what we get in the US. So, it was still palatable. I left a tip. Next time, I would like to try that same salad again at a more traditional Lyonnaise restaurant.

Big cities depend on tourism dollars, so staff are usually well trained in customer service. So friendly hospitality at hotels, restaurants, and retail stores is very important. Not often in these settings will you have a bad experience with the staff. Most service and hospitality industry employees are kind, considerate, and helpful. But respect and courtesy go both ways. Be mindful of how you treat others.

After lunch, we made our way to the tour bus stop around 3 pm. The bus appeared around 3:30, and our Hop on Hop Off Lyon City Tour began. It took over 1.5 hours to ride the entire route. I did not want to hop On and Off at the various stops so I stayed put until we returned to stop #1 where I originally boarded. This was a very insightful and enjoyable ride. The areas we toured were very clean and historic. Many sites I would not have reached on foot.

Lyon is in the Rhone Alps. So, it's hilly. This is a very pretty

2000-year-old city. Seems quiet but it's Sunday. Every city and village throughout France is quiet on Sundays. Unfortunately, there is a homeless population here which was very much in view (encampments on the streets) like in L.A. Regardless, the buildings here vary and are eclectic, especially the newer ones of modern architecture scattered among 16th and 17th century structures. We drove past Vieux (old) city Lyon, government buildings, and old army bases converted into schools.

The French know how to repurpose old buildings for practical use. In the U.S., old buildings are just torn down and replaced with some new structure. Next, we rode up the hillside to see several churches (Basilicas and Cathedrals), which can be seen from the city street below and the Roman ruins where concerts are now held.

We crossed bridges over both the Rhone River and the Saone River to see the confluence where the two rivers eventually meet. It's a well laid out city and seems easy to navigate by foot. Sad that I won't have enough time to really walk through different neighborhoods to get a better feel for this place.

After the tour, I reluctantly walked back across the bridge over the Rhone River into Vieux Lyon to visit this historic site. Most cities around the world have older areas where people first settled, France is no different. We found an antique street market with local vendors under popup awnings selling everything from antique serving sets to books which I videotaped while walking around that market.

Then we walked along the ancient streets of this area. Time was racing, it's now around 5:30 pm, I'm ready to head back to the hotel for a little rest. I hailed a taxi, which cost €14. I also found a restaurant nearby, just a 10-minute walk from the hotel. I'll go there for dinner after 7 pm. Thinking I want steak and fries or duck tonight.

Back to my room and to my normal routine, I removed my shoes, recharged my phone, fed Colonel, and relaxed in bed for a while. I'm fatigued but don't want to take a nap. At 7:30 pm, we made our way to the restaurant nearby. Colonel walks all the way before I put him in his carrier. I spot the male server and inquire,

"Bonjour, une table pour une personne, s'il vous plaît." *(Hello, a table for one person, please!)*.

He speaks a little English so throughout the night we helped each other with French and English. At this rate with all the language help I'm receiving; I may become fluent one day. No chance of that happening this year, because I still have a long way to go with this language learning process. The waiter brings me a menu apologizing that it's only in French. No problem, I can read most of it and if needed, you can help me decide.

"D'accord" (Okay!), I assure him,

My young waiter (late 20s) is from Lyon. He tells me about the fountain that I passed by which was made for the city of Bordeaux but that city did not want it and gave it to Lyon. We chatted a lot throughout my meal. I asked for un verre d'eau *(a glass of water)* and ordered un rouge vin *(a red wine)* to drink.

He tells me that one dish isn't available which looks like the one I had a craving for *(a beef stew type dish)* or optional Salmon *(not on the menu)*. He suggested steak, fries, and salad instead. This dinner costs €19. Wine €4. You'll also get free bread and tap water with every meal.

Okay, I'll have your suggestion. If you love steak, you'll love France. I always seem to get the nicest waiters helping me at these French restaurants. He was right, my medium steak was cooked perfectly and was very tasty. I needed the salad and was happy it came with this plat. So hungry. I ate, paid, and said, "Bonsoir!" I'm still over tired and need to lay down. It's my age. I'm no longer 20 with endless stamina. Old body, young mind. I have already used up my reserved energy on this trip. Still, I march on because there's too much left to see and do on this journey.

I was back at the hotel around 9 pm. Colonel passed out on the bed while I wrote about my day and the sweet experiences I had during my short stay in Lyon. I like Lyon, it too is only two hours from Paris by train. There are a lot of commercial businesses here around where I was staying on the right side of the Rhone River, and the city wasn't overpopulated with tourists. I did see numerous Rugby fans and a few players.

It's a busy city with a slower pace unlike Toulouse. It isn't as hot here since it's near the Alps, a bit windy but tolerable. I could live here. It seems very laid back and with a cool homey vibe. But then again, it's Sunday, when businesses are closed and people are sequestered away spending time with their families. So, I'm not seeing the city in its day-to-day active reality with the local people moving about and doing what they do here through the week.

Can't believe two weeks have sailed by so quickly. Tomorrow afternoon I leave Lyon to visit the last city on this journey. I bet you can guess where I'm going next. If you guessed Paris, you're right. I once considered living in Paris but I'm not so sure anymore even though I love that city very much. I'm looking for a less hectic and smaller environment to call home. We'll see if it's added or scrapped from my list after my five-night, six-day stay in that city.

After this scouting trip, I'm going to miss France very much. Telling the truth, I don't ever want to leave. This has been a wonderful experience. I have not been disappointed in the cities I've visited so far or in the French people. I wish I could really express how I feel about France. A little similar to the way I felt about moving to and living in California all those years ago.

Of course, I will always love California, my heart will never let it go. Though I feel that France is where I need to be living now at this time in my life. I very much enjoy visiting this country. It's familiar, it's warm, and it feels like home. I look forward to being able to move to France, to some city, sometime soon. I'm ready! Bonne Journeé!

Celestine Cooley

CHAPTER TEN

Exploring Paris

Monday, Sept 18, 2023 | Leaving Lyon for Paris

Day 17 – Hurry up and wait is the military's motto. Today would test this theory. Waiting for anything is not one of my stronger qualities. This morning at 8 am, I am awake after a night of tossing and turning from the anticipation and excitement of getting closer to my dream. My brain rarely shuts down at night. Usually, so many thoughts are speeding through my mind like NASCAR drivers trying to win their first race. This frantic competition stems from my mental planning about ending my current life in Los Angeles and beginning my future life in France.

I can't think of anything else. Everyday my dream of moving seems so far away because I must wait. If I had my way, I would move to France right now. Nevertheless, I cannot move across the ocean at this moment, not this year or even next year due to my current work obligation. I'm not the type of person who would just walk away from responsibilities but I will walk away from chaos. Thus, the reason for my frustration and ongoing mental agony. The strong impulse I have had these last few months to leave the United States sooner is completely overruled by my logic to stick it out a little longer. Additionally, I must meet a financial goal before leaving the country, which will require me to continue working for two more years through the end of 2025.

After that time, I should be financially able to retire and make this big life changing leap more comfortably. Although, now I am more confident about my plans to relocate after taking this insightful scouting trip. Very sure that I can easily make the transition. So, brain please stop racing, please slow down, release these nagging thoughts, and give me some peace. I'll figure it all out later. Right now, I must get up and get ready to check out of this hotel. It's on to my next city.

It rained overnight. Getting an early start this morning so I could walk Colonel, find a bank, and have a full breakfast at the hotel's restaurant before leaving. After taking Colonel out for a thirty-minute walk, it was clear to me that I desperately needed orange juice. Yesterday and this morning, people were coughing and sneezing all around me. Vitamin C usually helps protect me from catching any kind of bug. Surely while on this trip, I don't want any ailments. I must stay healthy to complete this journey.

After breakfast with Google's help, I located the nearest bank with an ATM that was a short 15-minute walk from my hotel. I could not find a closer bank. It isn't difficult to figure out the Bank ATMs in France. You can change the language to English (British) with a tap on the screen. I wanted to use my credit card to withdraw funds from this bank.

However, I forgot about the pin and chip method used at French banks. Oh man, I have one but who can remember their credit cards pin numbers? Naturally, I couldn't because I have never used it in the States, only the ones for my debit cards. Good thing I brought my bank debit card along so I can withdraw funds from my checking account instead. Took my withdrawn funds and walked back to the hotel.

Having cash handy was a must for needs like tips, snacks, and trinkets or anything else I desired. If anyone tells you that you don't need cash while traveling, don't listen to them; you'll need to carry some euros or another country's currency in your wallet, the amount you need is up to you.

Big tip, try to avoid using currency exchange bureaus; instead use any bank's ATM to withdraw funds in euros safely and economically. Also, decline the foreign bank's money conversion inquiry. Your bank will do a better conversion giving you the best rate of exchange and less bank fees.

In France, most of the merchants use portable contactless credit card readers so you just tap your card or insert the card. Besides using a credit or debit card, you can use your phone with payment apps to pay with Google Pay, Apple Pay, Samsung Pay or Visa Pay if those systems are set up on your smartphone. If you have a business PayPal account, you can use your debit card abroad. I have used my phone to pay merchants but this payment method has not yet become a habit. It's another convenient and flexible option.

We walked back to the hotel. Colonel enjoyed that walk more than me. I packed my loose bathroom essentials into my carryon bag, replied to some posts, emails, and then checked out of the hotel. This stay in Lyon was too short. I wanted to see and do more in this city. Sadly, I didn't get to have the full Lyon city experience that I imagined.

Now, I'm following Google's walking directions on my phone and am taking a different 11-minute route to the train station. This time pulling my luggage on even pavement wasn't as challenging as it had been on cobblestone. We strolled on a commercial scenic route through a very clean business or financial district with modern high-rise buildings. Lyon is a clean city. It was a pleasant stroll. Colonel sniffed his way to the train station.

Coming from this direction, I entered on the opposite side of the Lyon Part Dieu Gare *(train station)* landing inside Hall Two. This is an entirely different entrance from where I had exited on Saturday evening to find a taxi. The small station was bloated with passengers and station employees moving about frantically. I wiggled my way through the masses to get closer to the tracks. Now gazing at the departure board which showed all the arriving trains were *(retard)* late, some by more than 50 mins. Wow!

Sometimes train travel can be challenging if you are trying to keep to a schedule. Often these European trains are on time though and have very tiny delays. I was happy that my TGV InOui train was only five minutes late and left this station at 1:03 pm. Maybe just a small reward for the long delay I faced getting into Lyon on Saturday. My first-class train ticket to Paris costs €60 one-way which I purchased using the Trainline App.

Patiently, I boarded my train car last due to the crush of people all trying to board this train at the same time. Take it easy! Interesting to watch adults acting like children bunched up like grapes to squeeze through that narrow 'one person' at a time entry way. This hurried behavior demonstrated everyone's need to settle into their assigned seats quickly. I found a luggage area mid-train located near my seat to stash my carryon and my suitcase where I could keep a close eye on them both.

Even for this short two-hour trip, I welcomed the more comfortable seats and roominess of this upscale car. Anytime first class is offered on your route, spend the extra money for a first-class ticket for the upscale experience and because you'll better appreciate the train ride. I was happy with my single window seat on the lower deck in Car 11. I opted for this individual seat which meant no other seat nor person seated next to me. Seating charts are nice to view when making train reservations. Sometimes you can choose your seat, other times the company chooses a seat for you. I always specify downstairs window seating though.

Colonel is in his dog carrier tucked under my seat. He's resting and I'm more relaxed now. Grabbing my earbuds so I can listen to additional chapters of my audiobook, a crime mystery. I was excited to be on my way to Paris without any delays, hopefully. Fingers crossed. I said a few bonjours and pardons to a few passengers, but had no in-depth conversations on this train trip.

Like most trains, after passengers are all boarded, seated, and settled inside, after the train starts moving down the tracks a subtle stillness blankets the coach. I welcome this unexpected calmness after navigating through the rush of people at the station. Now we can relax somewhat before arriving into the pulsating city of Paris.

Our train arrived on time at 3:00 pm into Paris' Gare Lyon station in the 12th arrondissement, which is only a 15-minute drive to my hotel in the same district. Again, logistics matter. Struggling a little with the heavy suitcase, I plodded my way through the crowds and out of this train station.

Following the posted signs inside the station led me to the G7 taxi stand out front. The taxi line wasn't too long with about 15 passengers ahead of me, mostly couples. Slowly, Colonel and I edged closer to the taxi attendant who greeted and guided customers to the awaiting taxis. I appreciated the efficiency of this system. It's a very effective way to get awaiting passengers into these waiting cabs quicker as opposed to individuals fighting for the cabs.

After waiting in this line for about 10 minutes and inching closer, it was my turn. The attendant greeted me and guided me to a kind driver who took my bags and loaded them inside his trunk. I held onto Colonel's carrier and hopped into the back seat of his taxi. I was happy that I didn't have to hail or call a taxi. This is my last city stop on this tour. I could not wait to get settled at the hotel before venturing out for the day.

Just a tip about taking taxis upon arriving at a train station or an airport in France, avoid anyone approaching you to take their taxi. Many of these people are driving unlicensed and unregulated taxis without meters and usually are scam artists. Certainly, no one wants to begin a vacation by getting into a faux taxi operated by some nefarious character trying to rob you or even worse. So don't be too hasty to catch a cab when you first arrive in a big city. Find the signs leading to the legitimate taxi stands or ask someone working at the stations or airports to point you to the regulated taxis.

For your safety, stick to the regulated taxis operated legally in any city you visit abroad. Usually there is an app or website for taxis. In Paris, the App is G7 Taxi which you can download to your phone from the App store before beginning your trip. Also, for the Paris

Metro you can download the Bonjour RATP App for public transportation and schedules in Paris. This time, I didn't have to use the G7 Taxi App since the clearly marked G7 taxis were waiting outside the train station.

My driver was kind and courteous. I told him in French (the best I could) where I needed to go. He quickly whisked us away down a wide boulevard southeast of the city's center, through bottlenecked traffic to reach my hotel safely. Glad I'm not driving a rental car in Paris. I remember that driving experience all too well. No thanks! Within 20 minutes, we arrived at the hotel. I believe the cab drive cost approximately €15, plus a three-euro tip.

Moments later, I'm checking into Hôtel De La Porte Dorée, a small four-story boutique hotel in the 12th Arrondissement. This one I booked for five nights/six days directly on the hotel's website. My 2nd floor deluxe double room has a chic charm with windows facing the street. It's exceptionally clean. No dust bunnies in sight. The cost for this three-star hotel stay was €1,010 including taxes but without breakfast. It has a small cafe that serves only breakfast. Since I was staying longer, my preference was to have breakfast at cafes nearby which usually cost less too.

A few days later I met Christina, a pleasant American woman from Sacramento, California *(she with her French husband, Laurent)* owns this lovely hotel. The ambience and design of the hotel is modern contemporary with a bohemian chicness. It has a homey and comfy feel. I had a feeling it would have this quality.

The reception and rest of the hospitality staff were very polite, respectful, and professional. It was nice getting to know them all over my six-day stay. I chose to stay in this 12eme *(district)* to be far away from all the tourists' areas but still close enough to get into the center of the city and the other districts by subway or bus easily. The subway is on the corner, a short two-minute walk from this hotel.

In addition, there's a great beautiful Park with a lagoon nearby which Colonel was very excited about visiting when I mentioned we were going to the park. He loves spending time walking and sniffing around parks. Sensory overload. I guess he thought, "Grass, finally!" We hadn't seen any parks or even a patch of grass since leaving Bordeaux.

The sidewalk became his outhouse, he's not accustomed to doing his business on cobblestone or concrete, but from the French dogs, he picked up their scents and followed suit. I'd say that Colonel is adapting very well to this French lifestyle. I've already adapted. I knew even after all these years that I would I still love being here. I'm excited and ready to move to France much sooner than my projected timeline.

By now it's almost 4 pm, so I am going to relax in my hotel room for a few hours, unpack, then go out for dinner around seven o'clock. After that short outing we'll call it a night. I'd like to be rested when I venture out into the city of Paris tomorrow. Bonne Journeé!

Celestine Cooley

Tuesday – September 19, 2023 – Paris

Day 18 - Okay, apparently, I'm running on fumes from past energy I had stored up during this trip. We had a full day in Paris after leaving the hotel at 10 am and wrapping up this day at midnight. No kidding! It was a day full of fun and adventure. I am really pleased that I booked this leg of the trip in Paris to arrive on a Monday, so I'd have a full week to experience this city again.

Weekends aren't as important when visiting Europe because most locals spend time with their families. I want to get a true feel of a city's pulse and its people when I visit. Only during the weekdays do you get the full life experiences of the residents moving about their daily lives, mingling, speaking, and just doing normal human routines. Now that the French residents have returned from their long vacations, you can see and feel this city's rhythm.

First thing this morning, I met my friend Martin Jones for breakfast at the hotel. He flew into Paris this morning from New York and was so tired. I've known Marty for 30 years. We worked together at LIVE Entertainment *(a video distribution company)* in Van Nuys, California back in the mid-90s. It no longer exits.

Marty was the Director of Physical Production and I was his assistant after my previous boss left the company. Before Marty arrived, I worked for two other executives there, one in sales and the other in marketing. After Marty left LIVE and before I resigned, I assisted the VP of Film Acquisitions and then the VP of Family Home Entertainment and New Media.

LIVE Entertainment was the same company where Jose Menendez was the CEO until he and his wife Kitty were murdered in 1989. I didn't work at the company when that incident happened, but joined the company a few years later in 1993. When that tragic slaying occurred, I was working for producer-director Ivan Reitman who lived on Elm Avenue, the same street on the same block as the Menendez's in Beverly Hills. Before those murders I drove past the Menendez house often going to Ivan's house.

Another of my many small world - six degrees of separation - life experiences I had while living in Los Angeles and working in this industry. LIVE brought more drama, but that's for another book about my Hollywood experiences. You'd be surprised by all the craziness I encountered while working in entertainment. For over 50 years, I've had multiple corporate careers and worked as an Executive Assistant, Story Analyst, Literary Agent, Writer, and Producer in many areas of the entertainment industry including TV, Film, Cable, Music, and Video Production.

A year later, Marty and I would unite again when he called me to work briefly with him and Actor, Producer Tim Reid on several independent film projects they were working on together. Again, we had a blast and have kept in touch for all these years. I really do cherish my industry friends and the extraordinary experiences I have had with many of them.

Marty is in France to attend his friend Kevin's wedding in Nice this coming weekend. So, he's hanging out in Paris with me for a few days and at this same hotel which I recommended. I am overjoyed to be spending this time with Marty here in the city of lights for a few days. We will explore some of Paris together. I have maintained relationships with some incredibly smart and talented friends from my decades of working in show business.

The uniqueness of this small boutique hotel in Paris makes my short time left on this trip so very special. It feels like the right way to conclude this trip. This hotel has miniature everything, rooms, an elevator, and a dining room. So darn cute. The elevator is so skinny, very narrow, and only holds one thin person and some luggage. The American-like staircase was easy to walk up and down, so I used the stairs often rather than that elevator.

My cozy room faces the street so I can hear traffic and people talking below during the day. Plus, I can hear the subway rumbling below the hotel. Now I understand why we were given earplugs at reception when we checked in. Around midnight the rumbling sound diminishes, I think the Metro stops running around 1 am, but not certain. After a few days, I didn't notice any of those city sounds anymore. Plus, after a long day of walking and exploring the streets of Paris, once I was asleep, I heard nothing, nada, zilch.

Why are most French people so thin? Walking up and down stairs and by constantly climbing so many darn steps everywhere in the Metro, at train stations, and the airport. Okay, I'm getting fit, yes thanks to all the distances I've covered on these long walks. Trudging up and down stairs, then walking on sidewalks with changing elevations, and mostly on uneven pavements that wind through the many neighborhoods we visited. It did not take long for me to really get tired of dealing with all the stairs in this city. At my age, I prefer walking more on flat surfaces to avoid falling. Nonetheless, I endured all the stairs I treaded but not without regretting each step I took.

Still being mobile on foot everyday was what I relished most during this trip. I know that I am blessed to be able to walk still. But what turned me off from wanting to live in Paris was all the various staircases and uphill elevations among some other pet peeves. I prefer taking the buses above ground rather than the subways running below ground in this city. Although I love Paris, it's a magnificent city; there is no other city like it, but it is not my city.

Many museums and UNESCO World Heritage sites are here too. The people, parks, museums, shops, restaurants, and bakeries are other worldly. I fell in love with the fresh baked bread in this city decades ago. Gastronomy is everywhere you look; the food, cheese varieties, and pastries are incredibly tasty. The wine, Oh my! This is a very special city indeed.

After breakfast at the hotel, a jet lagged Marty decided to take a nap. I continued with my plans to go to the Latin Quarter and St. Germaine today. I bought a Navigo weekly pass for €30 (unlimited, all zones) to take public transportation *(Metro/subway and buses)* during my stay. It's a plastic rechargeable card I'll keep to use on my next visits to Paris. Just like my Nice Metro Card which is also rechargeable that I'm holding on to as well. You can purchase a day pass or buy single tickets to ride the bus and metro.

This 12th district where I chose to stay while in Paris is an off the beaten path area. There is a nearby Metro a few steps away from the hotel that makes getting around Paris easy. Yacine, who checked me in at the hotel yesterday, outlined my Metro map going from the hotel to the Bastille in the 11eme. Showing me what line to take and how to return. Today, I decided to do more riding and less walking. Still, I walked a lot despite my decision not to go up and down too many Metro stairs. Unavoidable at times in this city.

Around 12:30 pm, I made my way to Notre Dame then took the Big Bus 'hop on hop off' tour around Paris. The driver handed me earphones in a plastic bag. Found a seat on the first level, near the front, plugged in my earphones on the console. Now I was ready to listen to the audio guided tour while seeing the sites we rode by: the Arc de Triomphe, the Champs-Élysées, Tour Eiffel, La Louve, Bastille, D'Orsay Museé, the American Church, the Opera, and so much more for over 2 hours on this bus.

Then I hopped off at my original stop near the Notre Dame Church. Colonel is on lease so we walked a few short kilometers to see Shakespeare and Company, the famous book store. I did not go inside since there was a long line to enter the store. I took pictures of the exterior and its next-door cafe. Paris has many wonderful bookstores like this one.

This English-language bookshop was first founded in 1919 by American Sylvia Beach who operated it until 1941 during the occupation of Paris by the Germans. In 1951 another American, George Whitman, revived the bookshop first calling it Le Mistral at a new location on the site of an old Monastery, across from Notre Dame. In April 1964, on the four-hundredth anniversary of William Shakespeare's birth and in honor of bookseller he admired, Sylvia Beach, he changed the name to Shakespeare and Company.

The bookstore was a famous gathering place for the expat literary community in Paris. Famous American writers in the 1920s known as the lost Generation, such as James Joyce, Ernest Hemingway, Gertrude Stein, F. Scott Fitzgerald, T.S. Eliot, and Ezra Pound as well as some leading French writers, André Gide, Paul

Valéry, and Jules Romains gathered here.

In the 1940s, prolific American writers such as Anaïs Nin, Richard Wright, William Burroughs, William Styron, Allen Ginsberg, Julio Cortázar, Henry Miller, James Jones, William Saroyan, Lawrence Durrell, and James Baldwin found kindred spirits among the books at this iconic shop. I bet many of their discussions focused on their literary lifestyle in Paris. Most writers today can find inspiration from the volumes of work from these legendary masters.

I spent the rest of the afternoon walking leisurely from district to district through various neighborhoods such as the Marais, St. Germain, and the Latin Quarter. Of course, I missed lunch again while riding on the tour bus. I'm determined to have a formule lunch before I leave Paris. Looking forward to ordering la formule, a fixed-price *(a prix fixe)* meal.

Usually, it's a multi-course meal that includes two or more courses at a set price. For instance, from the special menu posted out front, you could order three items, an entree, plat, and desert or an entree, plat, and drink or whatever the special of the day is which usually costs between €14 to €19, depending on the restaurant of course. Lunch is cheaper than dinner. I'll try to make it to a recommended restaurant for lunch on Thursday for this la formule lunch special.

Colonel and I made it back to the hotel around 6:15 pm when I noticed a text from Marty asking what time I usually have dinner. I replied back, "Usually around 8 pm." So, he made reservations for us at Chez Paul in the 11th arrondissement, which was recommended by his friend, a United Airlines flight attendant. We had more than an hour to just chill before dinner. I fed Colonel and watched a French series.

We left the hotel together around 7:20 pm heading to the Metro. Those dreaded subway steps again. Only one train and six stops away to reach our destination. Pretty convenient. Metro travel in LA is not short or easy. Often, I'd have to take a slew of buses and subways to get to one destination. Can't avoid taking a bus to get to and from the LA metro with different lines that run throughout the city and even out to Long Beach. The city is so big and spread out. The city planners didn't expect the explosive population growth.

Although I complain about so many steps, the Paris Metro is not at all bad. It is very efficient here. You can get from one part of town to another in minutes using this spider web of subways throughout the city. The buses take a little longer but you can see all the sites above ground. I don't mind taking public transportation in other places, much cleaner and with friendlier more considerate passengers.

In Los Angeles, I detested taking public transportation because buses and subways became a haven for crazies and crime. Often terrifying experiences for passengers who were unlucky enough to be victims of assaults, muggings, or stabbings which happened regularly at a few Los Angeles Metro stations.

There is so much crime all around, you just don't know when you leave home whether you will return in one piece or at all. Sometimes it felt like being in the trenches surrounded by enemies and predators, this is the LA that I was experiencing in the mid-2000's, in the middle of the mix without a car. I walked all over the city and went from place to place on public transportation for eight years.

When you are secluded inside your car driving around the city you aren't exposed to the same elements and don't feel the impact of the nutty outside environment like you would walking around the streets of L.A. The dramatic changes in this city brought me such sadness. It certainly was no longer the safe and jubilant LA I knew as a young adulthood and mother. I had outgrown the city of angels.

Those adverse changes forced me to buy a car so I could get to work safely and mentally intact every day. After a while just driving in rush hour traffic began to wear me down. I couldn't even take the 405 freeway because it was usually a bottle-necked dead zone and often a frustrating drive. Driving the canyon routes south going over the hills made for a better morning drive experience, much calmer and more scenic.

We're in the Bastille area and just a short walk to Chez Paul. This Bistro is very popular with locals. The tables inside and outside of this restaurant were never vacant for long. We chose to eat inside. Perusing the French menu, we decided to first split a plate of six escargots and a bone marrow entrée *(appetizers)*.

Marty ordered a Spritzer, and I ordered a glass of Bordeaux (red wine). Marty chose the *"dramatic"* pepper steak. I say this because there was a lot of drama served with his dinner order. I ordered Duck Confit and potatoes, a non-dramatic choice at this bistro.

Our petite waitress was a character. When Marty asked for his steak to be *'well done,'* the waitress said,

"No, only medium rare or rare."

Marty insisted on his steak being well done. Silently, like a sitcom, I'm watching this funny scene play out, knowing how this episode will end.

She responded adamantly with,

"Only one and one, but not well done."

"Okay, okay!" He responded and then asked for a 'medium' steak.

The waitress shook her head and wasn't kidding when she told him one *(rare)* and one *(medium rare)*.

When our appetizers arrived there was a hint of a salad that came with the bone marrow, so we split that too.

Politely *(not wanting to get on her bad side)*, I asked for,

"Une bouteille d'eau (a bottle of water), s'il vous plaît (please)

The waitress asked,

"No fizz?"

I responded,

"Oui, non-fizz, non minerale."

She said,

"D'accord!" *(Okay!)*

After she left our table, I quietly mentioned to Marty that the medium steak he ordered will be medium rare when it arrives. Still in denial, he insisted that he was going to get his way. I snickered and knew that he had lost that battle way before it began.

Then I said, "You'll see."

When his steak arrived, I swore I heard it *'moo.'* It was seared dark brown on the outside *(an illusion)*, but when he cut into it the very red meat on the inside oozed blood. It was so rare.

I added, "Told you!"

Disappointedly, he looked at the steak then at the waitress.

She replied to his expression,

"One and one!" she snapped and then marched away.

I think she runs the joint. To me, *"One and one!"* meant *'one way only' 'rare.'* Poor Marty, he couldn't eat the center of that rare steak. So, he gave the rest of it to me for Colonel to eat once we were back at our hotel. I'll recommend this restaurant. It was entertaining and the food was awesome.

Dinner was fabulous despite the drama. I enjoyed this dining experience. My duck was moist and very tasty. Marty then ordered dessert, vanilla ice cream with a chocolate sauce which we shared. So good! The wine was of good quality too. I'd go back to eat again.

We ended dinner around 11 pm. As we're walking back to the Metro, I spotted a narrow side street that looked like an alley crowded with people. We took an à gauche (a left) detour to walk down and check out this lively street. It was long, slender, and full of bars lined up on both sides of this street. One bar after another, I called it 'Bar Alley.' What an enjoyable stroll we took down this long pathway of good cheer, while feeling the joy and energy of the young exuberant patrons.

People crowded inside these small bars, drinking, laughing, and listening to music. Some were standing out front on the sidewalk talking, drinking, and greeting us as we walked by them. A few food stands were crammed between the bars. We walked to the end of this street, rounded the block, and then made our way back to the Metro.

By now, we are both zapped of energy and had to deal with more of those damn steps. Some of the subways do have escalators, but not enough. I carried Colonel in my arms after letting him walk down a short flight of steps. He's out of the carrier so he can stretch and relieve himself. We arrived back at the hotel around midnight. Our hotel is traditionally French, when you're leaving you must turn in your room key *(cle)* at reception. Then pick it up again when you return. I loved that!

We picked up our keys then parted ways, off to our separate rooms to happily settle in for tonight. Marty is on the first floor. Looking forward to catching a good night of sleep. I gave Colonel some of the leftover steak and he was most appreciative. Thanks, Uncle Marty. We had a full fun day. Created more memories. It's now 1:30 am in Paris as I complete writing this post. Colonel is out and I'm ready to do the same. Bonne nuit! A Bientôt!

Six French Cities

Wednesday September 20, 2023 – Morning

Day 19 - I'm using WhatsApp a lot on this trip. Of course, Google still drives me crazy, because I'm so directionally challenged. This morning, I met Marty across the street at McDonald's for breakfast. Don't laugh! It's located on the corner near our hotel. We're sitting by the window eating a burger and talking when I see flashing lights and hear sirens outside. I jumped up to run outside to take a video with my phone. Leaving Colonel with Marty.

Right place, right time to catch this very formal military-like procession of men in uniforms riding on horses trotting down the middle of the street. Curious about this event, I asked a few people who were standing on the sidewalk,

"What is going on?" (in English).

They had stopped to watch this parade pass by. No one really knew. But a young woman declared,

"Just extravagance, it's Paris!"

I laughed and soon remembered Marty mentioning that Charles, the King of England was visiting Paris today. So, all this fanfare marching down the center of this boulevard was in preparation of his visit. I would later learn that this procession was headed to the Champs-Élysées where the main event was taking place.

This state visit to France by their Majesties King Charles III and Queen Camilla was being received by France's President Emmanuel Macron. Celebrating the alliance between the UK and France. They were also attending the France-UK Climate and Nature Finance Mobilisation Forum.

After breakfast, Marty, Colonel, and I walked across the street from the hotel to visit Vincennes Park. It's so beautiful! Paris has many lovely parks located strategically throughout the city. Our mission on this bright sunny day was to walk, enjoy nature, and relax. We found the water, a small lagoon, that we had spotted on a map upon entering the park.

Nature walks are a soothing way to really unwind and unplug from the daily grind. Seeing these sights and listening to the sounds of nature delightfully impacted that park visit and was extremely peaceful. It's a nice feeling not having to rush around a place, to take the time to unplug, and just being present to fully enjoy this natural setting and tranquil environment like we were doing now.

After walking for a while we sought out a bench, sat down, and just chilled for over an hour. Taking the time to appreciate the beauty and the park's lovely assortment of foliage, floral, and the sounds of fauna. We watched local people run or stroll by on this mild mid-morning. Since Marty rarely has time to take such a break this downtime was special.

Plus affording us the quality time needed to catch up since our last meet up in Los Angeles a few months ago. It was a pleasant way to spend a morning in Paris. Right before noon, we returned to the hotel to prepare for our day of activities. For lunch we wanted to eat something different. So, asking Google, I found us comfort food, Mama Jackson's Soul Food restaurant in the 12th arrondissement.

Marty and I hopped on the Metro. This place was just three stops away. We split a chicken and waffles plate. Ordered peach iced tea and a bottle of tap water. The food was pretty good. I wrote a review for Google. Here is an excerpt of that review:

Authentic American Soul Food is not easy to find in Paris, France. So, when a Google Search of breakfast restaurants in Paris gave me several selections nearby, I was surprised and delighted to discover Mama Jackson's Soul Food. A small family-owned cafe located on a side street in the 12th arrondissement. Inside, the ambience of this black owned cafe was soulfully decorated with a collage of black American musicians posted on the walls. The vibe was a mixture of French and Caribbean. The service was wonderful. The owner, a young woman, was lovely. It's unfair to compare *"Soul Food"* made in other countries to similar dishes made at Black American restaurants in the states but I will.

Granted, soul food in the USA can be hit or miss, generally there is a distinct look and taste to most black regional dishes. At Mama Jackson's, sadly many of those flavors were missing. Her fried chicken, although crispy and well cooked, was a bit bland, missing a few familiar spices that would have elevated the chicken's natural flavor for a much more appetizing taste.

The chicken was crispy and tender but a bit bland for me. The waffles were light and very good yet bland. It was not at all like what you'd find in restaurants like Roscoe's back home in the States. Still, I'd give her a good passing grade for her effort. My peach iced tea was great, not too sweet. On a sweetness scale of 1 to 5, it was a 3. Nonetheless the food here was a little different but still very good, we ate every bite. It really is unfair for me to compare.

Still, I did recommend this cute little restaurant on Google. And I do encourage anyone visiting Paris who's familiar with chicken and waffles or wants to try this cuisine to please patronize Mama Jackson's version of Chicken and Waffles to decide for yourself. You may feel differently than I. Would I return for another go, sure I would like to try something else on her menu. I believe she's on the right track. So, I wasn't entirely disappointed, just somewhat surprised.

We thanked the owner, paid our check, then walked back towards the Metro. On our way to a gallery opening Marty was invited to, I'm tagging along with Colonel. Before hopping on the Metro, we nixed the opening after Marty received a message. Instead, Marty decided to go to the Cinematheque museum and a movie. I wanted to go to Sacre Coeur. We parted at the Metro station after lunch going in opposite directions.

Six French Cities

Wednesday, September 20, 2023 | Paris Afternoon ~ Evening

Day 19 - It may rain tomorrow so checking this tourist site off my list now is better than waiting. I took three Metro lines to reach Montmartre located in the 18th arrondissement. It's a magnificent Basilica to see in person. Perched high on a hill, above the city, it overlooks other surrounding neighborhoods. This tourist attraction was packed to the guild with people moving about and standing everywhere around this church.

From a distance, you could hardly see a semblance of the steps leading up to Sacre Coeur. It looked like an invasion of cicadas covering the length and width of the steps. Not at all what I was expecting. I thought that most of the tourists were gone. I was wrong. Now, I'd have to take my chances of not catching some crazy bug and getting sick.

You have two ways of reaching the church at the top of the mound, either by Funicular or the very long staircase starting from the street below. Bet you know which way I chose. Once inside, I realized there was no fresh air circulating within this packed Funicular, it was hot, stuffy, smelly, and an agonizingly slow yet short ride to the top. It seemed to take forever. I just wanted to get off and be back outside in fresher air. Next time, I'll take the stairs. I think I could have managed them slowly one step at a time.

Once off this car, I noticed more steps still to climb to reach the front of the church. To myself, 'ah, I don't need to go up there. I can get some great shots from right here.' I took some pics of the vast city below, an aerial like view, and snapshots of the church above. After walking halfway around the building, I saw them...those famous steps cascading down. The ones I did not take to ascend to this level. Glad I didn't attempt the steep climb that those numerous steps demanded. I would have been out of breath for sure.

However, I did take my time to walk down those stairs without dread just for the heck of it. Some people who were brave enough to walk up these steps seemed to be regretting their choice by taking small breaks at each landing to catch their breath. I laughed as I congratulated a few for their determination as we passed. Colonel and I walked around that district for a while, checking out the various shops. I couldn't find the little square dotted with cafes where some artists hangout. I bought some candy to take back home. Window shopping, I gazed inside a few antique and boutique shops.

Colonel and I followed the crowd down to a main street where the Metro was waiting. There was some police activity near the entrance. Several young men were being questioned and protesting being stopped. We climbed the stairs to reach the metro platform above the street and waited for our train. It was now five o'clock and time to return to our hotel to unwind. We needed some downtime after all the walking around this district. Plus, Colonel was hungry and sleepy. I just needed to get off my feet and get flat for a few hours.

Back in my room, it felt good to finally slow down. I know I've been pushing myself a little too much but I feel okay health wise, just a bit fatigued. My long walks with Colonel in LA are not this intense. Tomorrow shouldn't be so hectic. Marty texted that he was still at the Cinémathèque and enjoying himself. Around 8 pm, I wanted something light to eat nearby within walking distance of the hotel, no Metros to take tonight. So, I ambled across the street from the hotel where there are two restaurants.

After perusing both menus, I chose the restaurant C'Sters Café, closer to the park. It had the meal selection that I was craving, onion soup and a Chicken Caesar salad, a glass of Rosé, and tap water. Fresh bread came with my meal. I was so tired I feared I'd fall asleep face down in my salad, which was a lot that I couldn't finish. The onion soup was delightful, cheesy, and robust. I think the wine was acting like a sedative, because after having a few sips I could barely keep my eyes open throughout that meal.

We returned to the hotel around 10 pm. I can't do these late-night meals every day. Currently, I'm on intermittent fasting so all meals are eaten by 7 pm usually, but not on this trip. My body doesn't like ingesting or digesting food so late. Afterall, I'm not twenty anymore. My metabolism is slower now. Once living here though, I'll stick to cooking meals at home and eating between 5-6 pm, my routine time for dinner.

Actually, I prefer having a heartier lunch, maybe a light breakfast a few times a week but not daily and an even lighter dinner each evening. I'll not attempt to keep up with the after 7 pm French dinner meal times. Speaking of lunch, I am hoping to catch a proper lunch tomorrow or Friday, before leaving France.

Marty sent me a text message about the film he watched in French and the restaurant where he dined in Bercy, same name as his mother's "Roberta." He was still out and about enjoying himself. I was dead on my feet and beat. Tomorrow will be a lighter day for me, only a few hours of walking. Marty leaves in the morning to travel south to Nice. He is attending his Friend Kevin's wedding there on Saturday.

Tomorrow, I hope to visit and walk with Colonel along the railway park that inspired New York's Highline. Then visit some of the warehouse shops located below it called the Viaduct. These attractions are near my hotel here in the 12th. So, I don't have to deal with Metros. Instead, I can walk or take the bus to reach those Viaduct shops. It's getting a bit chilly in Paris and may rain later tonight and into tomorrow which may change my plans to visit any attractions. I knew I'd need the light jacket that I packed.

Since I've spent these past weeks in France, becoming familiar with cities, living in neighborhoods, being around the residents, riding public transportation, and walking all over the city, I have noticed a lot, especially how the average French citizen dresses. One thing I know for sure is that the non-expat YouTubers are wrong in their assumption about Parisians' attire. I dislike misinformation and think there is too much of it going around social media.

These influencers on various social media platforms are providing erroneous information about what French women are wearing daily in France. To set the record straight, French woman dress like us American women. French men are mostly in jeans. The teen kids have adopted a more western style of daily attire from black hip hop America. The U.S. has had a major influence on kid's styles and music around the world from Europe to Asia.

For example, these young influencers claim that you won't see French women in leisure wear *(sweats, leggings, or athletic wear)*, yet I've seen a lot of leisure wearing women not only coming from the gym or jogging but in general like running errands, in the markets, picking up kids from school, and on the Metro. These French women also like to be comfortable. There is no dress code in France. You don't have to wear designer fashions to fit in this or any other French city. Everybody wears jeans and sneakers. Very relaxed, casual, and comfortable. Dressing up for dinner is a norm.

I have yet to see women walking down the streets in France wearing designer brand couture straight off the runway. Working women dress very business casual like we do in the U.S. They wear either sensible sandals, not flip flops, but flats, or tennis/athletic shoes, not heels. Rarely, have I seen women here wearing heels walking down the street. That kind of apparel is better left for evenings out or major events or perhaps French celebrities going to award shows. It's just not the norm here.

Women who do wear heels end up carrying them anyway and walking barefooted. Cobblestones were not designed with high heels in mind. In my opinion, high heels are medieval torture devices that I stopped wearing decades ago. Young people on YouTube seem to have a distorted view of reality or are creating their own. It's apparent that most who visit France never venture beyond the city centers.

The French dress casually. They wear sweatshirts, hoodies, T-shirts, nice tops, and jeans or slacks. Women wearing white jeans were big this summer and very colorful light summer dresses. They don't wear just black attire every day. The French love Nike's. The only women I saw wearing designer brands, decorative bobbles, and carrying expensive handbags were foreigners, including millennial Americans.

These young people are copying what other influencer are saying, and have really bought into this false fashion hype. They are unknowingly setting themselves up to be targets of theft and who knows what else. Wearing expensive jewelry around the streets of Paris or any big city isn't very smart, advisable, or even necessary during the daytime. Jewelry and dressing up is more geared for nighttime events. So, anyone traveling to France just know to dress the way you like to dress and pack what you want to wear. No fashion police or judgement from anyone.

Okay, now I'm on a rambling rampage it looks like delirium is setting in and my brain is shutting down. I'm going to go to sleep now. Have an awesome day!

Six French Cities

Thursday September 21, 2023 | Paris ~ Morning

Day 20 - I woke up to a cold and rainy Paris morning. This weather is giving me an excuse to settle down, stay in and just rest. Today Colonel and I will just chill in our room at the hotel. No more sightseeing. I've decided not to venture far from the hotel after taking Colonel for a short damp walk this morning. He does not like le pluie *(the rain)*.

Plus, I think he needs a full day of rest as well. I'll have to see the sites and neighborhoods that I'm missing on another visit to Paris. No big deal. I can use the rest. The pace of this trip has been brutal. I know that I've really pushed myself more than someone my age should be doing. But I can't help myself. I must keep moving. My mind and adventurous spirit are young.

Marty checked out of the hotel at 10:30 am. We met him in the lobby to say our farewells for now. It's my turn to visit him in Austin. He calls me his big sister. After Marty left, I spent more time hanging out in the lobby chatting with Donovan, our hotel desk clerk today. He's worked at this hotel for about a year and really enjoys his work, especially meeting people from all over the world.

Donovan is from Congo, Africa. He's a very pleasant and respectful young man. Donovan is a photographer, a very talented one I might add. I browsed through some of his work on his phone. How can anyone not enjoy making these "new people" from all walks of life connections. Most of all, I encourage young people to follow their dreams, trust their intuition, and never give up because if you truly believe in those dreams, they will be realized with lots of hope, effort, and determination. This I know as fact from my experiences.

Marty gave Donovan his business card because I mentioned to Marty that Donovan wanted to come to the US and visit Texas first and then California. Marty lives and works in Austin. Not only is he the Head of Austin Studios but also an independent producer and director. I can't help but love the entertainment business, I always will. From that business I developed many incredible friendships, family-like relationships, strong bonds, connections, and collaborations. It is a special business and now has become very diverse which wasn't the case when I started working in TV and Film production in the 70s.

The hotel's owner, Christina, appeared in the lobby. Donovan began teasing her about showing up for work. Apparently, she hadn't been feeling well. So, she took a day off to rest. Donovan introduced us. I remarked how much I loved her cute and cozy boutique hotel. She asked where I was from.

"California!" I responded.

"Me too!" she shot back.

I told her that it's good to take a break, your body tells you when you need to lay down and stay down. We laughed. She looked as if she had recovered well and even had a bounce in her step.

Then Christina, upon seeing Colonel in my lap, mentioned him and that she saw us in the dining room on Tuesday morning. She was impressed at how well behaved he was and how handsome he is too. He really makes me proud that I can take him anywhere without worrying about his obedience. Colonel receives these types of compliments often. He's just a very loveable little dog.

Colonel is a special, smart, and remarkable canine. He was so easy to train for my medical needs. He was 2-years old when I adopted him from my disabled neighbor. Colonel wasn't trained at all and didn't know how to sit, stay, or lay down on command. I knew his mother, Princess, and saw him right after his birth. The tiniest puppy I've ever seen.

He was the runt of the litter and the only survivor. Colonel has a big dog's mentality and a strong survivor's instinct. So proud, cute, lively, happy, and free spirited *(like me)*. Very determined to live and strive. He's fearless. Naturally he thinks he's my big protection dog. Colonel certainly has turned out to be a great service dog and my best companion ever.

Yesterday, Yacine told me that they all work 12-hour shifts to cover the 24/7 reception desk duties. So far at reception, I've met Yacine, Jerome, and Donovan. And Allie works in the dining room. I'll have to remember to take their pictures. Yacine should be here on tonight's shift. Jerome was last night. Donovan today.

All the hotel's staff have been very hospitable, helpful, and kind. I bet you didn't know that the hotel staff with the most clout at any hotel is housekeeping. I learned that fact as a travel agent. They rule the roost according to hotel General Managers. I respect hospitality a lot. Always remembering to leave them a good tip in my room at the end of my stay.

Of course, I left my umbrella at home in another carryon that I was originally going to use on this trip. Thankfully our hotel has a supply of umbrellas for their guests to use. Classy! Around 11 am, we scooted back to our room so that Colonel could take a proper nap and I could respond to text messages and Facebook comments. I watched a little French TV too. It was a laid-back kind of day. I didn't feel rushed or in need of doing anything special. It was nice to just chill for a change.

Then around noon not wanting to miss lunch, I opted for a Bistro just a block away. I sat inside. Each time I order food at a French restaurant, I never know exactly what I'll get. It's always a delightful surprise when the dish arrives. Here's a tip, refuse the English language menu, request the French one instead because although it's the same menu, it's not always the same prices. Use a translation App. Sometimes the English menu will cost you more per dish. I like a challenge and opted for the French menu.

At this lunch for the formule, I ordered blood sausage *(very delicious)* with mashed potatoes. The Bistro was out of the green beans, the vegetable garnish I wanted, so I asked for vegetables and they substituted a small legume bowl consisting of edamame, green peas, and chopped cabbage, which had a very happy marriage of delicate flavors. I had been feeling a little vegetable deprived in France.

I wondered why vegetables aren't always served with French meals in restaurants. You may get salad on the side, but rarely will you see broccoli, Brussel sprouts, asparagus, carrots, peas, or green beans served. Produce is widely sold at markets. Corn on the cob is very rare here; you will not find it at most markets or have it served at meals.

Later I found out why vegetables are not served at restaurants. It seems that the French customarily eat so many vegetables at home during the week that they don't want to eat any vegetables when they dine out. This information was stated to me by a French person when curiously I asked this question.

Don't know how true that statement is but that was the reasoning I received when I asked. In restaurants, I have asked for vegetables, sometimes I get them, other times none are available. I think all French restaurants should provide a vegetable on the menu for people who want vegetables with their meals.

For my drink, I asked for a glass of Red Rhone wine and a bottle of tap water. Remember, tap water is free but Perrier mineral water, Evian or Vittel will cost you a lot. You may as well order beer, wine, or soda for the same price as mineral water. But I understand if it's a preference. I'll order a Perrier occasionally. My meal was presented so well, smelled like "my goodness" and looked so appetizing that a French guy at the next table took notice. Very tasty too.

I said to him, "C'est bon." *(It's good.)*
Then everyone at his table responded in French,

"Elle a dit que c'était bon."
Wow, I understood that - *'She said it was good.'*

So, he nodded to me and ordered the Blood Sausage plat when their waiter returned. After being served this dish, he devoured it so fast. Then I noticed a few other people sitting at nearby tables who after listening to our brief conversation were also ordering the Blood Sausage meal too. See what I started.

My brain gets so tangled sometimes when attempting to convert English into French on the spot that I told Marty most of the time I feel like I'm speaking Spanglish but in French.

Then Marty said, "Franglish."

"Yes," I said and laughed because it's a mixture of both French and English.

You must remember very much about the French language when learning vocabulary, grammar, past tense, verb conjugations, nouns, pronouns, gender-masculine, and the feminine in French. It makes me crazy, but I still try giving it a whirl. Marty did a great job of speaking French. He's very good! I'm getting there very slowly.

I very much like dining out in France because you can relax and enjoy your meal at your own pace. The wait staff won't bother you. You don't feel rushed to finish or give up your table right away. I had time to begin writing about my day so far while sitting there having lunch. This was an awesome meal. I turned down dessert. Glad I braved the rain to experience it. This medium sized restaurant had a very nice vibe. I think my meal was like €22 including the wine. To pay your bill, you must beckon the waiter or you'll pay at either the counter or the bar. Leave a €1 or €2 tip.

It's still raining as we head back to the hotel. I'm carrying the little dog; heaven forbid his paws touch the wet ground. Although I had activities planned for today, it is too cold and too wet now to enjoy any outside activity. Maybe tomorrow I can see more of Paris and some other sites as planned. If not, I'll be back to this city again. No worries, right now I need the rest.

Tomorrow is my last full day in this city. I returned home on a Saturday morning flight. Then it's back to work on Monday. I plan to have lunch or dinner with Denise, a Facebook Friend, before I leave. She flies into Paris tomorrow morning to celebrate an early birthday. Her 40th which she is not ashamed to disclose. We plan to see the sparkling lights of the Eiffel Tower together that evening as well. Perfect visit for my last night in the city of lights.

Six French Cities

With all my heart and the energy, I have remaining, I thank all of you for joining me on this marathon journey through France, for reading about my adventures here, and most importantly for sticking it out with me for these three fast paced weeks. My virtual travel companions. And my heart is full from the comments attributed to my writing style, triple thanks. I was hoping that these posts would make you feel as if you were here traveling with me.

I hope to continue my travel writing as I visit more countries and cities in the future. Traveling and writing about my voyages have been two of my passions since I was a kid. Through all these decades, I've written something every day of my life. I kept notebooks and journals of my day-to-day life and activities for as long as I can remember. I have lots of stories to unfold.

Now that this trip is nearly behind me, realistically I can start to concentrate on formulating my move. When I return home, I have my Hollywood memoir to continue writing. It's a captivating, often funny account of how I turned my dream of working in the Entertainment Industry into a reality and my many adventures that followed.

Living in Los Angeles in the early 1970s, a young single black woman fresh out of the US Navy like a tadpole out of a lake, I faced many challenges and seedy characters. At first, I had so much to figure out and overcome. Navigating my way through life alone, I made important decisions about my future while raising my child. With much determination and resourcefulness, I broke into show business without any Hollywood contacts at a time when there were very few people of color working behind the scenes in Hollywood production. It's not a 'tell all' book -but I do tell a lot.

Those were astonishing years that impacted my imagination and creative mind. I witnessed much of old Hollywood talent pass the baton to a new era of actors, comics, and musical artists beginning their young careers in both black and white Hollywood. The many people I met, befriended, and worked with along the way helped to create my many memorable moments, and enriched experiences that provided oodles of surprises over the decades.

I used to joke that if I ever wrote a book about Hollywood, I'd have to leave the country. Well, I probably will be moving to and living in France around the same time that I finish writing and publishing that Hollywood memoir. Hilarious! Coincidentally, I'm still working in the entertainment industry but looking forward to retiring soon and having more time to write. It's time to retire! Another reason this scouting trip was very important to take.

Till tomorrow, right now it's time to rest my brain and my body. Oh, the rain stopped and the sun came out around 5 pm. This weather is changing; it's very chilly outside. Still, I'm not moving from this comfortable bed tucked under a warm blanket as I listen to my audio book. It's been a pleasant and restful day for us both. We needed the down time to simply relax our weary bodies. Tomorrow, we'll be back at it, outside and walking around the city to explore more of Paris. Merci et Bonne Journeé!

Six French Cities

Friday – September 22, 2023 | Paris

Day 21 - We got a late start this morning even though I felt surprisingly rested. First, I woke up around 7 am thinking about the bakery across the street. Looking out of my window, I could see that the bakery's lights were on, the front door was open, and someone was moving around inside.

At that moment, I thought about running across the street to snatch a pain du chocolat (chocolate croissant) but my body was not in agreement with my mind. If I could open my window, I would smell the fresh bread baking. Instead of getting up, quickly I surrendered to sleep for a few more hours, waking up around 10 am. This time, I had not bothered to set my travel alarm.

Denise, a former travel agent, is now an event planner who I met on Facebook several years ago. She flew into Paris this morning from Atlanta. I received a text from her when she arrived, her room wasn't ready. So, I suggested we meet at a restaurant near her hotel for lunch. The hotel would store her bags. Looking forward to having one last French formule lunch before I leave this country.

Together by text, from a Google search, we selected Afaria in the 15th, which serves traditional French cuisine. I met Denise at the restaurant around 12:30 pm. Colonel is in his carrier. After guiding us to our table, our French waitress, Celia (20s), turned out to be hilarious and sweet. She playfully showed us that French attitude of directness that Americans claim as rude. After bringing us menus and asking what we'd like to drink, her friendly and humorous personality made us feel at ease. We talked to her a lot (beaucoup) throughout our meal. Celia took a liking to us too immediately.

Because Denise and I were talking so much to catch up, we forgot to look at the menus which meant Celia had to interrupt us several times just to get us to select items to order. We thanked her and ordered a shared dish that included the three courses at €28: a starter, a main, and a dessert. On the other hand, we could have ordered the special of the day for €17.

We also ordered a starter each, an artichoke terrine gratinated with smoked bacon and comté. A shared main dish. These prices were a little steeper than you'd find in a local neighborhood restaurant for this kind of menu. But this French meal was well worth the cost, plus the ambience and entertainment was more than expected. Priceless!

Roasted duck breast on the bone, large fries and a green garlic sauce, served for two and we shared a dessert - Carambar crème brûlée. Made of chocolate and caramel which Celia said was a typical French dessert that her grandmother often made. We also ordered two glasses of red wine and a bottle of tap water. Denise had a glass of Champagne while waiting prior to my arrival.

At first, Denise wasn't sure about the duck or the small salade. But I encouraged her to try a little. Surprisingly, she liked what she was tasting, then telling me that she never would have tried this dish because it was unfamiliar. I told her to not be afraid to take a few chances with food you've never eaten before because you may be delighted. The point of traveling is to try new things.

This food was scrumptious. Flavors, oh the flavors, that green garlic sauce complemented the very tender duck so well. Crunchy fried onions on our little salad on the starter dish, the artichoke terrine was divine. Delightful! Denise paid for our lunch and thanked me for making her try something new *(this food)*. Merci! So sweet!

Of course, we were the last customers in the restaurant. Even the Chef had left. Celia was trying to clean the place and close. We chatted with her a while before leaving. She was also working the dinner shift at 7 pm this evening. She's a student and working at the restaurant to pay rent and survive while finishing her university studies. And she recently got engaged to a sweet, tall, and very muscular Tunisian guy with dark wavy hair. Our waitress is Parisian, she knows we're Americans.

Celia told us that French kids think that American kids on Tik Tok are very dumb because they don't know geography or their own history. And they ask dumb questions like, "What language do Europeans speak?" Why don't the French speak English in France?" Because they're French and they live in France. So funny. I had to agree. It seems that social media turns kids into morons or perhaps I should not blame social media but their less than adequate historical and geographical education.

We told Celia we would write a good review about the restaurant and about her, *"No, our waitress was terrible and rude..."* We laughed and said, she'd get a great review too. As we were leaving, I turned around to give her a big hug and she hugged back,

Celia said, "We French don't hug."

I replied, "I know, but we Americans do."

Then we exchanged the bise. Said our goodbyes and thanked her for being so sweet.

Colonel and I walked Denise back to her hotel but didn't go inside. We planned to meet up later to go to the Eiffel Tower. Heading back to my hotel by Metro, Colonel's in his carrier. Back in the 12th, first I took Colonel for a walk in the park. He really had to go and was relieved, now he's ready for a bite to eat and a little nap. We relaxed in our room watching TV until 7:30 pm. I packed the night before, so I'd only have a few things to put back into my carryon in the morning.

Celestine Cooley

Friday, September 22, 2023 | Last Night in Paris

Day 21 - Since Denise and I were still stuffed from lunch, we bypassed an 8 pm dinner, deciding to go straight to the Eiffel Tower instead. A night viewing of this well-known monument is spectacular, almost enchanting. We met at a Metro stop near Denise's hotel. It took a moment to meet up and find one another.

Earlier I had promised to show her how to use the Paris Metro System and how to purchase a rechargeable Navigo card. Since this seven-day Metro pass is only valid from Monday-Sunday, I suggested that Denise buy one on Sunday to use next week. In the meantime, she'd have to buy individual tickets through the weekend to take public transportation, the subway or bus, if needed.

Getting to the Eiffel Tower located in the 7th district from our meeting point in the 15th district was only three stops away on the Metro line 8. Using the map in the subway for reference, I explained the Metro system to Denise by showing how the train lines connected and pointing out that line M8 was the line she was closest to which would get her all over the city. From there she could make the Metro connections needed to get to other lines at various hubs.

The Metro stop near my hotel was on line M8 too. However, I was on the opposite end of the line from the Metro stop near Denise's hotel, there were 20 stops before we reached her metro stop. The Metro runs every 5 minutes it seems. The trains were very regular. We didn't wait long for a train to arrive.

Once off the Metro, we made our way to the iron lady which

was constructed by Gustave Eiffel in 1887 for the 1889 World's Fair to commemorate the 100th anniversary of the French Revolution. French history is fascinating and is often bloody, filled with twisted tales of families, conquests, and conquerors from Italy, Britain, and Spain. I've taken an interest in learning more about France, so have devoured many books on the subject which triggered memories of my studying World History in high school. Funny how memory works and what dormant information the mind recalls 'from way back when' just from hearing or seeing something familiar or significant from your past.

It took a little over two years to build the Tour Eiffel and just in time for the fair. Denise asked if I was going to the top.

I said, "No, I don't do heights."

She had reserved a ticket for doing just that which includes climbing the 674 steps to the second floor and then taking an elevator to the summit (top). I told her, she'll know if she wants to go to the top once she sees how tall it is in person. From the Les Invalides Metro stop, it was about a ten-minute walk to reach this famous tower.

As we grew closer, I told her to look to the left to get a glimpse of the lit structure just behind some trees. Suddenly, we're closer and there it was in full view, so large and magnificent. One of those "WOW!" moments for sure. It has been a long time since I've seen this tower at night. I forgot how breathtaking it can be in person. I don't think it sparkled back in the 80s. Nope, the sparkling effect began in 1999.

Upon seeing the structure's height, Denise changed her mind about going to the top of the tower at a height of 906 feet. At the top you will have a 360-degree view of the city. No merci, my view from the ground is just fine. As a kid, I went to the top of the Empire State building in New York and to the top of the Space Needle in Seattle. So *'been there done that,'* and I don't have to repeat that kind of crazy experience ever again. Just like ziplining, that was terrifying and fun, but once is enough for me.

We walked around the tower, weaving through loads of people going from the Eiffel Tower toward the Place du Trocadéro, this center is a short walk across the Seine. There we could get a different perspective and better picture taking angles of Madam Eiffel. We passed by people selling souvenirs, miniature Eiffel Tower replicas, some with twinkling lights and other Paris related trinkets. Gently passing on an opportunity to purchase any of those street vendor souvenirs.

On our way, we noticed a bunch of people standing in the middle of the main street that passes under the tower. These young people were defying traffic to take selfies with the tower in the background. I'm sure this activity which was interfering with the flow of traffic had a frustrating effect on the Parisian drivers. Lots of noise from the honking and shouting.

That chaotic scene was another spectacle that was beyond entertaining. Some of the young women posing for pictures were dressed up and had professional photographers who used umbrellas and huge lights to give off a more dramatic key light effect, which seemed too elaborate. All this photo activity was happening in the middle of a busy boulevard. We could not believe how many people were taking selfies in the center of traffic. Inconsiderate and from a safety point of view, just Crazy!

Denise and I stopped short of walking up a zillion steps at the base of the Trocadero, which is a modern multiplex center that has museums, fountains, sculptures, gardens, and restaurants. Events are also held here throughout the year. Instead of taking the steps we found a nice stoned ledge to sit on near the fountain. From this angle our view of the tower was clear and unobstructed. It could not have been more perfect. Wanting to see the sparkling tower in a full wide-angled view prompted our move to this location. Just in time, because the sparkling lights only happen for about 5 mins at the top of the hour after dust.

It was getting colder; my light jacket wasn't warm enough to combat this chill. My hands are now ice cold, I needed gloves. At 10 pm, the lights began to flicker and then sparkle. Lit up by 20,000 bulbs that twinkle for five minutes. So Beautiful! This unique display is one of the attractions that we come to Paris to see. We chatted more about France, life, friendships, and work until 10:45 pm, deciding it was time to leave. I had a morning flight to catch. Denise was now hungry and found a restaurant on our walk toward the Metro. We hugged and said goodbye. We'll keep in touch and have done so since our meetup in Paris.

Colonel and I made our way towards the subway, I thought. But as usual, I got lost after leaving Denise. My misdirection took 45 minutes to find the right direction to get to the Metro, unable to recall which way to go. Going in the wrong direction with Google's help. Finally, I asked someone how to get back to M8. I was very tired.

What a crazy night! Finally, we were back at our hotel after midnight. First stopping at McDonalds, I grabbed a fish sandwich and fries to go. Back in our room, Colonel went to sleep. I ate the fish sandwich, and completed packing around 1:30 pm, set my alarm, and turned off the light. Feeling sad, it's my last night in France. I'll miss this country. I had fun and I'll be back!

I have taken over 1800 pictures on this trip between my camera and my phone. Sorting through them chronologically, separating the videos from the stills, creating folders by city, and then adding them all into those individual folders on my laptop is never a task I look forward to doing. Eventually transferring all the photo folders to my external hard drive.

Back in the US I will have a lot to do in preparation for my move to France and the city I choose so that when I arrive, I can stay in France permanently. Tomorrow will be a long travel day. We must rest up. Bonne nuit and Au Revoir!

Six French Cities

Saturday, September 23, 2023 | Farewell France

Day 22 – Up at 6 am, I began charging all my mobile devices, took a quick shower, got dressed, and then packed the toiletries into my carryon. The dog is up, dressed, and ready to go. At 6:50 am, a call from reception, our taxi to the airport is here. I checked in yesterday for my flight and downloaded my boarding pass to my phone. I check on my 11:25 am flight, it's on time.

Quickly, I put my luggage in the narrow elevator and headed down the steps to meet it on the ground floor. Seamlessly, we checked out of the hotel, hopped into the taxi, and were off to Charles de Gaulle Airport. We arrived at our departure's terminal about 25 mins later. Cost 30 euros and a four-euro tip.

In the terminal, I attempted to get rid of my last euros by buying two bottles of water. Not thinking, I forgot about the liquid rule before clearing security. So, Colonel and I drank some water from one bottle. Then I gave the other bottle to a security agent nearby before going through the security check point. I think my delirium resulting from fatigue is now catching up with me. This trip was fast paced and exhilarating but so much fun. So, I'm hoping I can sleep on the plane.

First, I checked my large suitcase at American Airlines. Following the signs, I made my way to security. The French are serious about security; after scanning passenger's items in a bin, some carryon bags are sent back through the scanner again. Then those scanned bags are stripped of everything inside by agents who carefully check each item inside those bags. When security is finished with this searching process, the passengers are left with a pile of their personal items in the bin to reorganize and place back into their bags. I've never seen anything like this in any other airport I've passed through and I have passed through many in other countries with tighter security. So be aware of the Paris CDG airport's stringent security checks on departure from Paris.

After placing all my small personal and electronic items, my carry-on and Colonel's carrier in bins on the conveyor, I must go through Security first, Colonel stays and is called after me. An Agent holds him until I complete my security check. When I am done. The agent puts him down and I call him to walk through a magnetometer. He does it so well.

I can't count how many times I have had to explain to the TSA agents that I had total knee replacement surgery on both knees. So, the metal titanium in my knees always triggers the magnetometer. After that full body scan with the big magnetometer machine, then the hand-held body scanning device, and a quick pat down, I was able to wait in a lounge area until my bags were completely scanned and checked by an agent.

It took a while for all of us passengers to get through this tough security check system. No chance of TSA Precheck here in Paris. My carryon bag went through the scanner twice *(too many electronics)* then it's stripped apart and searched. In the meantime, I'm sitting nearby security while waiting for my bag and watching this process. A very pleasant lady from Glendora, California sits next to me, she is also waiting for her carryon's to be cleared. We chatted for a while. I tell her that I am traveling solo with my dog and the purpose of my trip. Suddenly she's livid about her boyfriend and begins to vent, adding that after this trip from now on she'll be traveling solo too.

We shared very transparent, relatable, and personal details about relationships and traveling companions. She's adamant about her feelings, voicing her dismay and unhappiness about being on this trip with her boyfriend *(travel companion)*, but mostly about his awful behavior.

"He was so needy and so jealous." She confesses.

I know the insecure type so I reply, "Get rid of him."

That is exactly what she plans to do when this trip ends and they are back in California. She went on to explain how she had lived a peaceful life for over 30 years before meeting him *(a widow)* over a year ago. This miserable relationship was not what she expected. She told me to look at him standing next to the agents going through the bags.

She asked, "Doesn't he look lost and pathetic?"

Chuckling inside, I nodded in agreement. Feeling her pain, I knew that coming to Paris with a companion like that would have made me want to climb and then jump from the Eiffel Tower. She could not enjoy her trip to France which was such a shame. Hearing her story, I was glad to be divorced and traveling solo. I did not mind listening to her vent. They were on my flight.

About 15 minutes later our bags were cleared and released. We were called to retrieve our messy pile and carryon's which we repacked before proceeding to our gate. This in-depth security scrutiny experience was a first for me. Hoping never to go through this process again. Next time, I won't carry so many electronics in my little carryon bag. Hopefully, that will resolve any security inspection issues.

Finding the right gate at any airport is always a little confusing. After figuring out in which direction to go, I took the escalator up to my gate and waited in the small lounge area to board our flight. Hunger hit me suddenly, the only food service around reminded me of a cafeteria setting without any seating. This small terminal did not have an assortment of eateries, so I had to settle for the only place available selling food.

It was like a miniature convenience store with a service counter that sold an assortment of readymade sandwiches, salads, soups, yogurt parfaits, drinks, and pastries inside a refrigerated case. I grabbed and purchased an orange juice, yogurt, Quiche Lorraine, and a bottle of water. I had some kibble for Colonel to eat. Then I settled down in a chair near our gate to eat and wait. This boarding area was packed with tourists heading back to the USA, first stop Dallas.

While waiting to board our flight, a nice couple from Texas sitting across from me revved up a conversation. They were both talkers, so from the wife I learned about their entire family history in one hour. When the wife began talking to another woman sitting nearby, her husband walked over to sit next to me. I seem to draw strangers to me like some conversational magnet but am usually captivated by their unrivaled stories and brief company.

Naturally, at first, we exchanged our views about the current conservative situation in our country, education, and a few other topics. He was a retired college professor who now worked for FEMA, the government disaster relief agency. I mentioned CERT being under FEMA. He was a very nice and very interesting man.

We were on the same American Airlines flight going to Dallas-Fort Worth and then I'd transfer to my connecting flight to LA.

By the time everyone boarded the plane, our "on time" flight left 15 mins late. Colonel and I boarded this plane early along with other disabled persons and parents with babies before the first and business class passengers. So, I don't have to worry about finding an empty overhead bin to store my carryon. Plus, we're settled comfortably in our seats before everyone else scurries into our plane. It's a nice perk, especially when I am worn-out like I am now.

I appreciate flying American Airlines. The flights are usually on time, and there is no unusual drama inflight. The flight attendants are friendly and helpful. Plus, I like their Advantage program where you can earn points for dining out as well as flying. Colonel is content and has his AA Service Dog ID. Plus being an AA frequent flier, there are even more rewards.

Although, I never had a chance to visit any airport lounges due to the short duration I had between my arrival at airports on this trip or I'm leaving from a different terminal than where the lounges are located. The Centurion lounge is in Terminal D near gate 12. My plane arrived at Terminal B at DFW. I had hoped to spend my waiting time in the lounge. No chance of that desire, my connecting flight to Los Angeles. Simply not enough time to clear customs, pick up my checked bag then recheck it. lounge.

Fortunately, when we arrived at DFW at 3:00 pm, I learned that our connecting flight was also delayed and now scheduled to leave at 4:45 pm instead of 3:38 pm. Although I had time to check out the Centurian Lounge, I didn't want to miss that flight by traipsing to another terminal.

My carryon was extremely heavy, so carrying it through the airport was difficult. Now, I wasn't happy about how far I had to walk again to reach my gate. We could only use the luggage carts for a short distance. I thought of taking the courtesy cart but didn't want to wait for that ride either. At the gate, we arrived with only 19 minutes left before boarding my flight to L.A. Once onboard, Colonel and I both slept on this leg of the flight.

After arriving at LAX, I took the Flyaway bus to Van Nuys, but I boarded the wrong airport bus which I discovered too late. Yep, I'm tired. This bus wasn't going to the Valley, instead it dropped me off at the Union train station in downtown L.A. So, from downtown Los Angeles, I needed to get to the San Fernando Valley. I could take the metro but contacted an Uber instead. It had been a long and difficult day. I just wanted to go home.

When the Uber driver arrived, he began arguing with me about my dog who was in his carrier. I told this driver that Colonel was a service dog and showed his service dog harness and ID. But the driver said that Colonel was too small to be a service dog. Oh boy, here we go. I explained to him that a service dog can be any size or breed. And that many people have disabilities that you can't see. So, he needed to be better educated. Then he said he could refuse to take any dog.

Obviously, he doesn't know the Uber dog policies either, especially about service dogs. I had no intention of continuing this conversation with him. Instead, I gave him a daggered look and said, "I've had a long flight and a long day. I just want to go home." He got the message, opened his trunk, then helped me put my bags inside it, and without further discussion he silently drove me to the Valley.

This was the second time that I encountered an uneducated Uber driver making that erroneous service dog size statement. I realize that these ride-share drivers really don't know the ADA laws or Uber's policies about service animals. In America, they can't refuse to drive a service dog and handler because the driver and Uber could be sued by the handler for violating the ADA which becomes a huge liability for Uber. This ignorance about the ADA laws is another reason to leave this country. People are not properly trained to do their service jobs. I really get tired of trying to educate people about service dogs or my disability status.

That ride home took about 20 minutes from downtown. The freeways were surprisingly clear. Still, I should have been home an hour earlier. Releasing a huge sigh of relief after unlocking my apartment door at 8 pm. Happy to be back home safely. Logistical mistakes I made on this trip were numerous. Now, really beat, I am still trying to be productive with so little energy left. Got my bags inside which I'll unpack later. Colonel and I were hungry. I prepared his meal and ordered a takeout for pickup by me. Why? I don't really want to drive anywhere right now. Habit!

In the parking lot, to my surprise, I can't unlock my car doors. However, I can open the lift gate for the cargo area. But I can't even start my car remotely. I had a difficult time logging into OnStar which sadly couldn't locate my account. Ugh! It's probably the battery since my car hadn't been started or driven for three weeks. Still determined and trying to get it started was a big waste of time. Maybe changing the battery in my car fob will help, still no juice.

Tomorrow morning, I'll try again to open the car and get it started or call OnStar for assistance via phone. I really can't deal with this car right now. Back inside, I called the restaurant to ask if they could deliver my order. They could and did. Colonel was coiled and snoring under the covers on my bed. So tired I could only finish half of my lasagna and garden salad before calling it a night. Lights out and me too by 10 pm.

Over the next two weeks I would experience chronic jet lag, extremely tired and barely able to function. In all my years of traveling, I've never experienced even mild jet lag, so this condition was unpleasant and debilitating for quite some time. Marty said he had jet lag too from his France trip.

Now, I have a lot to think about before deciding about the city I liked the most and would consider moving to in France once I retire. I don't know yet when I'll retire precisely but I am hopeful that it will happen soon. I am not getting any younger and I've waited long enough for this dream to come true. I miss France already. Have a great day! Bon Nuit!

CHAPTER ELEVEN

Choosing A French City

October 6, 2023

Back in Los Angeles, it took several weeks to recover from jet lag. However, I'm extremely happy that I planned my three-week scouting trip through France visiting more than six French cities. It was a very insightful and fun experience which gave me a different perspective on France. Although this trip went well, it was not without its challenges like my heavy bags and the long train delay to get to Lyon.

No trip is perfect, but this one was very close to perfection just from the people I encountered and I learned more about the cities I visited. I love France and appreciate this country even more after my exploratory visit last month. Most importantly, just going to France for three weeks has brought me closer to my dream. This trip has helped me decide on the region and on which French city I should move to when I retire in about two years.

In this chapter, I analyze each of the six cities I explored chronologically. However, I knew before leaving France which city I loved the most. Yet I waited until after returning home to make my city choice final. I don't have to explore any other regions. Plus, I wanted to read my notes and re-evaluate each city to give them all an equal chance.

This clear decision about which one would not have been possible without visiting these cities to get a true sense of each one for myself. It was important to wrap this matter up, and know where I wanted to land before preparing to move, and then applying for my French Visa.

No book, magazine, video, or movie can really give you a sense of what it's like to experience the sights, sounds, smells, and people of a destination unless you go there in person. Plus, you are guaranteed to have fun and many surprises in the process. I know now that two days isn't enough time to spend getting to know a city. Three days should be the minimum. Realistically, I learned that spending five days in a city was ideal. It gave me time to relax, adapt, and become familiar with a place.

FRANCE

France is large, a centuries old country in western Europe that shares borders with eight other countries and a coastline fronting the Mediterranean Sea, Atlantic Ocean, and the English Channel. It is made up of several regions of varying climates. Often, we forget that the people who live in France are not tourists but lifelong inhabitants.

Most residents are French natives while others are immigrants. My desire to live in France isn't unique. Numerous Americans have dreamed of living in France too. Today, it's estimated that over 200,000 American Expats *(up from 150,000 in 2015)* are living in France *(American Embassy 2023 statistics)*.

In 2024, over 13,000 Americans *(up 5% from 2023)* received their first French residency cards. Americans are the fifth largest nationality living in France, African Americans, Black Africans, and Caribbean Immigrants are approximately *(3.5 million)* 8% of the French population.

Monthly, countless U.S. Nationals continue to immigrate to France, choosing to live in various regions throughout the country from big urban cities to small ancient villages or out in the lovely countryside. France does not record racial census, officials saying that all people are one, so these estimates are gathered by other statistical data organizations.

France is a popular tourist destination that caters to all interests and ages. Its celebrated past and old-world charisma appeal to history buffs, yet all visitors appreciate the historical monuments, UNESCO Heritage sites, food, and architectural wonders found in many of its cities. Throughout France you will find a continuum of cultural attractions, tours of many kinds, annual events, activities, celebrations, antique fairs, many festivals, gracious people, splendid cuisine, and renowned wines. These delights are what draws many immigrants and tourists to this country above many others.

Initially these iconic attributes drew me to this country too. While visiting and spending time in France in my 30s and 40s, I felt at home there, comfortable with the surroundings, and was treated so well by people that I could not help but fall in love with France.

There are many ways to get to France but once you arrive finding transportation choices for connecting to different cities regionally is very easy. One can travel by train, plane, bus, or by renting a car. France has extensive roadways and railway systems; I chose the French railway as my major transportation link to travel from city to city. In the cities, walking and taking Trams was easy and efficient for exploring each place I visited.

BORDEAUX

Bordeaux is a port city on the banks of the Garonne River in Southwestern France. Well-known for its wine, it's here that the wine trade in France began. A must-visit destination for wine enthusiasts like me. Beyond the vineyards, Bordeaux is a UNESCO city with over 360 spectacular historical monuments and Roman sites dating back to the 15th century and some earlier.

In this city you will find stunning St. Andre Cathedral, two Basilicas, and other churches, sixteen museums, a stunning opera house Grand Theatre, multiplex cinemas including an IMAX, many British Pubs, an assortment of wine bars, fine dining restaurants and Chateaux galore.

Many urban vineyards are reachable by bus or tram. Those appellations out in the countryside surrounding the city are reachable by train or car. Bordeaux is also along the pilgrimage route of the Camino de Santiago trail. It's a fascinating city with lots of character and yes, charm.

This city is a mix of historic and modern with elegant architecture, including the spectacular 18th Century Place de la Bourse, Mirior d'eau (reflecting pool), and the newer Cite du Vin Museum with its permanent exhibition featuring global wine production which stands out among the attractions.

It's a multigenerational city blending young and old that has a huge and lively diverse population of approximately 260,000 residents. Bordeaux has a thriving cultural scene, the arts, fine dining, local activities, and festivals year-round.

After seeing enough of these six visited cities, my heart beats for

Bordeaux. Even after first researching those six French cities, Bordeaux remained at the top of my list. But I wanted to see it and then explore the other recommended cities as well to make sure. I fell in love with Bordeaux immediately on the first day of my visit. It felt warm, welcoming, and peaceful.

I really liked the laid-back vibe of this city. Plus, a big seller was it being mostly flat and only a two-hour train ride to Paris, Lyon, or other smaller cities nearby. I like that Bordeaux is closer in distance to Paris than Nice. It is only 90 minutes to the beach by train, car, or bus. Bordeaux also has an airport, so going anywhere inside or outside of France quickly is possible.

This city is smaller than Paris, less congested, less hectic, beautiful, and cleaner appeals more to me. Bordeaux is a quiet city with a big heart. It's flat with no steep hills to climb and no subway stairs to descend and ascend. Getting around town walking or using the trams and buses was much easier for me to manage. It's a very safe and walkable city, so convenient to get from place to place on foot in very little time. Colonel likes it better too. He wasn't anxious but felt safe and comfortable in Bordeaux more than the other cities we explored. Dogs know best.

Additionally, I felt safe and very much at peace in Bordeaux more than the other cities I visited on this trip. I really enjoyed the warm and friendly people I met and adored the Chartrons neighborhood the best where I stayed during my visit. Chartrons is like a small village within a big city.

Although Bordeaux is smaller in comparison to Nice or Paris, it still feels metropolitan. Bordeaux is an active city with numerous activities and attractions year-round. Full of culture: many museums, theatres, concerts, fairs, festivals, flea markets, antique shops, and other events to attend seasonally. Plus, Bordeaux is in the beautiful Southwest region of France, the heart of wine country dotted with many Chateaux and vineyards to visit for touring and wine tastings.

While walking to and from restaurants in the evenings, I felt safer. Bordeaux has many more English speakers and a large expat community which will be helpful for support. As I adjust to the French lifestyle, undoubtedly, I will develop friendships with like-minded people there. Many Parisiens have moved to Bordeaux because of its size, slower pace, affordability, schools, surrounding communities, and many to raise their children.

So happy to have discovered this city over ten years ago through a travel agent event held by Atout France, the French Tourist Board. My curiosity peaked after learning that Bordeaux is the sister city to Los Angeles. Many foreign cities and American cities share a sisterhood. This city's climate is more ideal for me; temperatures are just like in Southern California.

Boredom does not loiter in this small attractive city with plenty of events for me to do here. I will feel better about being outside in open spaces and around crowds. More comfortable. I can tell that Bordeaux is the right fit for me because it checks off all the boxes of my wants and needs. It's ideal, progressive, and very walkable with the right vibe. Looking forward to calling Bordeaux my new home.

Celestine Cooley

BIARRITZ

Biarritz is a small French city along the Basque coast bordered by the Atlantic Ocean. It's in the Basque Country, located near the Spanish Border. This elegant seaside city holds a rich history. Biarritz is a major surfing destination with long beautiful sandy beaches. Often referred to as "Little California," with similar beaches, it remains the European surfing capital.

Once a huge whaling city inhabited by only a few hundred people, today its population is around 25,810 residents. For decades Biarritz was a popular getaway for world renowned celebrities and wealthy Europeans. Today, European families and multinational tourists spent their summer vacations enjoying traditional cuisine and extended walks along the beaches.

I visited Biarritz because I had always wanted to see this city and experience the Basque Country. I never considered it to be a city in which to live but one never knows. Maybe this city would change my mind. However, visiting Biarritz had no effect on my choices. It could have been a contender but it seemed too small and just not my vibe. This short overnight trip was just a deviation from my plan and a city to scratch off my 'must visit' list. Still, it was worth the time I spent on this visit. Pleased that I added this stop to my agenda.

This seaside city is in the Pyrénées-Atlantiques department of the Nouvelle-Aquitaine region of Southwest France. It's a popular European resort area where a local mix of French and Spanish cultures collide. Here locals may speak both languages.

There is much to see and do here including shopping or just

relaxing on the beach. Walking around this city was easy, especially around old Biarritz. Going to the older sections of a city opens your imagination into what was or could have been. Still centuries old buildings stand among the ancient city settings, which you can't find in the younger U.S.A.

Walking around this unique city was a joyful experience. Glad I chose my one-night stay here. Additionally, I didn't mind the heat which was mild considering there was much sunshine and the sea. People I met were engaging and helpful when asking questions. I managed not to get lost in Biarritz.

I found that there are accommodations for every wallet in this city. Even though this city caters more to upscale European tourists, anyone on a budget can still enjoy the offerings here too. Dining here is exceptional with the traditionally prepared Tapas and a variety of fresh seafood dishes uniquely prepared which you can't find everywhere. I liked my afternoon dining out experience and my visit to Biarritz. Glad I took the detour.

France is known for their wines and champagnes grown in the various appellations throughout the country. In the Southwest, Red and Rose wines are heavily produced but you can find an assortment of white wines and sparkling wines produced at local vineyards. In the Basque Country a good variety of the wines comes from the Irouléguy appellation.

The Irouléguy wine is fruity and acidic, a blend of Cabernet Franc and Cabernet Sauvignon. I'm not a big fan of sweet wines but will drink them nonetheless, yet preferring Reds and Roses to White wines, unless they are White Burgundy's or Chablis of course. Can't find Chablis in the U.S. anymore.

Celestine Cooley

The weather was perfectly warm, not too hot in September. It isn't a flat city, with its proximity to the Alps. I walked up and down a few hilly streets. It was easier than most of the other mountainous cities I visited on this trip. I did not notice a homeless population.

Biarritz deserves another visit along with other cities in the Basque Country close to Spain. I wouldn't mind seeing the running of the bulls in Pamplona, Spain but safely from a balcony view. Biarritz is a pleasant getaway. I am looking for a city with more to offer me, a different makeup of diversity, community, and a good fit.

TOULOUSE

In the South of France, Toulouse sits on the banks of the Garonne River, while the Canal du Midi, a UNESCO World Heritage Site, traverses the city. It's famously known as "La Ville Rose" or "the Pink City" because the sun casts a pinkish hue over its stylish buildings. This vibrant city boasts historical sites, attractions, and annual activities.

With countless bars and restaurants, its lively youthful atmosphere is prominent. Toulouse is the fourth largest city in France in the Occitanie region to the south with an estimated residential population of 1,070,750. A big city not far from Provence that offers a blend of history, culture, art, and science. It is also the center of the European aerospace industry.

Toulouse is a large lively city with a younger vibe. It had many bars and plenty of nightlife. I found it to be clean and the people friendly. But it does have a growing homeless population of displaced immigrants. I walked a lot in three days so I didn't use public transportation. However, I can see why some expats like living there because it is a nice and pretty city with lots to do. And with the Canal du Midi snaking its way through Toulouse it just adds a little more finesse to the pink city's charm.

I could live there but it doesn't give me the same vibe as Bordeaux. So, I marked this one as a second favorite on my list of possibilities. I know that I wouldn't be as happy living in Toulouse although the food scene was excellent. I'll go back to visit as often as I can. I already miss that restaurant, "Meet the Meat." That duck liver salad was to die for; I can still taste it.

Walking around this city was not much of a challenge. I found it easier to find places of interest to visit. Taking the bus to explore the city of Carcassonne was the highlight of my visit to Toulouse. It was a positive experience in a friendly city which should not be missed. Next time, I'll stop by Aix-en-Provence and a few more cities nearby.

NICE

Nice is located on the Cote d'Azur (French Riviera), offering year-round sunshine, splendid beaches, a pleasant old town with interesting old buildings, and the lovely Promenade des Anglaise along the beachfront. It's a diverse city with a population of 351,011. It boasts lovely Haussmann and Italian-style buildings on clean wide streets.

There are monasteries dating back to the 14th-century, ancient sites, and monuments that showcase the city's rich history. Nice is a great base for exploring any of the other beautiful cities and villages along the French Riviera, while enjoying a luxurious and relaxed Mediterranean lifestyle. I felt relaxed in Nice.

Although I enjoyed visiting this city, there were a few negatives for me. I didn't like the uncomfortably high humidity and sticky heat like Florida's climate. Weather is an important aspect of where I chose to live. Although this city was easy to navigate on foot, I never got my bearings there or any sense of direction. As if this city kept telling me, 'No, not here.' One has to be cognizant of omens.

Unlike in Bordeaux where after getting turned around a few times I quickly learned my way around easily. Yes, I was often lost in Bordeaux, but I found my bearings there to navigate that city. Also, I didn't see any green spaces in Nice like parks but I'm sure there must be some. I'll have to seek out those open green spaces on my next visit to Nice.

I enjoyed strolling around old Nice and down the promenade along the sea when I could find it. The beach is okay but has pebbles to walk and lay on instead of sand, so no Nice doesn't work for me on any level. The neighborhood where I stayed those five nights was in a central area but off the beaten path, so I had no complaints about noise or other annoyances. Nice is hilly. Although, I appreciated the older and younger diverse mix of people and cultures. And I found the locals to be very friendly.

The tram system offered very good, convenient, and efficient transportation. I did not ride the buses since I stayed mainly in the city's center. Nice has a lot to offer for retirees and I hear there is an expat community for support. Although I didn't run into any expats while visiting Nice this time around. I was hoping to meet a few expats to learn their views on living in this seaside city.

Still, my overall experience of visiting and exploring Nice was pleasant. I remember this city from my first visit eons ago. It still holds that Mediterranean allure. I am a California girl so the sea always calls out to me. Even though I no longer like going into the sea or riding on a boat, I can still appreciate the views from land.

In the end, as much as I wanted to love this city, I could not. Nice is nice but not for me. I don't know why but this city didn't appeal to my sense of calm or belonging nor did it have that laid back peaceful "at home" vibe that I was seeking.

Also, Nice felt too small land mass wise and it was too crowded even in the fall. I heard that during the summer tourist season you really can't enjoy Nice because of the crowds. This city did not check off my 'must have' needs. Maybe I am not cut out for the Mediterranean lifestyle even though I appreciated being near the sea. However, I can see why other expats enjoy living in Nice. Anyway, I'm glad I gave Nice a shot.

One other negative for me is that Nice is too far from Paris by train, six hours with a change of trains in Marseille. Not feasible for a leisurely day trip to Paris. After my train delays from Nice to Lyon, I'm still traumatized so I would hesitate before thinking about taking that train route again. Flying to Paris from Nice makes more sense, since the cost is often less on Air France for a one hour and thirty-five-minute non-stop flight than it is to take the train when you are on a schedule. Convenience is better.

Although there are many expats living in Nice, I just couldn't make myself like Nice enough to want to live there. I like Cannes much better but would not want to live there either, like Monaco, which is too small and hilly. I prefer to just visit this Mediterranean region occasionally. Visiting the south of France at a different time of year without the heat and humidity would be more ideal for me. I would enjoy these coastal cities much more than I have at this time of year.

Nice is a lovely city. Anyone who likes the sea or ocean will appreciate all that this city has to offer. I encourage a visit to see this city for yourself and form your own opinion. Indeed, the only way to know if a city fits your style is by visiting it and having a few local type experiences such as dining out, talking to locals, and shopping. I know I'll go back to Nice for visits and to visit the other towns and villages nearby. Plus, I want to visit Corsica. Nice is a big No, so it was scratched off my list.

Celestine Cooley

LYON

Lyon is the gastronomic capital of France located in the Auvergne-Rhône-Alpes region. Smaller than Paris. Lyon has a well-known culinary scene that boasts numerous Michelin-starred restaurants and its traditional Bouchons. Once a major silk trading center, Lyon rests on the confluence of the Saone and Rhône rivers.

This small city with a population of 520,774 residents is the third largest city in France. Lyon felt smaller and is definitely hilly. This city offers locals and tourists dozens of museums, unlimited attractions, and world-class events year-round. I'm sure there would be plenty of activities and events to attend here. And I know there is an expat community here too.

Lyon is a beautiful city that feels too slow. Maybe because it was a Sunday that the energy seemed very low. It's a large city but I didn't find a lot to do that would appease me or keep me engaged. Again, it was the weekend so not much was open and I didn't spend as much time in this city as I had planned. Because I only had one full day to spend, it's not fair for me to judge Lyon as a possible city for living.

Plus, I did not have a chance to experience any recommended restaurants, but did enjoy a few. I'll have to return at another time for the gastronomic experiences I missed and to walk more around this city, venture into different neighborhoods, and take the metro.

I rode the bus but not the metro *(subway)*. The buses were clean and efficient. It's a somewhat walkable city. I don't remember seeing a lot of bike riders. Since I was only in one part of this town for a few hours, I could not explore this city well enough to judge it. However, what I did experience was not my vibe. Lyon did not grab me at all. It felt cold, industrial, and very linear. I just didn't have enough time to really get a feel for all it has to offer or see other neighborhoods.

Plus, I need to be on the ground walking around and engaging with people to get a better sense of a place. The people I met were pleasant enough. Lyon's climate is cooler. Although the city tour took me to other areas, still I did not pick up that vibe anywhere while there we visited here. But one day is not enough time to get a good feel for a city.

Still for the reasons mentioned, I removed Lyon off my list of possibilities. I think the train delay was another factor that sealed that deal acting like an omen telling me this city isn't the one. I feel I made the right decision about Lyon even though I didn't have those two planned days to experience this city as I would have liked.

However, many expats love this city and have made Lyon their home. So, I encourage others to give Lyon a try and form your own opinion. And don't go on a Sunday or even a Monday when most retail stores, boutique shops, some attractions, and other activities are closed.

PARIS

Paris, in the Île-de-France region, is the capital known around the world as The City of Light. With a population of approximately 2.07 million residents, it is the largest city in France. World renowned as the global center for culture, art, fashion, gastronomy and UNESCO monuments, it lives up to its hype.

This energetic city's diversity, cafe culture, and designer boutiques are noteworthy. Its twenty districts are dotted with wide streets and boulevards, historic monuments, famous landmarks, and tall lovely Haussmann architecture. The River Seine divides the right and left banks of Paris. This major European city's "must-see sights" appeal to travelers of all ages, interests, wallets, and backgrounds.

Paris is a fun city, big, popular, full of energy, and fast paced. It's very busy and some areas are noisy and very congested. The district where I stayed in the 12th was less congested and quieter. I could easily live in Paris, especially in that area of the city where I stayed. I did not love the subways though. Not fun at my age.

This city is not entirely flat either. But I really enjoy visiting Paris and know that I will visit it often in the future. Overall, I was able to stick to my earlier decision about not wanting to live in Paris. Visiting this city is a true lifetime experience that all travelers to France should not miss.

Colonel and I loved the park and walking around the city. I could also take the bus from place to place easily. It's just too big, hectic, and too loud for me. Paris is as expensive as living in Los Angeles. So, for that reason, it's out. Anyway, I'll be able to visit

Paris whenever I want to since it's just over two hours from Bordeaux by train. There is so much I do enjoy about this city's ambience so I can't dismiss it completely. However, living in another big city is not what I desire anymore.

One more fact about living in Paris: if you're looking for affordable rental housing it isn't practical unless you want to live in a tiny studio on the 6th floor, with no elevator, but having to climb too many flights of stairs. I had a difficult time climbing up to the 2nd floor of that Nice apartment daily where I stayed without an elevator. Even Colonel was skeptical about those "scary" winding stairs in which he exhibited very little trust. No thanks!

There you have it. This chapter concludes my scouting trip to explore France and find my new home city. I plan to move to Bordeaux. If you get a chance to go to France don't just visit Paris, it's not the whole of France. Other cities throughout France offer a lot of charm, interesting sites, attractions, traditions, culture, and activities as well. You'll be pleasantly surprised at what you'll discover on a trip through France by train or car. Renting a car and driving through the countryside of France is a beautiful and amazing experience. Think about visiting France the next time you plan a trip. Au revoir!

EPILOGUE

Old Endings, New Beginnings

Once back in L.A., I realized that I had not missed this city, my neighborhood, or my little apartment in the San Fernando Valley. Clearly, my positive brush with France confirmed that I didn't want to live in California anymore. I could not have known then that my dream would be coming true sooner than I had planned.

Three days after returning from this trip, my boss told us that his position was eliminated. Sad about his leaving because Robert skillfully rebuilt our department from four to twelve, selecting a team of very talented individuals to run each division. Although I knew I would be next on the chopping block, I just didn't know when. So, I waited to be let go.

Over the next few months, I was so unhappy that I mentally and emotionally checked out of my job and this city. No longer feeling attached to MGM or to Los Angeles. Even though I enjoyed my four years at MGM before my boss's departure and certainly adored my teammates, that same joy lessened over time as new players entered the picture. I tried to hold on as best I could. The organizational changes, other co-workers leaving MGM, and Amazon's corporate culture, made me want to retire earlier than I had planned. Since I had pretty much achieved my goals of working in entertainment and living in Los Angeles over the last five decades, l was ready to check out. It was time to let go and move on. But I didn't want to quit my job, I knew sooner than later I would be laid off too.

During the Christmas holiday, I was very unhappy, feeling totally conflicted, impatient, and trapped in L.A. Desperately I needed peace of mind and a change of environment. Instead of screaming, one day while sitting in front of my computer at home, I just closed my eyes, saw the city where I wanted to live, and wished that I could move there before the upcoming elections in 2024. Emotionally, I could not let the feeling nor the idea of moving to and living in France to start my life's new chapter go. This strong unwavering feeling nagged at me daily; I could not shake it.

At the time, I only hoped but didn't know that in January 2024, my dream would come true in the form of an email notification sent to me from Amazon-MGM. It stated that my position had been eliminated. YES! Was my immediate reaction. It was like hearing soothing music in the distance. Suddenly I felt absolutely free. Opening that email was like being a kid at Christmas unwrapping a gift I had waited for and hoped to receive.

Rather than working two more years by applying for a lateral position at Amazon which was offered, I decided to retire. Many MGM employees were let go on that glorious day. Elated, I notified my team, and then I put on my tap shoes and danced. That next day, I began packing boxes. I was prepared for this moment and I knew all that I had to do moving forward. YIPEE!

It's truly amazing how life works out and gives you what you deeply want and need when you ask and are ready to receive it. So, don't give up on your dreams. Because you are never too old to follow your dreams nor is it ever too late to pursue your long-awaited passions. I believe that "Obstacles are merely opportunities waiting to be discovered." I am truly grateful to still be alive in my 70s, enjoying life, and equally pleased that finally I realized my lifelong dream of moving to France. I never knew what peace truly felt like until I moved to Bordeaux.

Sometimes life is full of unexpected surprises like writing this first book. It's not the one I had in mind. Soon after finishing Six French Cities, I began writing my second book in this series, A Boomer in Bordeaux, about moving to Bordeaux and adapting to my new life during my first year of living in France. Moving to France was quite an experience but what I needed to begin my next life chapter on this illustrious journey.

If you enjoyed reading this book, please tell your family and friends, and if you have time, please leave an honest review online where you purchased this book. Reviews very much help other readers to find my book. I read all the reviews. Á Prochaine!

~ END OF PART 1 ~

ACKNOWLEGEMENTS

I would like to thank my many supportive friends and family on Facebook who, like virtual companions, followed my French adventures and to Stephanie Schuster who encouraged me to write this book.

To Tricia Davey, Kimberly Meyers, and Shirley Vivion whose critiques after reading my book proposal helped me narrow down my theme and rethink my book's title.

To Jana Davis Middleton who helped retrieve some of my lost Facebook posts that are included in this book.

To Alexis, Sharon Olson, Desi Darris, Shirley Monestier, Danielle Tolhurst, and GeVonna Fassett, whose keen eyes and positive suggestions helped me rethink this book's cover design.

To Elaine Jessmer who sparked the idea for me to self-publish this book even when I first resisted.

To expats Oliver and Lina Gee, Jay Swanson, and An and Jeff Scott who through their YouTube Channel Vlogs and Podcasts shared their knowledgeable information about moving to and living in France. Their helpful tips enabled me to make informed decisions and have a much smoother transition when I moved to France.

And lastly, to all those earlier dreamers who dared to follow their dreams, you all inspired me to keep believing and follow mine.

~ Merci Beaucoup! ~

ABOUT THE AUTHOR

Celestine Cooley is a published poet, writer, and producer from Los Angeles. She began writing about this scouting trip and her French adventures on social media in the fall of 2023. She retired from an extraordinarily long fifty-year career in the entertainment industry.

She happily moved with her Chihuahua, Colonel to France in 2024. Currently, Celestine is writing her second book in this French adventure series, A Boomer in Bordeaux. A memoir about her experience of moving, adapting, and living her first year in France.

In her spare time, Celestine enjoys walking with Colonel, exploring medieval cities, attending local events, spending time with friends, reading a good mystery, and relaxing with a glass of wine and a bowl of popcorn.

Six French Cities

Colonel enjoying the passing French landscape
©Photography by Celestine Cooley

Six French Cities

Colonel and I going down into a Paris Metro
©Photograph courtesy of Martin Jones

Six French Cities

THANK YOU FOR READING

Celestine Cooley, Six French Cities *(My Magical Medieval Journey)*, a travel memoir.

©Cooley Communications, 2026, 314 pages.

The Paperback book is available on Amazon and other online book retailers for $21.99, plus shipping.

The eBook is available on Amazon and other online book retailers for $9.99 as a digital download.

Join my Newsletter for updates about upcoming book events, new books, and general information. Visit my website:

www.celeste-cooleycommunications.com

Book two in this French series, A Boomer in Bordeaux, *(My First Year Living in France)*, launching in the Fall of 2026.

If you enjoyed reading my book, please leave an honest review on Amazon or online where you purchased the book. Your reviews will help new readers discover my book. *I appreciate reviews and read every one.*

SIX FRENCH CITIES

www.ingramcontent.com/pod-product-compliance
Lightning Source LLC
Chambersburg PA
CBHW071955290426
44109CB00018B/2027